Sanderson's Fiction Writing Manual

Sanderson's Fiction Writing Manual

Jim Sanderson

LAMAR UNIVERSITY press

ISBN: 978-0-9915321-2-4
Library of Congress Control Number: 2015931099
Manufactured in the United States of America

Lamar University Press
Beaumont, Texas

For all writers who seek ways to improve their writing

Other books from Lamar University Press Include

For more information go to
www.LamarUniversityPress.Org

CONTENTS

Student Stories

Introduction

No one is a natural born writer. No one is naturally gifted as a writer. Every good writer had a teacher in some form or fashion, and all successful writers had to struggle to learn their craft. Note that I did say "craft," for a beginning writer should see writing as the manipulation of craft, sort of like bricklaying or plumbing. Maybe regard it as something few people like to do, for almost no one likes to write. Writing is hard, lonely work, and most writers, while disliking the process of writing, like only having written well.

The market for writing is terrible, so it is impractical for anyone to plan on growing up to be a writer. Very few people who take a creative writing course will become a writer, though all who sign up have legitimate reasons for taking the course.

From taking the course, students will get a little better at writing (not just in fiction but in all forms of writing), and, I hope, a lot better at reading, for fiction-writing courses emphasize learning to read more critically.

Those who take fiction writing and really like it should follow up with more classes, for courses such as the one for which I wrote this manual are introductory. Also it is a good idea to join or create a writers' group, or start exchanging manuscripts with reliable critics.

Writers struggling with learning to write short fiction can find a useful metaphor in Marv Newland's two-minute animated cartoon, "Bambi Meets Godzilla," found in numerous sites on the world wide web.

Even if not drawn well, Bambi is a delicate creature, dependent upon staying true to his own nature. Such are working stories. So if a Godzilla shows up, that Godzilla can crush poor Bambi. Consider Godzilla as the writers' intent (what the authors think their stories mean, what the writers wants their stories to mean, what really happened, what genres they have read, what genres they want to write, what they think literature should be).

So the lesson to all of us is not to let the Godzilla inside of us squash poor, delicate Bambi. Don't let what you want your story to be (or what you think fiction should be) squash what's working.

A second useful metaphor comes from a story told by my mentor, Gordon Weaver: a guy walks into a bar and starts swinging a baseball bat or a sledgehammer. Blood and guts fly. Heads are bashed in. The place gets messy. Another guy walks into a bar, goes up to his enemy, pulls out an ice pick, puts it against his enemy's ear, and then pushes.

In which scenario did you gasp more? So the metaphor is to use an ice pick, not a sledgehammer or a bat. Don't overwrite. Don't beg. Earn your emotion. Use an ice pick, not a sledgehammer.

Aristotle, Burroway, and Others

Janet Burroway, most other fiction writing textbook writers, and writers mention that a story must have a character who *wants* something and then confronts something that stands in the way of that *want*. Sometimes, these same writers say that the character should be *likeable*. Then they elaborate. But the basis for all of this discussion is Aristotle's "Poetics."

So why not search the internet, the Lamar library, or your local library for "Poetics" and see if you find it or something about it. Here is one: http://classics.mit.edu/Aristotle/poetics.1.1.html

Aristotle, unlike Plato, is a realist, a mechanic. Think of him as a plumber or auto mechanic. Think of your fiction, at least for a while, as a craft, like bricklaying or carpentry. So Aristotle first asks what art is. For him, "*Art imitates reality by adding order and harmony to chaos.*"

That statement makes a big philosophical statement. So let me digress a bit and warn you about what it implies. First, reality is chaotic. Second, we know it only through imposing something on it, such as art. So art is mimetic. Art imitates and thus informs us. It thus has a direct relation to reality. Third, literary critics, especially modern ones, debate this statement. Some post-modernists say that we have lost Coleridge's "willing suspension of disbelief." Coleridge says that when we read a poem, we know that it is not real, so we suspend our disbelief to enjoy it, savor it, learn from it, transcend with it. Some critics say that we have reached the point where, as a culture, we know that we are watching a movie, reading a poem or a book and that we cannot suspend our disbelief. In other words the art or the craft is no longer mimetic.

So now ask yourself what a writer might find better to believe. Writers, for the most part, are Aristotelian. Most writers want to believe that they have something to say about the real world, that they and their craft are not just constructs of society, and that they have adroitly imitated reality.

So, for the sake of efficiency, let's side with Aristotle. After stating what art is, Aristotle asks what is the best type of art. He has statues to look at, music to listen to, lyric and epic poems to read or listen to, and dramas to watch. He decides that, because they have more movement, immediacy, and sensuality than the other art forms, dramas are the best art form.

He now has two types of drama to choose from: comedy and tragedy. Aristotle then says that the best type of drama and thus the best art form is tragedy because, more so than any other art form, including comedy, tragedy more fully *excites pity and fear*. So, according to Aristotle, the best art form is tragedy because it best adds *order and harmony to chaos*. Thus it *creates and excites pity and fear*. Comic actors, dramatic actors, and comedians often cite the following quote, attributed to any number of actors: "Dying is easy, comedy is hard." Can you see why, given Aristotle, this is ironically true?

When we watch a tragedy, we are more emotionally involved because we fear for the protagonist and pity him when he falls. We get a certain amount of *delight* in seeing this all work out. Notice that, according to Aristotle, we do not escape from reality—as many movie and TV viewers say of their preferred art form. We aren't just entertained. We are emotionally aroused, and we see our real worlds make some sense. For those folks who just want to escape and thus want their entertainment or art to be merely an escape from their reality, then I'd suggest that they stop reading or watching and get a lobotomy. For, if we take Aristotle at his word, as writers do (or as folks who are going to write something at the end of this semester should), then we should see narrative—whether tragic or pathetic, funny or sad—as an emotional engagement with some non-real people who resemble real people. In other words, we want to see characters who, like us, want what we want. We want to see characters whom we don't necessarily like but who are like us.

The next step for Aristotle is to explain how the tragedy arouses pity and fear. Unlike a comedy that presents a character who is less than we are, who is not as smart or as capable as we are, the tragedy presents a protagonist who is "greater than the average man." *Basically, Aristotle says that a tragedy does the following. An* appealing protagonist *who* is greater than we are *because of his* nobility *moves through a series of* united scenes *where* no part is greater than the whole *toward* an insurmountable obstacle *and fails to overcome that obstacle as a result of some* tragic flaw, *and in his* fall *the protagonist realizes or* recognizes *his mistake or his tragic flaw.*

So there it is. You should try to memorize that sentence. You should paste it to your work desk. But let's look at it more deeply.

1) A character is *appealing* if we recognize him as being like us. Note that Aristotle does not say that we have to like her, as in applauding her actions, but we should see parts of ourselves in her. What makes this noble person like us is her weaknesses.

Test yourself on this point. Ask yourself how emotionally involved, how much pity and fear you have, for a superhero. If a protagonist is better than you—Rambo, Superman, etc.—just how much do you worry about him. But if a protagonist has a vulnerability that he cannot see, though we in the audience can, then don't you have an emotional investment, more suspense, more surprise, more pity and fear? When John Milton published his epic poem *Paradise Lost*, many of his fellow Calvinists criticized it because the most well-rounded and "sympathetic" character was Satan. Satan displays all sorts of weaknesses despite his power, so readers tend not to just empathize but sympathize with him because he is like the readers. A protagonist's warts makes him "like" us.

2) Yet, Aristotle says that this protagonist must be noble or *high born*—primarily for two reasons. The mechanistic Aristotle reasons that the greater the fall, the more pity and fear are engendered. Since a tragedian can only kill, blind, or otherwise torture a protagonist, the bottom has a limit, but not the top. So the tragedian can raise the top. He can make the hero high-born. Thus, secondly, because the protagonist is high born, his fate affects his country or culture. His fall and his story have a *certain magnitude*.

In "Tragedy and the Common Man," Arthur Miller, the playwright who gave us Willie Loman in *Death of a Salesman*, takes Aristotle to task. He says that the same amount of pity and fear can accompany the fall of a common man. Loman does awful things in the play and is not at all admirable, but Willie tries to maintain his dignity in the face of everything that threatens to take it away. Miller claims that this "want" gives Willie dignity and nobility.

Similarly, as a culture, we no longer believe in the rights of kings or the natural superiority of royal birth. So for us, nobility should probably take some emotional, intellectual, ethical, or moral intensity that is greater than ours. And in fact Aristotle implies that the protagonist's high birth or outward nobility mirrors some spiritual, moral, emotional, nobility. Perhaps we should think that the hero is like us in that he is weak but unlike us because of his nobility.

3) The *tragic flaw* is the most difficult of Aristotle's terms and is the most often debated. Many critics define *tragic flaw* an "error in judgment." But for the writer this error must be the result of the protagonist's nobility, not his weakness. Think about the irony here. A character who is better than we are fails precisely because of what makes him superior to us.

As the play moves along and we start to find the character appealing because he is like us, what makes him better than us is what pushes him closer toward some insurmountable obstacle. We see this irony; the protagonist does not. We want to shout out at him to watch out, to suppress his own character. We fear for his safety. Knowing what the character does not know is called *dramatic irony*. However, suppose that he can somehow hear our warnings and stop his quest, his search, his inquiry, his want. Suppose that he simply gives up. Now he has committed an even greater crime, for he has stopped being himself. He no longer appeals to us, and he is no longer better than we are, so we disengage, leave the play. All the tragic hero can do is to move toward the obstacle, which will defeat him but give him recognition of how he was fated to fall —as he eventually does.

Audiences say that Oedipus's pride doomed him. His intellect—he solved the riddle of the Sphinx and became a hero to Thebes—pushed him onward. His need to know who murdered the king, to solve all of life's riddles, and to save the city pushed him onward. His error resulted from his intellect, his nobility.

Audiences say that Hamlet failed because he couldn't make up his mind. Although he is a prince, his indecisiveness is not noble. Like Oedipus he is a leader and an intellectual. As he moves through the play, often in his soliloquies, he debates appearance and reality, cause and effect. Can he trust what a ghost told him? Can he trust any of his advisors? What act will best accomplish his purposes, will best help

Denmark? So he delays to think, reason, and figure. How can he do otherwise and still be better than us?

Audiences say that jealousy doomed Othello. But on the other hand, he simply trusted the wrong people too much. In other words, these tragic protagonists' virtues—not their vices—doom them. The tragic flaw may be an error, but it is a flaw that comes from that virtue. See the irony?

If tragedy presents men as better than they are, then a character who is superior to the audience fails because of those very qualities that make her better. And ironically, if a comedy presents a character as worse than we are, then that character overcomes the obstacle through luck or circumstance. Can you see the way the Greeks saw a fateful, ironic, tragic world?

4) Obstacle. Notice that in this scheme Aristotle does not present a villain—or an *antagonist*. He simply says obstacle. A person can be the obstacle and thus become an antagonist, but the obstacle need not be a person/character. An obstacle is the goal, task, construct, threat, character, dilemma, etc. that "kick starts" the tragic flaw. With a character firmly in mind, a writer should create an obstacle that challenges what the protagonist wants, that forces the character to resort to his very nature to overcome the obstacle. Actually, choosing an obstacle is relatively easy. An audience will accept almost any obstacle—if the audience members see that that obstacle best reveals the protagonist's noble traits. A baseball card could be an obstacle if it reveals character. A character's desire to collect baseball cards could reveal his tragic flaw.

5) But the protagonist must realize his own mistakes. He must have *recognition*. He must make sense of the chaos in his life, see the order and harmony, and understand his own destruction.

6) Thus through this recognition, the protagonist suffers more than is warranted, more than he deserves, but all is not gloomy. While we have feared for the protagonist and pity him once he has fallen, we, like the tragic figure, see the world rendered understandable. Order and harmony have made chaos intelligible. By figuring this out and seeing the protagonist figure it out, we feel a sense of delight because we've learned something. But we have also felt something. Our pity and fear have given us an emotional investment in the narrative. The tragic fall purges us of emotion. The purging is a *catharsis,* as Aristotle says. Basically then, if the

protagonist does not realize his complicity in his own downfall, then he is pathetic rather than tragic. (A comedic character, who is less than the audience, may overcome an obstacle through no nobility of his own, but he remains pathetic.)

A note here is appropriate. Arthur Miller and others say that, if the audience recognizes the tragic flaw and the protagonist does not fully realize it or even realizes the wrong pattern, then the audience's recognition is enough for a "tragic effect." This point is open to debate.

Applied specifically to a short story, this recognition has a relation to what James Joyce calls an *epiphany*. Borrowed from religion, *epiphany* means, for Joyce, that sudden moment when the character suddenly sees the world differently. Just as important to Joyce is the way that that epiphany is presented. Usually some physical action or object "triggers" the epiphany. So for Joyce a short story brings the protagonist to a moment when she suddenly realizes her mistakes or her mistaken view of her world.

7. The manner in which the protagonist moves toward the obstacle is through a *series of unified scenes* in which *the parts are not greater than the whole*. If we look back at Aristotle's formula, we can see that it fits Gustav Freytag's curve of rising action to a point of denouement, or falling action. On a stage or in a movie, that rising action is literally a collection of spaces seen one after the other. What moves the action forward are units of space/times that take place on a stage or screen. Fiction tries to approximate these space/times or scenes. The difference between performance mediums like stage/screen stories and fiction is that the performance mediums have immediate, tangible, limited scenes. They are linear and clearly defined by space and performance time.

Fiction, a rhetorical medium, is not as linear as drama or film and does not require a clear space and time. People born after World War II have grown up surrounded by visual images—TV and movies. As a result, when we think of narrative, when we imagine our lives as stories, we do so in visual images, in scenes.

So a lot of writers create a story using some narrative logic and imagine it or plan it as a series of scenes. Knowing Aristotle can help with both the overall plan and the scenes involved. Of course, writing the story changes everything.

Let's look at some of Aristotle's pointers. First, he says that the drama, should start *in medias res* (in the middle of things). He implies that the complications and conflict have already started. The background, the explanations, the backstory have already taken place. We see the backstory through ongoing actions. One difficulty for any writer is deciding with what scene to start the story. What space or time will efficiently propel the story forward?

Deus ex machina means "god from the machine." In Aristotle's time a playwright sometimes had difficulty knowing how to close a play. His hero is in trouble, is facing a dilemma, but the play needs to end. So the bad Greek playwright might simply solve that problem by having an actor raised or lowered by means of a crank, pulley, and rope. If the actor were raised, that would mean that the gods had rescued the protagonist.

Today such a story would seem contrived. The ending (usually) isn't deserved. Cliff Huxtable of *The Cosby Show* just wraps everything up for the family. In others the hero and heroine are reunited at the last minute. The protagonist sees the error of his ways and then rights them all. Or worst of all, some coincidence rights all the wrongs or saves the protagonist.

Aristotle does indeed say that a drama must contain "surprise," not A SURPRISE. When the ending to a story happens, the viewer or reader should indeed be surprised. But after that ending takes place, the viewer or reader should see that that ending is the only one for that particular story. As Burroway says, there are no accidents in fiction.

And contrary to popular belief, O. Henry stories are mostly not too good. They depend upon the irony of the ending, upon the twist. They are like one-trick ponies. The ending should complete the story, should show the logical consequences of character. Without the demented narrators who expose themselves as murderers, perverts, or monsters, Poe's stories work toward the trick ending. So do not write a story just to provide a trick ending. Earn the ending.

Aristotle has another reason for requiring that the protagonist be high born. He says that the drama must have a "certain magnitude." The city, a great family, a culture, a state should be at risk. So the protagonist's fall affects the entire kingdom, community, family, or civilization.

But Aristotle's views do not always fit modern narratives.

Clearly, we no longer view nobility in the same way as Aristotle. In fact the term "high born" to us seems either prejudiced or archaic.

1. In realistic and naturalistic literary movements, characters are governed by society or environment. Today sociology and psychology suggest that human motives are influenced inwardly and outwardly, so we have a hard time seeing someone as endemically noble. We have a hard time believing that people are autonomous. We explain people in terms of their sociological or psychological impulses. Further, we tend to believe that people can't fully know themselves, that their id, their true motives, and their genetic makeup make them act as they do. Thus we don't believe very much in recognition. So to us, people, and thus characters, seem more pathetic than tragic.

2. Aristotle says that the most important element of the drama is plot and then character. Today, especially with literary realism behind us, we want to see character. Realistic novels were frequently long because they followed characters around, recoding their actions and thoughts, and were not confined to a strict plot. However, plot and character are intertwined. Henry James stated that plot was watching the character move through the story toward his doom and that plot is the revelation of character through movement. So the two are interchangeable.

3. Next, the obvious point is that Aristotle is writing about drama, not fiction. The play is presented through a unified series of actions on a stage—scenes. While fiction surely has scenes, fiction can flashback, show a character thinking while simultaneously doing something, and even jump around in time. As a result a fiction is less linear than a drama. The end of one scene and the start of another is often hazy. The edges may be fuzzy. In fiction the arrangements of scenes may not be chronological.

4. Voice or point of view and the situation of the telling of the story will affect how the reader views character and consequently plot.

So why do we continue to study Aristotle's *Poetics*?

1) In itself, *Poetics* is good to know because it is adaptable.
2) *Poetics* does apply more readily to movies and dramas and thereby helps us understand those mediums.
3) Many people start writing without a clear sense of narrative, drama, or irony. *Poetics* is a pretty good place to start.
4) Most folks don't have a clear understanding of how to organize a story, how to outline, or how to think about "what happens" other than chronological order. *Poetics* offers a way to start thinking about what happened.

So what can we conclude?

Present day stories—delivered in whatever form or format—may not be strict tragedies because their characters are generally more pathetic than tragic. But Aristotle offers us a guide. We prefer a story that depends upon a character who is real to us, a round character—that is, more than one dimensional—who might be dynamic, as a tragic character surely is.

In modern narratives what the character wants, needs, or is driven to have taken the place of nobility and his appealing nature. We have trouble seeing nobility, but we see the strength of desire, even when it is misdirected, and view it as an admirable quality, even if we disagree with the specific desire. If that character is true to what she wants, then we will give her empathy and perhaps our sympathy.

A dynamic character, because of his psychological, emotional, intellectual, or spiritual makeup, faces an obstacle that challenges who he is. In other words, he is complicit in his own conflict and fate. He moves toward this obstacle through a series of scenes and overcomes it or falls to it because of who he is. He may recognize his complicity although, if he doesn't recognize it, he is more likely to be pathetic than tragic. This recognition may be a sudden epiphany. Thus, the overall tone of the story may be tragic, pathetic, or even comedic.

Some points about the interaction of plot and character:

1) When talking about a whole story, we frequently start with a "what if." John Gardner advises that a writer might choose an incident, a headline, a memory, or a witnessed scene and then move forward

from it to a climax or work backward to see what caused it.

Gardner quotes a headline: "Woman runs over and kills flagman." He asks how the event could have caused drama. So he makes up some scenes. In the first scene, an aging stripper is fired from her job to make way for younger strippers. Her sleazy male boss with diamonds on his pinky and gold around his neck fires her. Next she goes to the bank to ask for a postponement of her auto loan since she is now without work. Another man, this one a courteous but aloof loan officer, turns her down. Going home on the freeway under construction, a flagman tries to flag her off the road. But he is another man trying to tell her what to do, so. . . .

2) Gardner, like a screenwriter, discusses the organization of the scenes.

    a. They can be chronological, like most plays, *Hamlet*, for instance.

    b. They can be logical. The books in *Gulliver's Travels* are arranged according to logic. Together they show what mankind is not.

    c. They can be arranged symbolically or imagistically, in which recurring sensual appeals unite the scenes. The links between the scenes can be dramatic, ironic, or emotional, and the links between scenes can have more than one connection.

    d. Or (I add) they can combine these methods.

Starting a Story.
Burroway distinguishes story and plot by stating that story is essentially a retelling of "what happened," but a plot is the arrangement of scenes for the most dramatic effect. So here are some suggestions.

1) Think about a story that you may have heard from a mother, father, grandfather, wife, or some relative. This story has probably circulated around the family for some time. Now try to write down the basis of the story. Write something like "My _____ always talked about the time that my _____ did _____." Elaborate just a little. What type of shoes did

that person wear? Where did he work? Try to get some distinct scene of what happened.

2) Write a character sketch of some person you know or a person you imagine. Stick to the physical details — looks, appearance, dressing habits, speaking, etc. Now elaborate on some emotional, psychological, or social history for this person. What does this person think? Consider what event or person might threaten that person in some way. Write the first scene that would push that person toward the obstacle, then a scene in which the person confronts that obstacle. Then write some scene or scenes in between.

Once you start to understand "story," Aristotle, narrative, and other aspects of form, you may begin to see conflicts—and thus stories—everywhere.

Warning: Avoid Godzilla and sledgehammers.

1) Sentimentality is a sledgehammer. It is unearned emotion. Rather than creating an emotion, it appeals to emotions that we already have. Puppies, kitties, small children shouldn't be hurt. TV preachers, advertisers, politicians, and propagandists frequently use sentimentality as a tactic because it is easy. Commercial television and movies are full of sentimentality. Sex, violence, and romance are often other forms of sentimentality because they beg for an emotional response.

2) Genre fiction is like Godzilla. The monster lives inside you, right next to what you enjoy. So when you try to duplicate what you are fond of, it often comes out as heavy-footed as Godzilla.

3) Most of us lead passive lives, but our fiction should create some form of movement. If not physical, at least emotional or psychological. Consequently, as Burroway advises, we should avoid totally passive characters.

Terms from Tragedy, Plot, and Character

Learn the following terms in order to critique later stories.

1. imitate reality through adding order and harmony to chaos
2. excites pity and fear
3. insurmountable obstacle
4. appealing protagonist
5. high-born or noble
6. tragic flaw
7. recognition
8. pathetic and tragic
9. certain magnitude
10. suffers more than is warranted
11. antagonist
12. comedy presents men as worse than they are
13. tragedy presents men as better than they are
14. uunity of parts (scenes)
15. no part greater than the whole
16. in medias res
17. Deus Ex Machina
18. delight
19. catharsis
20. situational, dramatic, verbal, and cosmic irony.

Other terms from narrative:
1. epiphany
2. static and dynamic characters
3. flat and round characters.

Description and Narration

With a knowledge of Aristotle's *Poetics*, you have an idea of form. You know where the scenes are supposed to go. But how do we fill up these scenes? George Bluestone, a film critic from the 1920s, in comparing film and novels, commented that fiction is organized according to time and appeals to time, and film is organized around space. He goes on to say that, because its bearing is on time, fiction is much more successful in conveying thought. In fact, fiction is better than most dramatic mediums at approximating thought and showing the past and present working simultaneously on a character.

Think about what you do when you read. You probably resist the temptation to skip ahead to see what happens because the story that you are reading is taking place through time. If you go to a movie, you don't want to skip ahead. You want to look at what is happening NOW in front of you. You want to see and enjoy the images on the screen.

In *Annie Hall*, Woody Allen disrupts chronology, but we really aren't bothered because we like looking at the scenes, the spaces. But when Faulkner disrupts chronology in *The Sound and Fury*, we are terribly confused. So the screenwriter knows that we will watch those spaces, those details, the onscreen IMAGE. And any time a cinematographer or director points a movie camera at some target, even if it is just a short close up, that moviemaker knows that dozens of details will show up on the screen. If you pause a movie and study the "stilled" picture, you can see the details that you might have consciously missed. Details aren't the problem for the screenwriter. She wants to keep the story going and provide context. When the screenwriter writes, "The armies clash," the director, producer, and studio heads have headaches and heart attacks. But they forget that the able screenwriter has supplied the context that makes that clash important. So the screenwriter does not merely write a blueprint for a movie but also provides the drama's overall importance. As a result, the screenwriter is less concerned with the details, which are the strength of the movie, and more concerned with the "time," the overall drama.

The fiction writer, however, does not a have a camera to fill a screen with details. He must provide those details. And those details will never be as immediate as a movie's. So the fiction writer must cheat; he must supply—THROUGH WORDS—those details. These details should take the form of emotional appeals—or images. Tangible things that, as poet Richard Hugo says, "trigger" an emotion. Fiction, as with any art form, works through emotion, and the way to emotion is through sensual detail, images, and references to the five senses.

So as Hemingway said, and every writer and writing instructor repeats, SHOW DON'T TELL. Use details, use the elements of direct character presentation—appearance, dialogue, thought, and action—to create the story. And as Burroway says, these details should be more than just a bombardment of sensual appeals. Rather, they should be significant details, ones that work to give a dramatic impression.

Story writer Laurie Drummond explains that individual scenes cannot hope to provide the whole plot. At best a scene or parts of a scene provides *tension*. So a scene within a short story uses significant details (sensual appeals) to build conflict.

Flannery O'Connor, speaking to cadets at West Point, said that the start of every story—indeed the first paragraph—should appeal to at least three of our senses. Sensual appeals create imagery, and imagery need not be solely visual. We have to get through time in a fiction, but fiction relies on actual scenes. Summary tells us background, what happened; scene puts in the midst of the action.

Remember Freshman Comp

Most textbooks discuss *description* and *narration*, but the terms can be confusing. Teachers have told us our writing should be "descriptive." Yet they also said to tell a story. The two rhetorical modes, description and narration, are very close together and almost self-evident in any writing. Nouns in our language describe something that we see in Newtonian terms as a fixed spatial object. Verbs are used to show motion. Thus any sentence is likely to contain both narration and description; that is, it occupies space and designates some time.

On one hand, *description* is a term that teachers use to describe a quality in writing. This quality is specificity. Writers should use concrete nouns and active verbs if they wish to write descriptive essays. On the other hand, *description* as a rhetorical mode organizes the essay spatially while *narration* seeks to organize it around chronology. However, given the nature of our language and the way we use it, narration, like any other rhetorical mode, must have description to be effective. So stories need some description, some spatial specificity, as well as narration, because we see, feel, and think mostly in spatial terms.

To restate, *description* arranges writing according to space. It will employ transitions like *over, beyond, across, under, over,* etc. Narration, conversely, organizes an essay or a section of writing according to time. It will have transitions like *after, before, during, while, meanwhile, three months later.*

Description is vital to writing because it emphasizes place. It appeals to the five senses, uses imagery, and shows rather than tells. Narration is not as vital as description because all stories fundamentally concentrate on a limited number of spaces. Many students write narrative like kids describe an exciting movie. The description comes back as time: and then, and then, and then, and then. There is no detail, no showing, no senses; it just jumps from one time to another. While a narrative may be organized around a series of times, each time ought to slow down, stop, and *describe* some spaces.

Look at this chart.

Time	Space
Fiction (so we must cheat to get space)	Film (so we must cheat to get time)
Narration	Description
Tell	Show: significant detail, sensual appeal, imagery
Summary	Scene
Indirect Character Presentation (telling about a character)	Direct Character Presentation —appearance, action, appearance, speech, thought.

As the left hand column shows, because fiction is necessarily governed by time, it is a part of any writing. But the idea is to cheat to the right, to try to include as much space as possible.

Figurative Language: Its Care and Use

Metaphor, symbol, allegory, and imagery are vital to all sorts of writing. In fact, even technical writing depends upon metaphor. Think about your car. It has shoes, drums, diaphragms, chokes, and throttles. Circuitry has male and female plugs.

The use of figurative language, especially in technical writing, makes ideas and things more vivid. Concrete nouns and active verbs make for good writing in that they make a sentence vivid. They do so because they create images. We respond best to images because they have sensual appeal. We respond to what we can sense: taste, feel, see, hear, or smell. Poetry tries to communicate primarily through imagery, so poetry is the most concrete and specific language that we have. Before they understand a poem, readers frequently sense the poem. Poetry can teach the fiction writer, the technical writer, and the wise manager a lot about communication. Using concrete nouns and active verbs offers a good start to writing poetry.

Fiction too, as we've seen, relies on vivid imagery. However, when students turn to writing essays about ideas, concepts, or theory—as they are asked to do in history, science, business, computer science, sociology, etc.—then active verbs become scarce. Then concrete nouns go. Writing about the United States' foreign policy during the 1950s might not bring to mind active verbs and concrete nouns, but the rules still hold. Like all exercises, training and repetition are important.

But sometimes those verbs and nouns aren't there, so the writer should illustrate through modification. The writer should get specific through modification. The writer should start to create images in adverbial and adjectival constructions. Look at the following sentence:

The Soviet Union, a wounded, starving tiger after World War II, clawed its way to being a superpower by the 1960s.

1) The appositive "a wounded, starving tiger" compares the Soviet Union to a tiger. It attaches an image to the Soviet Union. So it is acting as a metaphor.
2) What does "clawed" suggest? That's right, a tiger. "A wounded, starving tiger after World War II" suggests a fierce cat.
3) This is a *submerged metaphor*. Active verbs can readily create submerged metaphors. But don't overdo this technique. As with

any figurative device, if used too much, it calls attention to itself. Using active verbs that give human qualities to inanimate things can get syrupy, cloying, overly sweet, bad for diabetics—creating what John Ruskin called the *pathetic fallacy*. Too much of this humanizing of inanimate objects is like taking steroids: the muscles show but don't look natural.

4) Notice that these "metaphors" illustrate the Soviet Union, but they prove nothing about it. The deductive method—syllogistic reasoning—proves. The inductive method—examples, facts, figures, data, statistics, experiments, tests—offers evidence, suggests likelihood. Allegories and metaphors illustrate but prove nothing. To prove, a writer needs the nitty-gritty, the sweat, the hard work, the hours in the gym lifting. Terrible decisions are sometimes made based on analogies rather than proof—the domino theory in Southeast Asia, America as a cowboy or a gunfighter. In reading and writing, the writer and the reader must wade through the research.

Here is a near cliché. A cliché usually starts out as an image or metaphor, but it gets used so much that it becomes practically meaningless. You should avoid clichés, but I'm going to use one.

In 1962, during the Cuban missile crisis, Kennedy and Khrushchev, representatives of two views of the Western world, stood eyeball to eyeball, hands at their sides, about to draw. After thirteen tense days, with U.S. military urging Kennedy to draw, Khrushchev blinked. Thus, the two men averted a catastrophic shoot out.

1) This is a cliché because the metaphor of an old west shootout for the Cuban missile crisis has been used extensively.
2) Look at the submerged metaphors.
3) Are any of the metaphors mixed? That is, do I introduce any images that create a different metaphor?
4) Do you see how I extended the metaphor?
5) Does this metaphor work, or is it a cliché?
6) Is there any modification that adds information without necessarily adding to the metaphor? (Look at "blinked." This submerged metaphor almost mixes the metaphor.) *Do not mix*

metaphors. If you start an extended metaphor, don't shift to another.

Remember, the basic strengthening exercises are important. One way to add imagery is to use concrete nouns and active verbs whenever possible. This practice first takes strain, then repetition, and then some heavy lifting.

I have been comparing writing to weightlifting, but I never say the word *weightlifting.* I use *metonymy,* words closely associated with weightlifting, or *synecdoche,* words that are a part of weightlifting. I never name the figurative term itself. Did this extended metaphor help your understanding? Does it distract? Did I use it too much? Did I mix any of it?

Image, Symbol, and Metaphor

Image

At the basis of any figurative writing is the image, which is an appeal to one of the five senses: touch, taste, smell, sound, sight. Imagery starts with specifics. It starts with concrete nouns and active verbs. With the sensual appeal comes an emotional response, a vivid transfer of information through words. In sensual appeals, language transcends itself, as John Gardner says. Thus, with imagery the reader goes through the words to a nearly-direct experience. A person gains experience without having had the direct experience himself. A reader gets vicarious experience. His life gest larger without experiencing the difficulties that he reads about. This vicarious experience is among the attributes that art provides.

Symbol

A symbol is not something that requires a decoder ring. It is not something that the writer or the reader makes up. It is something that the writer *creates* and the reader *discovers*. A symbol is first and foremost an image. It never stops being an image. However, through repetition, placement, context, and associations, an image gathers meaning beyond the literal. Throughout *The Great Gatsby*, Fitzgerald refers to the green light at the end of Daisy's pier. Jay Gatsby stares at the light from his mansion across the bay from Daisy's mansion and pines for her. Fitzgerald mentions this light several times. At the end of the novel, he mentions that the original settlers, the Dutch sailors, were inspired beyond their imaginations by the "fresh green breast of the new world." Fitzgerald then reminds us that their view was much like Gatsby's. Thus, through repetition (lots of reference to *green*), association (Gatsby and the sailors), placement (at the end of the novel), and context (the longing embodied in looking at green), the green light at the end of Daisy's dock becomes a symbol in the novel. The color green becomes symbolic. But the symbolic value of green is closely related to the literal color and to the light at the end of that pier. The more that we respond to the color and to the light at the end of pier, the richer its symbolic value becomes.

Some advice to writers about symbolism: Do not set out to create symbols. Intention usually spoils the symbols. Symbols come about when the writer looks at what he has written and sees what his consistent imagery suggests. Symbolism comes about in later drafts.

Metaphor
(Here I borrow liberally from Laurence Perrine's
Literature: Structure, Sound, and Sense)

A metaphor has a *literal side* (the subject or term actually being discussed) and *a figurative side* (the illustration of the term).

1) The literal term is usually an abstraction and becomes clearer when the abstraction is compared to a more concrete or specific term.

2) Now, if you are ahead of this game (there's a metaphor), you know that an image is specific and concrete. So an image is the figurative side of a metaphor. If the writer says that the literal side "is like" the figurative side, then this is a *simile.*

    When Robert Burns says, "my love is like a red, red rose," *love* is the abstract literal term. *Red, red, rose* is the more specific figurative term. The more we look at the specific figurative term, the more we know about love. Love is perfectly beautiful, like a rose. Love is perfectly symmetrical, like a rose. Love is red, like a rose. Thus love is hot, like a rose. Love has thorns. . . . That simple metaphoric comparison shows us about love and adds complexity to it. However, don't use Burns's line. So many people have used it so many times that it has become a cliché.

3) The literal side of the metaphor can be named or implied. The figurative side of the metaphor can be named or implied. Two ways to imply are

    a. *synecdoche* (implying by appealing to a part of the whole) and

    b. *metonymy* (implying by appealing to something closely associated with the term).

In my extended metaphor about writing being like weightlifting, I named *writing* (the literal term), but I used things closely associated with weightlifting or a part of weightlifting—"toned," "buff," "muscles," "strengthen," "lift"—to imply the figurative side of my metaphor. *Notice that these associative terms or parts for the whole are concrete nouns, active verbs, or adjectives.*

In his classic poem the "Love Song of J. Alfred Prufrock," T. S. Eliot says the following famous lines:

> I should have been a pair of ragged claws
> Scuttling across the floor of silent seas.

In these lines, Prufrock compares himself to a crab by using "ragged claws," a part for the whole, synecdoche. Then he writes, "scuttling across the floor of silent seas," something associated with a crab, metonymy. Prufrock sees himself as a crab. So? Crabs are scavengers, living off what sinks to the bottom of the sea. Crabs don't really think; they act on instinct. Crabs move backwards. Some people may find crabs lowly, disgusting creatures. You get the idea.

Figurative Language Abbreviated:

1. Try to be as specific as possible. Use concrete nouns and active verbs.
2. If the content robs you of concrete nouns, use modification to add specificity and illustration.
3. Use similes, submerged metaphors (being careful to avoid cuteness and triteness), extended metaphors, and implied metaphors to illustrate, explain, and clarify.
4. Remember that illustration is not proof.
5. Use symbols sparingly. If you use them, let them arise out of your writing, in the second, third, or fourth draft.

Warning: Be wary of Godzilla.
Godzilla lives inside you, and he wants to stomp Bambi. You will be tempted to TELL us what to think in order to make sure that we are getting it. You will also want to write "pretty." You will want to use similes and adverbs. Don't—or use them sparingly. These Godzillas are monsters that all writers have to deal with.

Warning: Don't use a sledgehammer.
Don't bludgeon us with violence, aliens, etc. Be gentle.

Showing, Even in Telling

[I make comments in Verdana font and set off in brackets.]

Read through these excerpts and note the writers' use of what Burroway calls "significant detail," the fact or image that captures the tension or movement within a scene. Then read through these passages again and try to note whether they are primarily scene or summary and note whether they show direct or indirect characterization. If they show direct characterization, do the writers use *appearance, action, speech,* or *thought*? If the passages are *summary,* are they primarily *telling*? If so, note how, for the authors of these passages might also *show* you something.

Finally, in preparation for the next section of the course, note the nature of the speakers in these passages. What do they know, how smart are they, what quirks to they have?

F. Scott Fitzgerald, *The Great Gatsby*

"Daisy! Daisy!" shouted Mrs. Wilson. "I'll say it whenever I want to! Daisy! Dai—"

Making a short deft movement Tom Buchanan broke her nose with his open hand.

[Tom Buchanan, a former college football player, gives Myrtle a classic forearm shiver. He is married to Daisy and has asked his mistress, Mrs. Wilson, not to mention his wife's name. She defies him. What does this one sentence show us about Tom?]

Ernest Hemingway, "The Killers."

"That's right," George said

"So you think that's right?" Al asked George.

"Sure."

"You're a pretty bright boy, aren't you?"

"Sure," said George

"Well, you're not," said the other little man. "Is he, Al?"

"He's dumb," said Al. He turned to Nick. "What's your name?"

[Look at the start of the dialog and especially at "You're a pretty bright boy . . ." Should Nick be scared?]

Flannery O'Connor, "A Good Man is Hard to Find."

It came to a stop just over them and for some minutes, the driver looked down with a steady expressionless gaze to where they were sitting, and didn't speak. Then he turned his head and muttered something to the other two and they got out. One was a fat boy in black trousers and a red sweat shirt with a sliver stallion embossed on the front of it. He moved around on the right side of them and stood staring, his mouth partly open in a kind of loose grin. The other had on khaki pants and a blue striped coat and a gray hat pulled down very low, hiding most of his face. He came around slowly on the left side. Neither spoke.

The driver got out of the car and stood by the side of it, looking down at them. He was an older man than the other two. His hair was just beginning to gray and he wore silver-rimmed spectacles that gave him a scholarly look. He had a long creased face and didn't have on any shirt or undershirt. He had on blue jeans that were too tight for him and was holding a black hat and a gun. The two boys also had guns.

[Notice the rhythm and pace of the passage. O'Connor tracks the men as they come out the car. This view is from a family that has just had a car wreck. The one boy in a sweat shirt seems childish or addled. Now look at the second paragraph. O'Connor gives nothing threatening about the driver, nothing very threatening about any of them. But look at the next to last sentence. O'Connor—in parallel sentence structure lists that the man had on blue jeans and held a gun. You would think that the gun would be more important. But she hides that fact from us by not putting in a main clause. Now she gives us the information about more guns in a full clause. We now know that the family members looking at these strangers are in very deep trouble.]

Flannery O'Connor, "A Good Man is Hard to Find"

The grandmother didn't want to go to Florida. She wanted to visit some of her connections in east Tennessee and she was seizing at every chance to change Bailey's mind. Bailey was the son she lived with, her only boy. He was sitting on the edge of his chair at the table, bent over the orange sports section of the Journal. "Now look here, Bailey," she said, "see here, read this," and she stood with one hand on her thin hip and the other rattling the newspaper at his bald head. "Here this fellow that calls himself the Misfit is aloose from the Federal Pen and headed toward Florida and you read here what it says he did to these people. Just you read it. I wouldn't take my children in any direction with a criminal like that aloose in it. I couldn't answer to my conscience I did."

Bailey didn't look up from his reading so she wheeled around and faced the children's mother, a young woman in slacks, whose face was as broad and innocent as a cabbage and was tied round with a green head-kerchief that had two points on the top like a rabbit's ears. She was sitting on the sofa, feeding the baby his apricots out of a jar. "The children have been to Florida before," the old lady said. "You all ought to take them somewhere else for a change so they would see different parts of the world and be broad. They never have been to east Tennessee." The children's mother didn't seem to hear her but the eight-year-old boy, John Wesley, a stocky child with glasses, said, "If you don't want to go to Florida, why dontcha stay at home?" He and little girl, June Star, were reading the funny papers on the floor. "She wouldn't stay at home to be queen for a day," June Star said without raising her yellow head.

[Again, look at movement, speech, and appearance, or direct character presentation. How does O'Connor characterize these people?]

Flannery O'Connor, "Good Country People"

Besides the neutral expression that she wore when she was alone, Mrs. Freeman had two others, forward and reverse, that she used for all of her human dealings. Her forward expression was steady and driving like the advance of a heavy truck. Her eyes never swerved to the left or right but turned as the story turned as if they followed a yellow line down the center of it. She seldom used the other expression because it was not often necessary for her to retract a statement, but when she did, her face came to a complete stop. . .

[Look at the imagery. Now look at the words that connote a car or driving a car. See how, without naming a car, O'Connor compares Mrs. Freeman to a car. Now, through that submerged or unnamed metaphor, how is Mrs. Freeman characterized? Again, how smart is she?]

Flannery O'Connor, "Greenleaf"

The next morning as soon as Mr. Greenleaf came to the back door, she told him there was a stray bull on the place and that she wanted him penned up at once.

"Done already been here three days," he said, addressing his right foot which he held forward, turned slightly as if he were trying to look at the sole. He was standing at the bottom of the three back steps while she leaned out the kitchen door, a small woman with pale near-sighted eyes and gray hair that rose on top like the crest of some disturbed bird.

"Three days!" she said in the restrained screech that had become habitual with her.

Mr. Greenleaf, looking into the distance over the near pasture, removed a package of cigarettes from his shirt pocket and let one fall into his hand. He put the package back and stood for a while looking at the cigarette. "I put him in the bull pen but he torn out of there," he said presently. "I didn't see him none after that." He bent over the cigarette and lit it and then turned his head briefly in her direction. The upper part of his face sloped gradually in the lower which was long and narrow, shaped like a rough chalice. He had deep-set fox-colored eyes shadowed under a gray felt hat that he wore slanted forward following the line of his nose. His build was insignificant.

[How does O'Connor characterize Mr. Greenleaf through his actions, the way he stares at his foot? By the time she says that his build was insignificant, why do we already know this? How smart is he? Has he ever stood up to Mrs. May, the "she" of the first sentence?]

Larry McMurtry, *Lonesome Dove*

When Augustus came out on the porch the blue pigs were eating a rattlesnake—not a very big one. It had probably just been crawling around looking for shade when it ran into the pigs. They were having a fine tug-of-war with it, and its rattling days were over. The sow had it by the neck, and the shoat had the tail.

"You pigs git," Augustus said, kicking the shoat. "Head on down to the creek if you want to eat that snake." It was the porch he begrudged them, not the snake. Pigs on the porch just made things hotter, and things were already hot enough. He stepped down into the dusty yard and walked around to the springhouse to get his jug. The sun was still high, sulled in the sky like a mule, but Augustus had a keen eye for sun, and to his eye the long light from the west had taken on an encouraging slant.

Evening took a long time getting to Lonesome Dove, but when it came it was a comfort. For most of the hours of the day—and most of the months of the year—the sun had the town trapped deep in dust, far out in the chaparral flats, a heaven for snakes and horned toads, roadrunners and stinging lizards, but a hell for pigs and Tennesseans. There was not even a respectable shade tree within twenty or thirty miles; in fact, the actual location of the nearest decent shade was a matter of vigorous debate in the offices—if you wanted to call a roofless barn and a couple of patched-up corrals offices—of the Hat Creek Cattle Company, half of which Augustus owned.

[Snake-eating pigs? You just have to keep reading, don't you? And those are some tough pigs and an unlucky snake. By the second paragraph we're back with Agustus McCrae and learn that he just wants to keep cool. He wants the porch. In the third paragraph, look at the details and the way that the narrator uses them to show just how hot south Texas is.]

Oscar Casares, "Chango"

Bony was walking back from the Jiffy-Mart when he found the monkey's head. There it was, under the small palm tree in the front yard, just staring up at him like an old friend who couldn't remember his name. It freaked him out bad. The dude had to check around to make sure nobody had seen him jump back and almost drop his beer in the dirt. It was still lunchtime and cars were parked up and down the street. For a second, it looked like the head might be growing out of the ground. Maybe somebody had buried the monkey up to its neck the way people did to other people at the beach when they ran out of things to do. Maybe it was still alive. Bony grabbed a broom off the porch and swung hard. He stopped an inch away from the monkey's little black eyes, and it didn't blink. He poked the head with the straw end of the broom and it tipped back and forth. The short black hairs on its head were pointed straight up at the cloudy sky. The nose was flat and wrinkled around the edges like it'd been a normal nose and then God decided to push it in with His big thumb. The ears were old man's ears with whiskers growing on them and in them. And it kept smiling. It smiled from one monkey ear to the other. [How does the monkey's head come to suggest Bony's nature and character?]

Tim O'Brien, *Going After Cacciato*

It was a bad time. Billy Boy Watkins was dead, and so was Frenchie Tucker. Billy Boy had died of fright, scared to death on the field of battle, and Frenchie Tucker had been shot through the nose. Bernie Lynn and Lieutenant Sidney Martin had died in tunnels. Pederson was dead and Rudy Chassler was dead. Buff was dead. Ready Mix was dead. They were all among the dead. The rain fed fungus that grew in the men's boots and socks, and their socks rotted, and their feet turned white and soft so that the skin could be scraped off with a fingernail, and Stink Harris woke up screaming one night with a leech on his tongue. When it was not raining, a low mist moved across the paddies, blending the elements into a single gray element, and the war was cold and pasty and rotten. Lieutenant Corson, who came to replace Lieutenant Sidney Martin, contracted the dysentery. The trip flares were useless. The ammunition corroded and the foxholes filled with mud and water during the nights, and in the mornings there was always the next village; and the war was always the same. The monsoons were part of the war. In early September Vaught caught an infection. He'd been showing Oscar Johnson the sharp edge on his bayonet, drawing it swiftly along his forearm to peel off a layer of mushy skin. "Like a Gillette Blue Blade," Vaught had said proudly. There was no blood, but in two days the bacteria soaked in and the arm turned yellow, so they bundled him up and called in a dustoff, and Vaught left the war. He never came back. Later they had a letter from him that described Japan as smoky and full of slopes, but in the enclosed snapshot Vaught looked happy enough, posing with two sightly nurses, a wine bottle rising from between his thighs. It was a shock to learn he'd lost the arm. Soon afterward Ben Nystrom shot himself through the foot, but he did not die, and he wrote no letters. These were all things to joke about. The rain, too. And the cold. Oscar Johnson said it made him think of Detroit in the month of May. "Lootin' weather," he liked to say. "The dark an' gloom, just right for rape an' lootin'." Then someone would say that Oscar had a swell imagination for a darkie.

That was one of the jokes. There was a joke about Oscar. There were many jokes about Billy Boy Watkins, the way he'd collapsed of fright on the field of battle. Another joke was about the lieutenant's dysentery, and another was about Paul Berlin's purple biles. There were jokes about the postcard pictures of Christ that Jim Pederson used to carry, and Stink's ringworm, and the way Buff's helmet filled with life after death. Some of the jokes were about Cacciato. Dumb as a bullet, Stink said. Dumb as a month-old oyster fart, said Harold Murphy.

In October, near the end of the month, Cacciato left the war.

"He's gone away," said Doc Peret. "Split, departed."

Lieutenant Corson did not seem to hear. He was too old to be a lieutenant. The veins in his nose and cheeks were broken. His back was weak. Once he had been a captain on the way to becoming a major, but whiskey and the fourteen dull years between Korea and Vietnam had ended all that, and now he was just an old lieutenant with the dysentery.

He lay on his back in the pagoda, naked except for green socks and green undershorts.

"Cacciato," Doc repeated. "The kid's left us. Split for parts unknown."

The lieutenant did not sit up. With one hand he cupped his belly, with the other he guarded a red glow. The surfaces of his eyes were moist.

"Gone to Paris," Doc said.

The lieutenant put the glow to his lips. Inhaling, his chest did not move. There were no vital signs in the wrists or thick stomach.

"Paris," Doc Peret repeated.

"That's what he tells Paul Berlin, and that's what Berlin tells me, and that's what I'm telling you. The chain of command, a truly splendid instrument of ... Anyhow, Cacciato's gone. Packed up and retired."

The lieutenant exhaled.

Blue gunpowder haze produced musical sighs in the gloom, a stirring at the base of Buddha's clay feet. "Lovely," a voice said. Someone else sighed. The lieutenant blinked, coughed, and handed the spent roach to Oscar Johnson, who extinguished it against his toe-nail.

"Paree?" the lieutenant said softly. "Gay Paree?"

Doc nodded. "That's what he told Paul Berlin and that's what I'm telling you. Ought to cover up, sir."

Sighing, swallowing hard, Lieutenant Corson pushed himself up and sat stiffly before a can of Sterno. He lit the Sterno and placed his hands behind the flame and bent forward to draw in heat. Outside, the rain was steady. "So," the old man said. "Let's . . . let's figure this out." He gazed at the flame.

[Look at the opening paragraph. How many of your senses are assaulted? What is your emotional response to some the details: a leech on the tongue?]

Tim O'Brien, *The Things They Carried*

First Lieutenant Jimmy Cross carried letters from a girl named Martha, a junior at Mount Sebastian College in New Jersey. They were not love letters, but Lieutenant Cross was hoping, so he kept them folded in plastic at the bottom of his rucksack. In the late afternoon, after a day's march, he would dig his foxhole, wash his hands under a canteen, unwrap the letters, hold them with the tips of his fingers, and spend the last hour of light pretending. He would imagine romantic camping trips into the White Mountains in New Hampshire. He would sometimes taste the envelope flaps, knowing her tongue had been there. More than anything, he wanted Martha to love him as he loved her, but the letters were mostly chatty, elusive on the matter of love. She was a virgin, he was almost sure. She was an English major at Mount Sebastian, and she wrote beautifully about her professors and roommates and midterm exams, about her respect for Chaucer and her great affection for Virginia Woolf. She often quoted lines of poetry; she never mentioned the war, except to say, Jimmy, take care of yourself. The letters weighed 10 ounces. They were signed Love, Martha, but Lieutenant Cross understood that Love was only a way of signing and did not mean what he sometimes pretended it meant. At dusk, he would carefully return the letters to his rucksack. Slowly, a bit distracted, he would get up and move among his men, checking the perimeter, then at full dark he would return to his hole and watch the night and wonder if Martha was a virgin. [Jimmy Cross nearly becomes obsessive about these letters. They matter the most to him. Eventually his concern for this girl will lead to the death of a soldier. See why O'Brien starts with Jimmy Cross]

The things they carried were largely determined by necessity. **[Keep reading, but then come back to see how the meaning of necessity changes. These items represent emotional, moral or spiritual necessities—or obsessions]**. Among the necessities or near-necessities were P-38 can openers, pocket knives, heat tabs, wristwatches, dog tags, mosquito repellent, chewing gum, candy, cigarettes, salt tablets, packets of Kool'Aid, lighters, matches, sewing kits, Military Payment Certificates, C rations, and two or three canteens of water. Together, these items weighed between 15 and 20 pounds, depending upon a man's habits or rate of metabolism. **[First, the narrator lists the standard military issued necessities and even their weight]**. Henry Dobbins, who was a big man, carried extra rations; he was especially fond of canned peaches in heavy syrup over pound cake. **[Look at the relative clause, the *who* clause, see how this is buried but explains Henry's obsessions]** Dave Jensen, who practiced field hygiene, carried a toothbrush, dental floss, and several hotel-sized bars of soap he'd stolen on R&R in Sydney, Australia. Ted Lavender, who was scared, carried tranquilizers until he was shot in the head outside the village of Than Khe in mid-April. **[Look at all the *who* clauses and then note how they set up what these men carried.]** By necessity, and because it was SOP, they all carried steel helmets that weighed 5 pounds including the liner and camouflage cover. They carried the standard fatigue jackets and trousers. Very few carried underwear. On their feet they carried jungle boots—2.1 pounds—and **[SOP, military issued, but now look what comes up in the same sentence]** Dave Jensen **[hygiene remember?]** carried three pairs of socks and a can of Dr. Scholl's foot powder as a precaution against trench foot. Until he was shot, Ted Lavender carried six or seven ounces of premium dope, which for him was a necessity. **[Look back above at what he carries and look at the irony that for him dope would indeed be a necessity.]** Mitchell Sanders, the RTO, carried condoms. **[Who is he going to meet out in the junge?]** Norman Bowker carried a diary. **[Egotistical, isn't he?]** Rat Kiley carried comic books. Kiowa, a devout Baptist, carried an illustrated New Testament that had been presented to him by his father, who taught Sunday school in Oklahoma City, Oklahoma. As a hedge against bad times, however, Kiowa also carried his grandmother's distrust of the white man, his grandfather's old hunting hatchet. Necessity dictated. [Look at the irony here. Look at how necessity gets new meaning] Because the land was mined and booby-trapped, it was SOP for each man to carry a steel-centered, nylon-covered flak jacket, which weighed 6.7 pounds, but which on hot days seemed much heavier. Because you could die so quickly, each man carried at least one large compress bandage, usually in the helmet band for easy access. Because the nights were cold, and because the monsoons were wet, each carried a green plastic poncho that could be used as a raincoat or groundsheet or makeshift tent. With its quilted liner, the poncho weighed almost two pounds, but it was worth every ounce. In April, for instance, when Ted Lavender was shot, they used his poncho to wrap him up, then to carry him across the paddy, then to lift him into the chopper that took him away.

[Look at how SOP becomes really emotional. You now have the idea about what O'Brien is doing. Now he going to repeat sentence structure, content, manner, and characters. Try to note the revealing details that *shows* by creating irony. Note too that O'Brien is *showing* through his *telling*.]

They were called legs or grunts.

To carry something was to hump it, as when Lieutenant Jimmy Cross humped his love for Martha up the hills and through the swamps. In its intransitive form, to hump meant to walk, or to march, but it implied burdens far beyond the intransitive.

Almost everyone humped photographs. In his wallet, Lieutenant Cross carried two photographs of Martha. The first was a Kodacolor snapshot signed Love, though he knew better. She stood against a brick wall. Her eyes were gray and neutral, her lips slightly open as she stared straight-on at the camera. At night, sometimes, Lieutenant Cross wondered who had taken the picture, because he knew she had boyfriends, because he loved her so much, and because he could see the shadow of the picture-taker spreading out against the brick wall. The second photograph had been clipped from the 1968 Mount Sebastian yearbook. It was an action shot—women's volleyball—and Martha was bent horizontal to the floor, reaching, the palms of her hands in sharp focus, the tongue taut, the expression frank and competitive. There was no visible sweat. She wore white gym shorts. Her legs, he thought, were almost certainly the legs of a virgin, dry and without hair, the left knee cocked and carrying her entire weight, which was just over one hundred pounds. Lieutenant Cross remembered touching that left knee. A dark theater, he remembered, and the movie was Bonnie *and Clyde,* and Martha wore a tweed skirt, and during the final scene, when he touched her knee, she turned and looked at him in a sad, sober way that made him pull his hand back, but he would always remember the feel of the tweed skirt and the knee beneath it and the sound of the gunfire that killed Bonnie and Clyde, how embarrassing it was, how slow and oppressive. He remember kissing her good night at the dorm door. Right then, he thought, he should've done something brave. He should've carried her up the stairs to her room and tied her to the bed and touched that left knee all night long. He should've risked it. Whenever he looked at the photographs, he thought of new things he should've done.

[This piece is almost all *telling*, but notice how the concrete items that each man carries becomes a sign or symbol or indicator of what most scares him, characterizes him, or concerns him. So these objects, even with O'Brien's narrator telling us about them, show us the men. We could spend several weeks looking at this passage.]

David Rhodes, *Rock Island Line*, 1975, as quoted in John Gardner, *On Becoming a Novelist*, 1983

The old people remember Della and Wilson Montgomery as clearly as if just last Sunday after the church pot-luck dinner they had climbed into their gray Chevrolet and driven back out to their country home, Della waving from the window and Wilson leaning over the wheel, steering with both hands. They can remember as if just yesterday they had driven by the Montgomerys' brownstone house and seen them sitting on their porch swing, Wilson rocking it slowly and conscientiously back and forth, Della smiling, her small feet only touching the floor on the back swing, both of them looking like careful, quiet children.

Della's hands were so small they could be put into small-mouth jars. For many years she was their only schoolteacher, and, except for the younger ones, they all had her, and wanted desperately to do well with spelling and numbers to please her. Without fail, screaming children would hush and hum in her arms. It was thought, among the women, that it was not necessary to seek help or comfort in times of need, because Della would sense it in the air and come. The old people don't talk of her now but what a shadow is cast over their faces and they seem to be talking about parts of themselves—not just that Della belonged to the old days, but that when she and Wilson were gone it was unnatural that anything else from back then should go on without them.

[This passage is mainly summary, but look at the "habitual details." These details are what happened again and again, not just once. Look at the first sentence. Look at how Rhodes keeps the action moving through participle ("steering with both hands) and absolute phrases ("Della waving," "Wilson leaning over the wheel"). Now ask yourself, as John Gardner does in *On Becoming a Novelist*, how fast does Wilson drive? Now look at the second sentence. Again notice the absolute and participle phrases. The phrases keep the action moving. Who is deliberate, methodical, careful? Who is frantic, jumpy, small?

Now look at the details and sentence structure from the next sentence. How small is Della now? She is not just small but almost magically petite. Her hands fit into small-mouth jars. And she has some kind of special effect on children. And she shows up through some special feeling. She is a magical sprite. The townspeople talk about the Montgomerys as though they were parts of the townspeople—like a liver or kidney? But this is all telling, and the Montgomerys are gone. And now, you want to sigh. See how even in summary, writers use scene? See how the voice is vital in this presentation. See how you get a picture of the person telling you about Della and Wilson? See how more succinctly Rhodes delivers his images than I deliver my critique?]

Wayne C. Booth

I first read Wayne C. Booth's *Rhetoric of Fiction* way back in the dark ages when I was in graduate school. After three years, I sort of understood this incisive but difficult book. For more than twenty years, I've made use of Booth's book in my teaching. So over years of using Booth, I'm not sure what's me and what's him (and what's common knowledge). (Notice that I use the wrong pronoun case above: *me* instead of *I*, *him* instead of *he*. But notice how my persona would shift if I used the correct pronoun. I'd sound uppity.) My point here is that the writer gets confused as to his influences. So writers do the best they can to document what they can.

In rhetoric or composition classes, you probably learned something like Maxine Hairston's map suggesting that any writing consists of a persona, an audience, and a purpose—as well as the content. Each influences the other. She draws squares.

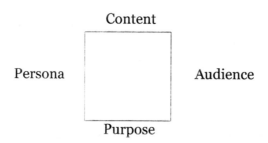

Content

Persona   Audience

Purpose

Persona is based on the term for the masks that Greek actors wore. These masks showed despair, anger, happiness, etc. The Greeks worried that, if an audience saw, say, Tom Cruise on the stage, the audience would say, "Hey, that's Tom Cruise," and totally forget that Tom Cruise is *acting* as though he is Oedipus.

I add that, given the situation or the writing task, this square would shift positions and become weird parallelograms. For instance, a person making a political speech may want to emphasize audience. Is it a friendly audience from the same party? Is it a news show or report? Is it an antagonistic audience? So the square could become any number of four-sided shapes.

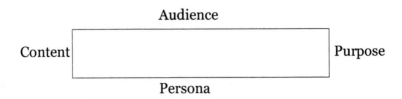

A newspaper report strives for "objectivity," will de-emphasize Persona and emphasize content.

Technical writing will have a similar shape to the above. It purports to be solely content.

Now think about some of the ramifications in this rhetorical setup. Scientists and students in lab reports use the passive voice in order to be, mistakenly, "objective." In other words they try to avoid saying "I." So instead of saying, "I injected the rabbit," they say, "The rabbit was injected." Who drugged that poor bunny? Journalists claim that a news report is objective. But as with the lab report, a news report is not objective. The reporter arrived after the fact. She was not a witness. She has a form to put the report in. The editor will cut, trim, or change, the story for style. So it is not objective. The report, like the lab report, *has an objective Persona*. Remember this idea. The idea of persona will influence all of your writing. For instance here is a typical college paper:

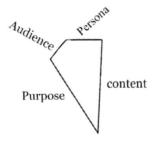

Now let's use another grammar or rhetoric to describe this idea about the interaction of purpose, content, audience, and purpose. This rhetoric or grammar was developed by Wayne C. Booth in *The Rhetoric of Fiction*, first published in 1961.

Look at the squares and shapes above. Suppose that I took one of those shapes and banged it into a straight line so that I had something like the diagram below:

Audience----------------Purpose-----------------Persona------------------Content

This is the shape that Booth uses to describe fiction. But he uses some different names since he is writing about fiction. Instead of content, he says *story*. By story, he means what most people assume fiction is: just "the what happens," just the basic plot. But as Booth well knows, plot is delivered to us through words; thus fiction is a rhetorical medium. A drama is a performance medium. The story is delivered through literal actions, dialogs, scenes. So to understand a story presented through a drama, a viewer needs to know about set design, acting, and staging. The same is true for a story presented through a movie. To fully understand the movie, the movie viewer must understand film technique. So to understand a story presented through writing, one must understand the rhetoric.

Controlling the story, manipulating it, in fact delivering the very words that form the story, is what Booth calls the *narrative persona*, or as most textbooks will say, the narrator. This narrator is some distance away from the story. Some time may have passed since the story took place. Perhaps the narrator is telling about a time when she was a girl. The narrator may be in a different locale from the story and may be missing that locale. The narrator may be talking about someone other than himself. The narrator may not even take part in the story or may not even mention himself (as what happens in third person limited omniscient point of view). The narrator may seem to know everything (as with omniscient point of view). So as you can see, in writing about a narrator or narrative persona, Booth is talking about what textbooks discuss in their chapters on point of view.

The point that Booth makes is that the narrator is at some personal, moral, emotional, psychological, spatial, or temporal distance from the story that he is telling. This distance equals irony. For instance, a narrator may lie, a narrator may be pompous, a narrator may not be of sound mind, a narrator may be bigoted. As some of you may have guessed, now I am talking about the reliability of the narrator. But it is not just the reliability of the narrator that concerns Booth but the whole nature of the narrator. We should be concerned with how he tells the story, with what is on his mind, with what he chooses to discuss (yes, this is true even of omniscient narrators).

However, the author ultimately controls the narrator. And the author has a point, a *purpose*, a theme. When we talk about the theme of a fiction, we say the author's name and use a present tense verb. We attribute what the fiction means to the author. This theme is not the flesh and blood author. So Booth says that we ascribe a controlling force to the fiction. He says that this is the *implied author*—or purpose, theme, point. Like most professors, I use the names of authors and professors as the names of themes, purposes, or ideas.

The implied author is at some moral, emotional, psychological, temporal, chronological distance from the narrator. The implied author may be younger or older than the narrator. The narrator may be unreliable, may be a bigot, may be a liar, may smell bad, so we should trust the implied author more than the narrator. If a reader thinks that narrator Huck Finn is implied author Mark Twain and that Mark Twain agrees with him, then *The Adventures of Huckleberry Finn* is not a very funny book. But if one sees the distance between Mark Twain and Huck Finn, if one sees how the implied author manipulates and controls Huck so as to satirize society, then the book becomes very funny.

Controlling everything is the Reader—or the audience. The Reader can shut the book, can quit reading, so the Reader has the most power.

Now what Booth is doing here, see, is he's saying we don't get the whole story if we just think the happenings is all that a story is. A story ain't just plot but gots a lot more to it than the happenings. That lots more gots to do with the thing what tells the story, which is a narrator thing. And then there's this force, this guy, behind that narrator making him jump through hoops and saying things so as to make some theme. The narrator, see, is like this ragged ol' puppet boy and the implied author is the fella pulling the strings.

What on earth did I do in the paragraph above? Why do you want me to stop? Why did I ruin my essay? I switched narrators. The narrator above uses a more colloquial language than the narrator or persona that you are reading now. Perhaps, because of your associations with that type of language, you assume that the narrator above wasn't as smart, as sophisticated, or as literate as the previous narrator. You were probably annoyed. The distance between the implied author and the narrator became greater. So you were wondering more about how I talked than about what I was saying. Now that my guise, my persona, my narrator is closer to the content and to the implied author and is in a language you would associate more with a textbook, you can trust me and look more closely at what I am saying, rather than how I'm saying it.

So once you establish a method of telling your story or your essay, once you establish a persona, don't change it. If I had started out talking like I do in the italicized paragraph above, you might have been confused, but you would have eventually gotten used to it.

What Booth says is that the rhetoric of fiction depends upon these distances. The following maps of some stories use these terms:

I.A= Implied Author, which equals theme, intent, point, meaning of story

N.P= narrator, which is synonymous with point of view

Story=plot, which is "what happens"

The idea behind these maps is that if the writer slides N.P. slightly toward I.A., then the story changes. The same is true with sliding the N.P. toward the story.

In the following, the narrator would be close to the story, but she might be unreliable because she is so far away from the point of the story.

I.A   N.P.   story

In the following, the narrator is looking back at his story, weighing it, judging it. Perhaps he is commenting and making fun of what happened. But we can trust him because he is close to the I.A.

I.A.   N.P.   story

A note on satire and sarcasm

In the first example, the distance between the N.P. and the I.A., shows what happens in satire. The speaker, the narrator, doesn't realize that he is showing himself to be foolish. In the second example, the narrator is aware that he is making fun, so that narrator may be sarcastic. The difference is in the speaker's awareness. (Remember, sarcasm is neither a crime nor a moral fault).

In the following example, the plot, the content, or "the what happens" is most important. We can generally trust what happened.

I.A.   N.P.   Story

In the following, perhaps a narrator tells about someone else, but we can't trust all that the narrator says, or we don't really know what to make of his own story.

I.A.   N.P.   story

Think of this arrangement between the I.A., N.P. and story as an accordion, stretching out and shrinking, with the middle, the N.P., being the most important.

The point is that there are as many different relations between the I.A. and the NP. and the N.P. and the story as there are stories. You may have noticed that I left off the term reader. Generally, very generally, if there is a great distance between the reader and the I.A., the theme, the point, the purpose of the fiction, the reader quits reading. Now of course, many contemporary literary critics will say that this is precisely what happens, but that point is best addressed by another writer in another course.

A note: Distance equals irony.

A note: Remember Aristotle? Aristotle said that the most effective way to achieve pity and fear, and thus an emotional response to a drama, was through irony. So drama needs irony. So if a story, as most people conceive, has the implied author, narrator, and story crammed up close together, like the following

I.A. N.P. story

Then, the irony must be situational irony arising from the story. How many popular fictions and boring stories have this arrangement without the situational irony.

Very few good fictions rely solely on this scheme. Remember, fiction is rhetorical, not dramatic, so fiction then should have some distance between these elements.

A note for other courses and other types of writing

Of course Booth is talking about fiction, BUT his ideas, which are more difficult to understand than Hairston's, can be applied to nonfiction. As writers, students will want their narrators to change with different assignments, just as their writing purposes may change. So they will want to look at the distances. For an essay in freshman composition that is about a personal experience a student may have the following arrangement.

    I.A.   N.P.   essay

A student may look back at himself and make fun of himself.

    I.A.   N.P.   essay

As student may be sarcastic and make fun of a fellow student or, God forbid, an instructor.

    I.A.   N.P.   essay

A student may write an editorial in which she attacks some local legislation.

    I.A.   N.P.   essay

Or the student may wish to appear to be perfectly objective, and emphasize the material.

    I.A.   N.P.   essay

A note on objectivity and passive voice

I would like to add that I believe that there is no objectivity, not in a lab report (passive voice does not make a lab report objective), not in a textbook. Someone, some intent has to make the narrator/persona/narrative persona choose what to write and how to write it. The only thing that is objective is an objective narrator. Objectivity is really no excuse for writing passive voice.

The point is that understanding Booth's concepts gives a writer more ammunition. Booth is simply looking at the age-old components of rhetoric and coming up with another way of presenting them. With Booth's idea about distance and narrators in mind, students might start reading newspapers, magazines, and editorials a bit differently. With

Booth as a guide, students might see satire, might see that the point that the narrator makes might not be the point of the essay at all. Students might also see the wondrous possibilities in writing. They might also see the wondrous ways that they might adapt their writing to the situation.

A note on traditional point of view

Instructors and eager students anticipating composition II may have noted that Booth gives more in-depth discussion of point of view. As presented by most composition II or introduction to literature courses, point of view consists of four different ways to narrate a story.

1) <u>First Person</u> An "I" narrates the story and, to varying degrees, takes part in the story.

2) <u>Third Person Limited</u> The story is sifted through the consciousness of a "he" or a "she." Some textbooks explain that the main character or the character delivering the story or the character who does the thinking is referred to as "he" or "she."

3) <u>Third Person Omniscient</u> The narrator is god-like, jumping from one "he" or "she" to another, commenting about the whole of creation, or going from commentary to the thoughts of a particular "he" or "she."

4) <u>Third Person Objective</u> The narrator looks only at sight, smell, sound, or touch common to anyone observing. The narrator does not go into any character's head. The narrator, as such, is like a camera.

According to Booth's logic, in first person, the "I" narrator is close to the story, but we might have to wonder how distant the "I" is from the implied author. We should wonder how much we can trust that narrator. A little more distant from the story than most "I" narrators, the third person limited, "he," narrator may be distant from the implied author—because the details and events are sifted through his mind, even though the narration is not in his words. An omniscient narrator can get close to the story or a character and then back up, but overall he still creates a way of telling the story that is his own. An objective point of view will not go into any character's mind, so he will be more distant from the characters than first or third person.

But Booth will allow that this point of view is like a spectrum, with as many "voices" or point of views as there are stories. As Moffet and McElheny say, "every story is first person, whether the speaker is identified or not" (588). That is, each narrator is distinct. Each story has a narrator that has a distinct way of telling the story. That narrator may say "I" or not, may take part in the story or not, may offer a lot of commentary or not.

Now, if you have followed this difficult concept, if you can see the rhetorical manipulation in these fictions, then you can better appreciate what happens in a fiction; you can come to see the difference between film and fiction; you see the "art" in fiction. And if you can manipulate this sort of principle in your own writing, not just in fiction but in all of your writing, then, whether paid for it or not, you may be on your way to becoming an effective writer.

Warning: Godzilla stomps Bambi when the I.A. tries to talk. The I.A. should never utter a word. All the words come through the narrator. However, the Godzilla deep down inside you will make you want to TELL us WHAT HAPPENS, or it will make you ask, "ARE YOU GETTING IT?"

Works Cited

Booth, Wayne C. *The Rhetoric of Fiction.* Chicago: The University of Chicago Press, 1961.

Moffett, James, and Kenneth R. McElheny. eds. *Points of View: An Anthology of Short Stories.* revised ed. New York: Peguin, 1995.

Examples of different uses of Voice

First, look back at the examples that I gave you for showing. Here is a very important question: how do those excerpts *show* the speaker? What is shown and the significant details and the manner in which they are delivered reveal the nature of narrator. Now that you have reconsidered the previous excerpts, *look at these excerpts, especially those that are primarily "telling" and see what they* show *(not* tell*) about the narrator.*

Jay McInerney, *Bright Lights, Big City*

You are not the kind of guy who would be at a place like this at this time of the morning. But here you are, and you cannot say that the terrain is entirely unfamiliar, although the details are fuzzy. You are at a nightclub talking to a girl with a shaved head. . . Somewhere back there you could have cut your losses, but you rode past that moment on a comet trail of white powder and now you are tying to hang on to the rush. Your brain at this moment is composed of brigades of tiny Bolivian soldiers. . . They need the Bolivian Marching Powder.

[This whole novel is written from the "you" point of view. However, does this *you* mean "a person," anyone, the general rhetorical term that we use when referring to people? Or is the narrator really referring to himself and avoiding responsibility and speaking colloquially, as we sometimes do with *you*?

This "you" is also exhausted and snorting cocaine, yet he is highly creative and dynamic. So how much can we trust him? What are we to think of him? These questions are the central issue of the novel

I.A.   N.P.   story]

Richard Hugo, "Degrees of Gray in Philipsburg."

[This is a poem, but look at how it works with voice]
You might come here Sunday on a whim
Say your life broke down. The last good kiss
You had was years ago. You walk these streets
Laid out by the insane. Past hotels

That didn't last. Bars that did, the tortured try
 Of local drivers trying to accelerate their lives.
[What does this *you* refer to? What is on the narrator's mind?
Isn't he repressing his part in the story? Doesn't he seem more
knowledgeable than McInerney's *you*?
I.A.   N.P.   story]

Mark Twain, *The Adventures of Huckleberry Finn*

You don't know about me, without you have read a book by the
name of *The Adventures of Tom Sawyer*, but that ain't no matter. That
book was made by Mr. Mark Twain, and he told the truth, mainly. There
was things which he stretched, but mainly he told the truth. That is
nothing. I never seen anybody but lied, one time or another, without it was
Aunt Polly, or the widow, or maybe Mary.
[Then Huck goes on to discuss Mary. He can't keep one thing in
his mind very long. And though cognizant of telling a story, he
doesn't do it very well. Similarly, Huck's chief concern is lying. All
adults lie, he says, as though lying is the classification for
adulthood. And through the course of the novel, he learns to lie
better and better.

Why might Ernest Hemingway say, "All modern American
literature comes from one book by Mark Twain, and that book is
Huck Finn"? If a reader misses Huck's voice, he totally misinter-
prets the novel. In the pivotal scene, "You Can't Pray A Lie,"
figuring that society is always right and that he is wrong, Huck
debates whether he should help Jim, his friend and also a slave,
escape from slavery. Society says that those who help slaves go
to hell. So Huck tries to pray to keep himself from going to hell.
He prays for "courage" so that he won't help Jim. But in the end,
he decides that he will help Jim, but he is also convinced that he
will go to hell.

Huck, then, does not fully understands the ramifications of
his story. However, he is aware of telling a story, and he tells
that story a year or so after it happens.
I.A.   N.P.   story

Gordon Weaver, *The Eight Corners of the World*

Jack, everybody gots to leave something behind when dead and gone, reet? Natural instinct of human animal schtik. Foto Joe Yamaguch ain't no exception. Best believe it, Jack!

So what to wataschi gots to bestow upon unborn generations of posterities of Nihon (a.k.a. Dai Nippon, reet?) much less global-wide to eight corners of the world? Plenty, Jack.

Foto Joe Yamaguch—me, how we say in nihonju, wataschi-gots stuff easy to itemize in last will and testament, being of venerable (pushing seventy, Jack!) age, sound mind in failing-fast body (obesity, emphysema, renal failure, rampant cancers!). Consider:

Gots me plenty money, how we say, genkin cash. Located in safe deposit vaoults here in Nihon, stateside, Switzerland (secret account numbers to be revealed only upon ceremonials reading of said will and testament).

No joke, Jack! Bread, dough, kale, cabbage, long green (not to mention also yellow, orange, red, currency speices of Nihon, France, United Kingdom, and Saudi Arabia in addition to legal tenders of U. S. of A.).

Not to fail to mention sizable quantities of bullion and Krugerrands as conservatie hedge against global inflations pressures arising from amidst incessant historical ebb-flow of international politico-economic flaps—I is talking big bucks, Jack.

Than which is not to fail to mention assets tangible than which is no sweat to convert to currency specie of choice if so desired, reet? Consider: domicile properties located in Tokyo Town (in which wataschi presently resides whilst awaiting arrival of Grim Reaper, Black Angel, etcetera blah, Jack!) Hokkaido Island, Hong Kong (lease not to expire except simultaneous with 1999 reversion of Crown Colony to People's Republic—Commie Chinks!—at which point in time situation is moot given wataschi's impending demise, reet?) City of Angels (L.A., Jack!) New York City Big Apple (condo in same edifice as ex-Prexy Nixon's)

[In my mentor's novel, Yamaguchi, as a child in Tokyo, helps New York Yankee catcher Moe Berg take photos of Tokyo. Moe Berg, of course, was a spy. Later, as a student at Oklahoma A & M University, Yamaguchi gets into trouble because of a girl and goes back to Japan. Having learned photography from Moe

Berg, he becomes a photographer for the Japanese Imperial army and takes photos of the bombing of Pearl Harbor. Later, when Americans bomb Tokyo, guided by the photos from Moe Berg, Yamaguchi's parents are killed. After the war, Yamaguchi takes pictures of G.I.s and earns the name Photo Joe. Later still, he becomes a Japanese movie maker. But this is also the backstory. Yamaguchi learns that Asian sailors tattoo their bodies during their voyages. They arranged it that when they died, they had themselves skinned, and then the skins would be displayed in a nautical museum, thereby accounting for their lives. Trying to account for his life, late in life, Yamaguchi goes to a tattoo artist and tells him story of his life, so that the tattoo artist can tattoo the story on Yamaguchi. The novel is this story.

So the narrator here is very aware of telling a story. He even has a distinct and specific listener. No doubt he will slant his story in his favor, but as with Huck Finn, we will be able to see through his slant. So actually with this story, with mine, "Boomtimes," with any framed or deliberately told story, we have two stories: 1. the events themselves (Yamaguchi's life) 2. the narrator's telling of those events (Yamaguchi to the tattoo artist). I.A   N.P.   story]

Edgar Allen Poe, "Ligeia"

And the will therein lieth, which dieth not, Who knoweth the mysteries of the will, with its vigour? For God is but a great will pervading all things by nature of its intentness. Man doth not yield himself to the angels, nor unto death utterly, save only through the weakness of his feeble will.   —Joseph Glanville

I cannot, for my soul, remember how, when, or even precisely where I became acquainted with the lady Ligeia. Long years have since elapsed, and my memory is feeble through much suffering: or, perhaps, I cannot now bring these points to mind, because, in truth, the character of my beloved, her rare learning, her singular yet placid cast of beauty, and the thrilling enthralling eloquence of her low, musical language, made their way into heart by paces, so steadily and stealthily progressive, that they have been unnoticed and unknown. Yet I know that I met her most frequently in some large, old, decaying city near the Rhine. Of her family—I have surely heard her speak—that they are of a remotely ancient date cannot be doubted. Ligeia! Buried in studies of a nature, more than all else, adapted to deaden impressions of the outward world, it is by that sweet word alone—by Ligeia, that I bring before mine eyes in fancy the image of her who is no more. And now, while I write, a recollection flashes upon me that I have never known the paternal name of her who was my friend and my betrothed, and who became the partner of my studies, and eventually the wife of my bosom. Was it a playful charge on the part of my Ligeia? or was it a test of my Strength of affection that I should institute no inquiries upon this point? or was it rather a caprice of my own—a wildly romantic offering on the shrine of the most passionate devotion? I but indistinctly recall the fact itself— what wonder that I have utterly forgotten the circumstances which originated or attended it? And indeed, if ever that spirit which is entitled Romance—if ever she, the wan, and the misty-winged Ashtophet of idolatrous Egypt, presided, as they tell, over marriages ill-omened, then most ply she presided over mine.

There is one dear topic, however, on which my memory faileth me not. It is the person of Ligeia. In stature she was tall, somewhat slender, and in her latter days even emaciated. I would in vain attempt to portray the majesty, the quiet ease of her demeanor, or the incomprehensible lightness and elasticity of her footfall. She came and departed like a shadow. I was never made aware of her entrance into my closed study save by the dear music of low sweet voice, as she placed her delicate hand upon my shoulder. In beauty of face no maiden ever equalled her. It was the radiance of an opium dream—an airy and spirit-lifting vision more wildly divine than the phantasies which hovered about the slumbering souls of the daughters of Delos.

[Read the opening lines very carefully. What does this narrator say? This is the guy whom we are going to have to trust to tell us "the story," the tale, the truth, and yet the first thing that he says is that he doesn't remember what he is going to tell us about. His memory is feeble. He mentions images of corruption and decay. What he does remember is "spirit," "demeanor," "musical language." He remembers the way that she made her way into his heart. What does all this romantic sensibility do to this narrator's credibility? Can we trust him? If we take him at face value, if we read what he says without considering his reliability, this is a supernatural tale of horror. If we pay attention to him, we see that he is a necrophiliac and a murderer. While this narrator doesn't designate a listener, I think that he does offer something like a dramatic monologue or a confession about what he *thinks* happened.

I.A.   N.P. story]

Sherman Alexie, "The Only Traffic Signal on the Reservation Doesn't Flash Red Anymore"

"Go ahead," Adrian said. "Pull the trigger." I held a pistol to my temple. I was sober but wished I was drunk enough to pull the trigger. "Go for it," Adrian said. "You chickenshit." While I still held that pistol to my temple, I used my other hand to flip Adrian off. Then I made a fist with my third hand to gather a little bit of courage or stupidity, and wiped sweat from my forehead with my fourth hand.

"Here," Adrian said. "Give me the damn thing." Adrian took the pistol, put the barrel in his mouth, smiled around the metal, and pulled the trigger. Then he cussed wildly, laughed, and spit out the BB.

"Are you dead yet?" I asked.

"Nope," he said. "Not yet. Give me another beer."

"Hey, we don't drink no more, remember? How about a Diet Pepsi?"

"That's right, enit? I forgot. Give me a Pepsi."

Adrian and I sat on the porch and watched the reservation. Nothing happened. From our chairs made rockers by unsteady legs, we could see that the only traffic signal on the reservation had stopped working.

"Hey, Victor," Adrian asked. "Now when did that thing quit flashing?"

"Don't know," I said.

It was summer. Hot. But we kept our shirts on to hide our beer bellies and chicken-pox scars. At least, I wanted to hide my beer belly. I was a former basketball star fallen out of shape. It's always kind of sad when that happens. There's nothing more unattractive than a vain man, and that goes double for an Indian man.

"So," Adrian asked. "What you want to do today?"

"Don't know."

We watched a group of Indian boys walk by. I'd like to think there were ten of them. But there were actually only four or five. They were skinny, darkened by sun, their hair long and wild. None of them looked like they had showered for a week. Their smell made me jealous.

They were off to cause trouble somewhere, I'm sure. Little warriors looking for honor in some twentieth-century vandalism. Throw a few rocks through windows, kick a dog, slash a tire.

[What do we know about the attitude and humor of this narrator? Look at his puns. Look at how he twists language around, how he is aware of the absurdities of our language, how he has a quizzical, yet ultimately pessimistic view of the world. Does it help to know that he is a Native American storyteller? Though he is not aware of a specific reader or listener, Victor, the narrator, is aware of telling a story. After all, in the story, what he wants to be is a storyteller. He is not fully aware of his ludicrousness, so he is distant from the I.A., yet his awareness gives him some distance from what he tells.

I.A.   N.P.   story]

Jim Sanderson, "Boomtimes"

June 10, 1981

My phone bill is going to have three very large digits. Russ is going to shit green twinkies when he gets it. I have called everybody back in Houston. Sometimes, I call my mother twice a day. Still, calling does not fill the whole day, so when I don't call, I write this. It is my book. Well, it is not really a book but a word processor file. I call it "my book" because it is just that, mine alone, for me only; no one else will ever read it.

I am beginning to feel like those pioneer women who moved out on the prairie and recorded their insanity and depression in journals and diaries. I now understand how, left at home, a woman is tempted to strip off her clothes and run naked into the open wilderness. Being a housewife (Oh God, a housewife is really what I am) in this barren, windswept place either dangerously numbs or excites your mind.

Jesus, I miss Houston. I remember the sour smelling drainage ditch behind our house that became just like one of the bayous when it rained. I used to be so bitchy about the humidity—the way it destroyed any

Jim Sanderson

way I fixed my hair and made me sweat through my make-up. Houston had nearly foot long mosquitoes. Now, I'd kiss a mosquito's stinger and bathe in a drainage ditch. I'd settle for Russ getting transferred to Lafayette or some other rotten Louisiana town to get out of this bone dry heat and back to civilization. I used to mock those middle-class women with Montgomery Ward charge cards, but now I want to walk in a mall and drive on a freeway.

[I wrote this story. It is an epistolary piece. When I got to Odessa, Texas in the early 80s, the town was in the midst of a boom. People were coming to the oil patch from all over the country, hoping for a job and quick money. As a result, people were living in tents. To rent or buy a place to stay, if he or she could even find a place, a person had to commit that day, that hour. Additionally, unlike Midland, Odessa was the oil field workers' town, but all sort of people were in town, and they were all thrown together.

So I imagined a newly married woman, just graduated from a prestigious school like Rice University, but brought to Odessa by her newly graduated husband, an engineer. They find the only available house that they can. Like a woman in the 19th century woman, left home while the man is at work, this woman grows listless and bored. So she watches neighbors—a wild, sexual, and sensual illegal alien couple. Instead of a diary or letters, this narrator types into her brand new, new fangled personal computer. She is lonely and disoriented and scared. All she has is her new p.c. So she very self consciously writes about her life and her neighbors and gradually, because she cannot bring herself to admit that her neighbors' lives are so much richer than hers, she becomes a racist. The story depends upon our discovering what she cannot see of herself, yet she is conscious of telling a story, and she is conscious of telling it in a particular form.

I.A.   N.P.   story]

[Read the following two passages together.]

William Dean Howells, *A Modern Instance*

The village stood on a wide plain, and around it rose the mountains. They were green to their tops in summer, and in winter white through their serried pines and drifting mists, but at every season serious and beautiful, furrowed with hollow shadows, and taking the light on masses and stretches of iron-gray crag. The river swam through the plain in long curves, and slipped away at last through an unseen pass to the southward, tracing a score of miles in its course over a space that measured but three or four. The plain was very fertile, and its features, if few and of purely utilitarian beauty, had a rich luxuriance, and there was a tropical riot of vegetation when the sun of July beat on those northern fields. They waved with corn and oats to the feet of the mountains, and the potatoes covered a vast acreage with the lines of their intense, coarse green; the meadows were deep with English grass to the banks of the river, that, doubling and returning upon itself, still marked its way with a dense fringe of alders and white birches.

Ernest Hemingway, *A Farewell to Arms*

In the late summer of that year we lived in a house in a village that looked across the river and the plain to the mountains. In the bed of the river there were pebbles and boulders, dry and white in the sun, and the water was clear and swiftly moving and blue in the channels. Troops went by the house and down the road and the dust they raised powdered the leaves of the trees. The trunks of the trees too were dusty and the leaves fell early that year and we saw the troops marching along the road and the dust rising and leaves, stirred by the breeze, falling and the soldiers marching and afterward the road bare and white except for the leaves.

The plain was rich with crops; there were many orchards of fruit trees and beyond the plain the mountains were brown and bare. There was fighting in the mountains and at night we could see the flashes from the artillery. In the dark it was like summer lightning, but the nights were cool and there was not the feeling of a storm coming.

Sometimes in the dark we heard the troops marching under the window and guns going past pulled by motor-tractors. There was much traffic at night and man mules on the roads with boxes of ammunition on each side of their pack saddles and gray motor trucks that carried men, and other trucks with loads covered with canvas that moves slower in the traffic.

[Notice that Ernest Hemingway essentially uses the same scene as William Dean Howells. Howells hopes to create this idyllic scene at the start of the *A Modern Instance* and then show the less than idyllic lives of the people in this area. But Hemingway changes the narrator. Frederick Henry in *A Farewell to Arms* is nearly shell-shocked, and he is trying to escape the war. Thus Hemingway's punctuation (or punctuation errors) not only runs the sentences and images together but runs them together in the narrator's mind. Thus, the tone is one that is dry, disengaged, and withdrawn. But the narrator is a first person narrator, so he is closer to the action than Howells' narrator, and that closeness to the war that is the problem.

For Howells, you would have the following rhetorical scheme:

I.A.   N.P   story

For Hemingway, you would have the following rhetorical scheme:

I.A.   N.P.   Story.

Look at the distance, see the irony? See how the theme and purpose of the story—the implied author—knows more than the narrator. Thus, we are examining the narrator, Frederick Henry.]

John Cheever, "The Pot of Gold"

You could not say fairly of Ralph and Laura Whittemore that they had the failings and the characteristics of incorrigible treasure hunters [yet in the finished novel, all that they do is quest for money], but you could truthfully say of them that the shimmer and the smell, the peculiar force of money, the promise of it, had an untoward influence [money controls their lives] on their lives. They were always at the threshold of fortune; they always seemed to have something on the fire. Ralph was a fair young man [sounds like a knight in shining armor] with a tireless commercial imagination [what is a "commercial" imagination? Does it make up jingles? And how imaginative can something done for commercial reasons be?] and an evangelical credence [like a religion] in the romance and sorcery of business success [how romantic can business be?], and although he held an obscure job with a clothing manufacturer, this never seemed to him anything more than a point of departure. [He never does go farther]

The Whittemores were not importunate or overbearing people, and they had an uncompromising loyalty to the gentle manners of the middle class. [The middle class has *gentle manners*?] Laura was a pleasant girl of no particular beauty who had come to New York from Wisconsin at about the same time that Ralph had reached the city from Illinois, but it had taken two years of comings and goings before they had been brought together. . . So true was Ralph's heart, so well did it serve him then, that the moment he saw Laura's light hair and her pretty and sullen face he was enraptured. He followed her out of the lobby, pushing his way through the crowd, and since she had dropped nothing, since there was no legitimate excuse to speak to her, he shouted after her, "Louise, Louise! Louise!" and the urgency in his voice made her stop. [Remember both had been in the city for two years and both had been lonely. So both are rather desperate. Notice that he tries the oldest pick up line in the book.] He said he was sorry. He said she looked just like a girl named Louise Hatcher. It was a January night and the dark air tasted of smoke, and because she was a sensible and a lonely girl, she let him buy her a drink.

[This excerpt clearly violates Hemingway's dictum: show don't tell, which again, most teachers and textbooks say without explanation. The showing here, the irony, the importance of the story is in the narrator's attitudes toward the characters and the plot. The narrator makes merciless fun of Ralph and Laura. Because the narrator knows that he is making fun of them, putting himself at an emotional and intellectual distance from them, he is aware of what he is doing. Therefore, this is verbal irony.

I.A. N.P.   story

Fielding, Richardson, Dickens, and Thackeray all have what critics call "authorial intrusion." It is not authorial but narrative intrusion. And it is not an intrusion but the whole scheme of the fiction. Those "authors," in almost post modernist fashion, remain conscious of telling a story. So they all work on a consistent way of telling the story. They also concentrate on the nature of the entity telling the story. So you have an intent creating a narrator. This narrator takes the guise of the author. Here is a passage William Booth quotes from Henry Fielding's *Tom Jones*. Look at how the narrator becomes a character and more or less begs us to stay interested in his novel. He is, perhaps, a little insecure about his story.]

We are now, reader, arrived at the last stage of our long journey. As we have, therefore, travelled together through so many pages, let us behave to one another like fellow-travellers in a stage coach, who have passed several days in the company of each other; and who, notwithstanding any bickerings or little animosities which may have occurred on the road, generally make all up at last, and mount, for the last time, into their vehicle with cheerfulness and good humour.

[I.A.   N.P.   story

The narrator in the passage above exhibits some foibles. He is not very confident in his story or his storytelling ability. However, the I.A. makes this insecurity a part of the tale.

Look again at the example from "The Things They Carried." What is this narrator's relation to his story?]

Tim O'Brien, *The Things They Carried*

First Lieutenant Jimmy Cross carried letters from a girl named Martha, a junior at Mount Sebastian College in New Jersey. They were not love letters, but Lieutenant Cross was hoping, so he kept them folded in plastic at the bottom of his rucksack. In the late afternoon, after a day's march, he would dig his foxhole, wash his hands under a canteen, unwrap the letters, hold them with the tips of his fingers, and spend the last hour of light pretending. He would imagine romantic camping trips into the White Mountains in New Hampshire. He would sometimes taste the envelope flaps, knowing her tongue had been there. More than anything, he wanted Martha to love him as he loved her, but the letters were mostly chatty, elusive on the matter of love. She was a virgin, he was almost sure.

She was an English major at Mount Sebastian, and she wrote beautifully about her professors and roommates and midterm exams, about her respect for Chaucer and her great affection for Virginia Woolf. She often quoted lines of poetry; she never mentioned the war, except to say, Jimmy, take care of yourself. The letters weighed 10 ounces. They were signed Love, Martha, but Lieutenant Cross understood that Love was only a way of signing and did not mean what he sometimes pretended it meant. At dusk, he would carefully return the letters to his rucksack. Slowly, a bit distracted, he would get up and move among his men, checking the perimeter, then at full dark he would return to his hole and watch the night and wonder if Martha was a virgin.

[Jimmy Cross nearly becomes obsessive about these letters. They matter the most to him. Eventually his concern for this girl will lead to the death of a soldier. See why O'Brien starts with Jimmy Cross]

The things they carried were largely determined by necessity. [Keep reading, but then come back see how the meaning of *necessity* changes. These items represent emotional, moral or spiritual necessities—or obsessions]. Among the necessities or near-necessities were P-38 can openers, pocket knives, heat tabs, wristwatches, dog tags, mosquito repellent, chewing gum, candy, cigarettes, salt tablets, packets of Kool'Aid, lighters, matches, sewing kits, Military Payment Certificates, C rations, and two or three canteens of water. Together, these items weighed between 15 and 20 pounds, depending upon a man's habits or rate of metabolism. [First, the narrator lists the standard military issued necessities and even their weight]. Henry Dobbins, who was a big man, carried extra rations; he was especially fond of canned peaches in heavy syrup over pound cake. [Look at the relative clause, the *who* clause, see how this is buried but explains Henry's obsessions] Dave Jensen, who practiced field hygiene, carried a toothbrush, dental floss, and several hotel-sized bars of soap he'd stolen on R&R in Sydney, Australia. Ted Lavender, who was scared, carried tranquilizers until he was shot in the head outside the village of Than Khe in mid-April. [Look at all the *who* clauses and then note how they set up what these men carried.] By necessity, and because it was SOP, they all carried steel helmets that weighed 5 pounds including the liner and camouflage cover. They carried the standard fatigue jackets and trousers. Very few carried underwear. On their feet they carried jungle boots—2.1 pounds— [SOP, military issued, but now look what comes up in the same sentence] Dave Jensen [hygiene remember?] carried three pairs of socks and a can of Dr. Scholl's foot powder as a precaution against trench foot. Until he was shot, Ted Lavender carried six or seven ounces of premium dope, which for him was a necessity. [Look back above at what he carries and look at the irony that for him dope would indeed be a necessity.] Mitchell Sanders, the RTO, carried condoms. [Who is he going to meet out in the junge?] Norman Bowker carried a diary. [Egotistical, isn't he?] Rat Kiley carried comic books. Kiowa, a devout Baptist, carried an illustrated New Testament that had been presented to him by his father, who taught Sunday school in Oklahoma City, Oklahoma. As a hedge against bad times, however, Kiowa also carried his grandmother's distrust of the white man, his grandfather's old hunting hatchet. Necessity dictated. [Look at the irony here. Look at how necessity gets new meaning] Because the land was mined and booby-trapped, it was SOP for each man to carry a steel-centered, nylon-covered flak jacket, which weighed 6.7 pounds, but which on hot days seemed much heavier. Because you could die so quickly, each man carried at least one large compress bandage, usually in the helmet band for easy access. Because the nights were cold, and because the monsoons were wet, each carried a green plastic poncho that could be used as a raincoat or groundsheet or makeshift tent. With its quilted liner, the poncho weighed almost two pounds, but it was worth every ounce. In April, for instance, when Ted Lavender was shot, they used his poncho to wrap him up, then to carry him across the paddy, then to lift him into the chopper that took him away. [Look at how SOP becomes really emotional].

[Do you have the idea about what O'Brien is doing? Now he is going to repeat sentence structure, content, manner, and characters. Try to note the revealing details that "show" by creating irony. Note too that O'Brien is "showing" through his "telling."]

They were called legs or grunts.

To carry something was to hump it, as when Lieutenant Jimmy Cross humped his love for Martha up the hills and through the swamps. In its intransitive form, to hump meant to walk, or to march, but it implied burdens far beyond the intransitive.

Almost everyone humped photographs. In his wallet, Lieutenant Cross carried two photographs of Martha. The first was a Kodacolor snapshot signed Love, though he knew better. She stood against a brick wall. Her eyes were gray and neutral, her lips slightly open as she stared straight-on at the camera. At night, sometimes, Lieutenant Cross wondered who had taken the picture, because he knew she had boyfriends, because he loved her so much, and because he could see the shadow of the picture-taker spreading out against the brick wall. The second photograph had been clipped from the 1968 Mount Sebastian yearbook. It was an action shot—women's volleyball—and Martha was bent horizontal to the floor, reaching, the palms of her hands in sharp focus, the tongue taut, the expression frank and competitive. There was no visible sweat. She wore white gym shorts. Her legs, he thought, were almost certainly the legs of a virgin, dry and without hair, the left knee cocked and carrying her entire weight, which was just over one hundred pounds. Lieutenant Cross remembered touching that left knee. A dark theater, he remembered, and the movie was Bonnie *and Clyde,* and Martha wore a tweed skirt, and during the final scene, when he touched her knee, she turned and looked at him in a sad, sober way that made him pull his hand back, but he would always remember the feel of the tweed skirt and the knee beneath it and the sound of the gunfire that killed Bonnie and Clyde, how embarrassing it was, how slow and oppressive. He remember kissing her good night at the dorm door. Right then, he thought, he should've done something brave. He should've carried her p the stairs to her room and tied her to the bed and touched that left knee all night long. He should've risked it. Whenever he looked at the photographs, he thought of new things he should've done.

[This piece is almost all telling, but notice how the concrete items that each man carries becomes a sign or symbol or indicator of what most scares him, characterizes him, or concerns him. So these objects, even with O'Brien's narrator telling us about them, show us the men. We could spend several weeks looking at this passage. The intent, the narrator is aware of these men's dilemmas and fear. Although not as severely as Cheever's narrator, O'Brien's narrator gently mocks these scared, doomed men. Thus you have more verbal irony.

I.A.   N.P.   story

63

[Now look again at David Rhodes's work. What does the narrator think about Della and Wilson Montgomery? The narrator could be one of the townsfolk who so fondly remembers Della and Wilson. As such, even though the narrator does not say "I," we get a sense of a distinct person or persona talking to us. So that, "all narrators are first person."]

The old people remember Della and Wilson Montgomery as clearly as if just last Sunday after the church pot-luck dinner they had climbed into their gray Chevrolet and driven back out to their country home, Della waving from the window and Wilson leaning over the wheel, steering with both hands. They can remember as if just yesterday they had driven by the Montgomery's' brownstone house and seen them sitting on their porch swing, Wilson rocking it slowly and conscientiously back and forth, Della smiling, her small feet only touching the floor on the back swing, both of them looking like careful, quiet children.

Della's hands were so small they could be put into small-mouth jars. For many years she was their only schoolteacher, and, except for the younger ones, they all had her, and wanted desperately to do well with spelling and numbers to please her. Without fail, screaming children would hush and hum in her arms. It was thought, among the women, that it was not necessary to seek help or comfort in times of need, because Della would sense it in the air and come. The old people don't talk of her now but what a shadow is cast over their faces and they seem to be talking about parts of themselves—not just that Della belonged to the old days, but that when she and Wilson were gone it was unnatural that anything else from back then should go on without them.

T. Coraghessan Boyle, "Greasy Lake"

It's about a mile down on the dark side of Route 8.
—Bruce Springsteen

There was a time when courtesy and winning ways went out of style, when it was good to be bad, when you cultivated decadence like a taste. We were all dangerous characters then. We wore torn-up leather jackets, slouched around with toothpicks in our mouths, sniffed glue and ether and what somebody claimed was cocaine. When we wheeled our parents' whining station wagons out onto the street we left a patch of rubber half a block long. We drank gin and grape juice, Tango,

Thunderbird, and Bali Hai. We were nineteen. We were bad. We read Andre Gide and struck elaborate poses to show that we didn't give a shit about anything. At night, we went up to Greasy Lake.

Through the center of town, up the strip, past the housing developments and shopping malls, street lights giving way to the thin streaming illumination of the headlights, trees crowding the asphalt in a black unbroken wall: chat was the way out to Greasy Lake. The Indians had called it Wakan, a reference to the clarity of its waters. Now it was fetid and murky, the mud banks glittering with broken glass and strewn with beer cans and the charred remains of bonfires. There was a single ravaged island a hundred yards from shore, so stripped of vegetation it looked as if the air force had strafed it. We went up to the lake because everyone went there, because we wanted to snuff the rich scent of possibility on the breeze, watch a girl take off her clothes and plunge into the festering murk, drink beer, smoke pot, howl at the stars, savor the incongruous full-throated roar of rock and roll against the primeval susurrus of frogs and crickets. This was nature.

I was there one night, late, in the company of two dangerous characters. I Digby wore a gold star in his right ear and allowed his father to pay his tuition at Cornell; Jeff was thinking of quitting school to become a painter, musician, or head-shop proprietor. They were both expert in the social graces, quick with a sneer, able to manage a Ford with lousy shocks over a rutted and gutted blacktop road at eighty-five while rolling a joint as compact as a Tootsie Roll Pop stick. They could lounge against a bank of booming speakers and trade "man's with the best of them or roll out across the dance floor as if their joints worked on bearings. They were slick and quick and they wore their mirror shades at breakfast and dinner, in the shower, in closets and caves. In short, I they were bad.

I drove. Digby pounded the dashboard and shouted along with Toots & the Maytals while Jeff hung his head out the window and streaked the side of my mother's Bel Air with vomit. It was early June, the air soft as a hand on your cheek, the third night of summer vacation.

[This is a story about teenage boys who meet some bad characters. But is the narrator a 'bad" boy? Look at his vocabulary. What is the narrator's attitude toward the characters and the story? Laying rubber in parent's station wagons? Reading Andre Gide? Fake cocaine? Look at the setting? This narrator, like

Cheever and O'Brien, mocks his younger self and those boys like him. See the verbal irony? How far is the narrator from the story? Can we trust him? So here, again is a way to express verbal irony.

I.A.   N.P   story]

Let me repeat myself from my presentation about Voice/Point of View/Wayne C. Booth:

But Booth will allow that this point of view is like a spectrum, with as many "voices" or point of views as there are stories. As Moffet and McElheny say, "every story is first person, whether the speaker is identified or not" (588). That is, each narrator is distinct. Each story has a narrator that has a distinct way of telling the story. That narrator may say "I" or not, may take part in the story or not, may offer a lot of commentary or not.

Now, if you have followed this difficult concept, if you can see the rhetorical manipulation in these fictions, then you can better appreciate what happens in a fiction; you can come to see the difference between film and fiction; you see the "art" in fiction. And if you can manipulate this sort of principle in your own writing, not just in fiction but in all of your writing demands, then, whether paid for it or not, you may be on your way to becoming an effective writer.

Student Stories

These are examples of stories that were turned in near the end of the semester. They are final drafts, yet they are not quite "press" ready.

Dwaine Augustine
Ebaye

As I was walking out to pick up the morning paper, I saw the sky reflecting off the sidewalk. I bent down, picked up the paper and shook off the water. While I was turning back to the house, I pushed down the plastic, took out the paper, and opened it up. I wasn't believing what I was reading in them headlines of the *Ville Platte Times*.

My eyes started rolling back, and the ground looked like it was moving up and down. I felt my eyes burning because they was filling up with water. There he was in that black and white picture, the kind we all take our last year of school, with that serious ass look on his face. They put him there so we could all see what had happened to him, the caption at the bottom saying, "Young militant hangs himself." Ebaye wasn't no fucking militant. I'd show 'em a fucking militant. Then a funny feeling started coming over me, making my legs shake and my hands tremble; and while I stood there thinking what a bitch it was to not have Ebaye around, all that anger and hope I had the night before was leaving.

* * *

The first time I saw Ebaye was in class. Them windows all fogged up, the lights looking all dingy and yellow, and them walls painted puke-gray. I looked about that classroom, and I saw 'em sitting there, the darkest nigga in class. He was—like my grandfather use to say—damn-black. The boy had skin the color of coal: coal that had been dipped in lacquer. When Ebaye was in the sun, his skin color changed from coal-black to deep purple when he walked, making him look like one of them crows parading around in the sun. And he did seem like one of them proud proud niggas. His nose was so wide open that I'm sure he could breath mo' air than the average nigga, and them lips of his was just the size to fit 'em around a small orange, but everything still fit just right on his face. He had some wide, serious eyes, that look like one of them boxers when they staring at you. Ebaye stood like a tree and was built like a damn tank. He shoulda been in stone in the park, 'stead of that Greek man that Ebaye said was there to give us some culture.

Me and Ebaye, we became close. We talked about everything. Well, he did most the talking, and I did most the listening. He said he was schooling me since I wasn't getting much schooling in school. Ebaye was one of them smart niggas; he read books like *The Republic*, *Communist Manifesto*, the *United States Constitution*, and the *Bible*— shit that most of us never even heard of, let alone read. People said Ebaye was like that because he wasn't from around here; he was from them West Indies Islands. His daddy had been some kinda lawyer and civil rights leader down in the West Indies—until somebody killed him. Ebaye didn't talk like us either; he talked in his West Indies way, all proper and shit. And he didn't say "nigga." As Ebaye put it, black folk helped the degradation of their character by calling each other "nigga." And he didn't say his words like we did; he said 'em the right way, and that kinda made us look dumb. But he never acted like he was more than us. Ebaye always talked *to* me, not around me, like some of them smart-ass white folk tried to do when we went to town. They just didn't know I was studying with one of them stark smart philosophers, John Washington, but Ebaye's what we called 'em, cause he was so damn black.

The first time we ever talked was at school when I said, "What's up, John."

"Nothing much, how are you my man?" Ebaye said in his West Indies talk.

"I'm fine, just thought I'd see what's up. You know, you ain't said a whole lot since you been at this school."

"I know," Ebaye said like he was hiding something. "By the way," he kept going, and now I'm thinking this nigga wasn't saying all he had to say. "It's okay if you call me Ebaye."

When he said that, I couldn't help but stare him in the face. It was his blackness that made me look at him. His skin was so smooth and slick, no light spots; he was all one color—black. And even though we poked fun by calling him Ebaye, that shit was okay with him. If he had been a nigga from 'round here he'd been pissed we called him Ebaye.

"We don't mean nothing by that 'Ebaye' shit. We always making up names to call people."

"No offense taken, I do not mind."

I sat there looking at his big, dark hands that was almost the same color all over—even his palms was dark. They had veins in 'em that look like plant roots, and I sat there thinking how bad this nigga could hurt somebody with them hands. But he was too polite to do that kind of shit.

From that day Ebaye and me stayed close. He told me how his daddy was a great man, and that he expected great things from people—all people. Ebaye told me his daddy said that all people was potentially great, they just needed somebody to show 'em how. He told me about his dreams and the things he'd like to do. About how he would like to change the world, and deep shit like that. Ebaye had everybody's respect, the black people, the white people, and the teachers. I think everybody respected him cause he said it like it was. Ebaye didn't pull no punches with anybody, white or black. Being black didn't automatically make you right with Ebaye. Just like that time Ebaye stopped Batman and Scooter from taking this white boy's lunch money; hell, Batman and Scooter had been taking his lunch money for years. They said it was payback for 400 years of slavery. And Ebaye was the first person that ever said anything, black or white. We all thought it was a shame, but what the fuck, they wasn't taking our lunch money.

And he was something to see at work. We all loved it when the teacher asked Ebaye questions in class. Every time he spoke, he stood up and you could almost feel the bass from his voice. The nigga had knowledge, so much knowledge it was scary. The only people we was used to seeing with that much knowledge was "Batman"—a nigga who could tell you anything about baseball you wanted to know—and Scooter, who was a motherfucker with some dominoes. Scooter had 'em all memorized, could count 'em before you played 'em, and knew where you were gonna put 'em. But Batman and Scooter was small time compared to Ebaye. Ebaye knew some real shit: philosophy, politics, and law.

"Mr. Washington," the government teacher called on Ebaye one day. "What do you think about the first amendment rights? Are they absolute? Do you think that people should be able to say anything they please?"

"Well, Mr. Breaux," Ebaye said, coming off smooth, "nothing is absolute, but I do think that people should be able to assemble and protest injustice so long as it is peaceful."

"So, are you saying that I can assemble and advocate the lynching of certain people, and that would be okay so long as it is peaceful?"

"Yes sir," Ebaye said while everybody in the class looked at each other.

We knew this shit was getting heavy. Ebaye said, "This country is based on the principle that people can assemble and express discontent, no matter how absurd, in a peaceful manner. I do not think the forefathers intended for liberties such as free speech and the right to assemble to be taken away simply because someone does not like what you are saying, or that authorities could force individuals off the streets by 11:00 p.m."

"Are you referring to the curfew, John?" Mr. Breaux asked, knowing damn well what Ebaye was talking about.

"Yes sir, I think it is unconstitutional to take away our right to assemble, no matter what excuse is used. I think that the students here should stand up and protest the curfew."

"But what grounds would you protest on, Mr. Washington?" Breaux asked Ebaye as if us students didn't have a leg to stand on to protest the curfew.

And to be honest I didn't think we did until Ebaye said, "Well, authorities use crime as a justification for the curfew, even before a crime is committed. That, I believe, is unconstitutional: to restrict an individual's freedom because they may commit a crime."

"You have a good point. Thank you, Mr. Washington," Breaux said.

And Ebaye stood there looking powerful, black like he knew he had a good point. And everybody, including Mr. Breaux, knew he had just said some shit that was even more powerful than his physique or his shiny black skin which was looking like the armor off one of them knights me and Ebaye had seen in one of them history books. Then Ebaye sat down.

Things like that happened all the time. Ebaye was a motherfucker with words. And I tried to pick up on some of 'em. Hell, I even watched my mouth around him. I just didn't feel right saying trashy shit in front of Ebaye.

We kept talking to each other, telling each other how we thought shit should be. And Ebaye kept telling me that we could change things in this town if we got off our ass—well he didn't say ass—and did something. He said we could change lots of things, from the curfew to the way whites treated blacks in what Ebaye called a "time warp"—Ville Platte.

We all complained about the new curfew that they put on us. The mayor said that it would help us to stop getting into so much trouble and from killing one another. Ebaye said that sounded good on the surface, but underneath, it was just another way to control black folks. He said they just want us to kill ourselves at a decent hour, 'stead of 1 o'clock in the morning.

One night, while we was sitting on the porch—which Ebaye called Plato's stage, after that Greek—Ebaye said, "You know, Earl, all I ask of myself in this world is that I leave something behind, something that people will remember and learn from."

"Don't worry, Ebaye. If you're gone before me, I'll make sure people remember you."

"That is not what I mean," Ebaye said, like he was teaching me it's this way, not that way. "I don't care if they remember *me*, Earl," he kept going in that voice that said this was important shit, and that I'd better listen. "I want to leave behind teachings that people can learn from, just like men in the past have left behind teachings for us to learn from."

I looked at him, and he was looking at the sky. Something told me that he wasn't finished yet. Then all of a sudden Ebaye changed the subject, just as he did every night when he felt that shit was gettin' too deep.

"Look at that moon, Earl," Ebaye said in a child-like voice. "It is full tonight and beautiful."

So I looked up to see for myself. The moon was bright orange, and if I didn't know any better I would've jumped up and tried to touch it. The sky was so clear I could see shapes of thin clouds that was close enough to the moonlight.

"You right, Ebaye, that moon is beautiful," and never looking at Ebaye, I kept going, "And this night, man, it's too nice to be sittin' on this porch," I said in a voice that sounded like a goddamn kid that was anxious to go somewhere.

"You want to take a walk?" Ebaye asked me.

A walk was against curfew. And the cops had a field day on niggas who broke curfew. Scooter Sonnier got his arm broke just last week in a scuffle with the police after they caught him out past curfew. Shit like that happen all the time—cops kicking folks around. That's the way it's been for years in Ville Platte, Louisiana, a town where niggas still worked in white folks houses and where niggas is more afraid of white folks than they is of the Lord.

"I don't know, Ebaye," I said after thinking about it for a little while. "I don't think that's a good idea."

"Earl," Ebaye said, like he was accusing me of something, "are you afraid to go? If so, we can stay here on the porch."

"I ain't 'fraid of a goddamn thing," I snapped at Ebaye, mad at him for realizing that I was just afraid as any other nigga in this town.

"Then let's go. Let's take a walk, my friend. The night is too beautiful to waste it on the porch."

"Okay, my friend, let's go."

The streets in Ville Platte was just wide enough for two cars to go down them at the same time. They was bumpy from all the potholes that had been filled in with asphalt. Me and Ebaye walked down those streets like there was no worry in the world, just laughing and talking and enjoying the night. The cool wind was blowing, and as we looked across the street into the field, we could see the tall grass dance from side to side in the moonlight. Then behind us we heard a car pull up. We turned around and there was two policemen with they guns out pointing at us.

"You two boys, on the ground now!" an officer said in a voice that pierced my ears.

"Get your hands out of your pockets," another voiced yelled out louder. "Spread your arms and legs." One of 'em came over and frisked us while the other one held his pistol on us.

"Goddamn, if it wasn't for your eyes I wouldn't be able to see you in the dark, boy," the tall, red cop told Ebaye, while his partner laughed.

"You right bout that. That's gotta be the blackest nigga I seen in all my life," the little fat cop said. And he had the nerve to criticize Ebaye for being *so* black when he wasn't that far from black hisself.

"Maybe because you spent your entire little life in Ville Platte," Ebaye said, shocking the hell outta them cops and me, too.

"What'd you say boy?" the cop asked like he didn't hear what Ebaye had said. And to be sure the cop didn't misunderstand him, Ebaye said it again.

"On your feet, both of you," the tall, red cop screamed. And turning to his partner, he said, "Write these boys a citation for breaking curfew."

"Okay, ladies, hand over some I.D.," the little fat cop said. And looking at him now for a second time, he was dark as me.

After the fat cop took our I. D.'s, his partner got in Ebaye's face, and before he could say a word, Ebaye said, "I know my rights. I do not want any trouble. You had no right to put us on the ground and point pistols at our heads. I have read Terry v. Ohio, and I know you have a right to stop us, but putting a gun in our faces was unnecessary and against the law."

"You done, now," the red cop said like he was bad.

I don't think a nigga ever stood up to a cop in Ville Platte. You just didn't do that to a policeman. But Ebaye wasn't from round here, and I guess somebody forgot to tell 'em. They stood there in the street while me and the little fat cop watched, half scared, half mad, but frozen. And everything was silent. It seem like for five minutes, but I know it couldna been that long. And about that time the cop pulled out his stick.

"I don't think you want to do that," Ebaye said with all the fucking confidence in the world, "Now, sir, you can give us our citation, and we will be on our way, or you can do what you think is necessary."

That cop was scared now. He knew that Ebaye wasn't fucking around, and hell, I think Ebaye knew more law than they did. None of us out there, cept Ebaye, knew shit bout Terry, and none of us was gonna act like we did.

The cop now had a look on his face like he was gonna hit Ebaye with his stick, but then he said, "This is your lucky night, boy," and walked away. Then they peeled off. It was a motherfucker to see Ebaye shame that cop, and I felt proud.

But, all the way back to the porch, me and Ebaye didn't say a word, and I couldn't wait to get home to smoke a joint to calm my nerves. I didn't know if he wanted to cry or fight. I know I wanted to do both. I'd been stopped times before, and this time was no different. I wanted to cry—cry like a baby and kick some ass all at the same time.

The next day in the school cafeteria, before everybody met up with girls and left campus, went to smoke a joint, or wash cars, Ebaye was up on stage calling everybody's attention.

"Listen, Earl and I were stopped by the police last night. And I know that all of you in here have been stopped from time to time. Some of you have even been beaten. This curfew is a vile attempt to suppress us. Enough is enough, people. If we let this town get away with these things, they will continue to treat us the way they do. I am calling on each of you to help put an end to the way we are being treated. Let's make a statement in this goddamn town, not just for better treatment by the police but equal treatment by everyone. Stand up sisters and brothers. Let's change this place. Let's show them who we are."

And everybody stood up, even the white people who I had never really paid much attention to until now. I think they hadn't paid much attention to us either, but with Ebaye saying the things he said the way he say 'em, nobody could help but agree. Then cafeteria busted into screams.

Batman screamed out, "Hell yeah."

And Scooter, broken arm and all, stood and said, "Tell it like it is, Ebaye."

"Now listen," Ebaye said, quieting down the crowd. "We have to do this peacefully. If we do not, they will discredit us, and we will accomplish nothing. Let us meet tonight at seven o'clock in the field behind Earl's house. Everyone be there."

Ebaye kept going. Not like he was trying to boss everybody around, but like he was concerned, like you might miss something if you wasn't there. And he was right. If you wasn't there you did miss something; you missed the best nigga Ville Platte ever seen at work. Mr. John Washington was organizing a bunch of wild negroes who didn't know shit, didn't care bout shit, and wasn't gonna do shit—til we met him.

Ebaye rallied us, laid down some ground rules, and made us stand up. So that's why we called the group *STAND UP*, (Students That Are Now Determined, so Unleash the Power), "STAND" for short.

We went out in the days and weeks after that first meeting and held demonstrations before school, after school, and on weekends. Them white folks couldn't go anywhere without seeing us niggas protesting, boycotting, or picketing someone, some business, or some institution. The old folks said we young niggas was crazy, and that we shouldn't be causing all this trouble in Ville Platte. They said things was good here, and that they had a lot of good white folks in this town.

But we didn't mind them, we just kept doing our thing. And a lot of folks still can't believe that Ebaye was even able to rally them young white folks in Ville Platte. Shit, they had gripes, too. They was even protesting, boycotting, and picketing they own folk's shit. Everything went fine, people started to listen to us, and it helped to have them young white folks on our side. Ville Platte was changing.

Until that Sunday, the day of the last march we ever had, the last time young black folks and young white folks got together to do anything, the last time people changed. The day started out gray, cold, and wet. And we all went to church, even Scooter who smoked more weed than anybody I ever seen.

By the time we got outta church, steam was rising from the streets and like the weather man on the radio said, "This is the hottest day in April I have ever seen."

This was going to be our biggest march yet. We was marching down main street in front of city hall, in front of the police station, and in front of the parish jail where a lot of our school mates was already. It was a bad motherfucker. We had more people than ever before and more young whites than ever before. Some people say they came from as far as St. Landry and Jefferson Parish to march with us, to change things, and Ebaye leading it all.

The street was just wide enough for two cars to pass down it at the same time, and we filled it from curb to curb, a river of people carrying signs and banners, singin' and chantin'.

Ebaye was in front of it all: me and him, because I was his right-hand man, studied underneath him, and helped bring all these people together.

By the time we got halfway down main street, the police were in the middle of the road in helmets, shoulder pads, and shotguns in hand. All five of them just standing in front of a crowd of bout a hundred people, like they knew something we didn't. They walked backwards a ways, telling Ebaye he was under arrest for disturbing the peace and inciting a riot. They handcuffed Ebaye and pulled him away. Ebaye screamed to me to lead the march, and "press on." Just about that time, somebody busted out a window in a car, and then the window in a store shattered. It was Scooter and Batman. Those two crazy motherfuckers, breaking windows and yelling, "Let Ebaye go!"

Following them was about 20 people. I kept marching, me and most of the group, and Scooter and 'em kept tearing shit up.

* * *

I was visiting Ebaye in jail for about a year. They kept him there waiting on trial and all this shit. I couldn't keep seeing him like that, so I quit going. The next time I saw him was on the front page of the *Ville Platte Times* in that school picture, looking serious like he always did, his eyes saying, "Press on."

That was a year ago. Now nobody march in the streets. Nobody stand up no mo', and the young white people and us don't even talk.

Ebaye's mamma give me all his books he had. She said she won't be needing 'em, and that Ebaye would want me to have 'em. I hadn't read none of 'em, and I don't talk philosophy no mo'. I just pick up the paper every morning, turn around, walk back to the porch where me and Ebaye used to talk, and fire-up a joint. Ebaye's dead.

Gayla Chaney
Piracy

Barbara Davis stared at the open eyes of this stranger, the gaping mouth, the still chest, the motionless tattooed arms, and the bloody hole in his forehead. This was the total impotency of the dead, Barbara realized, and she began to tremble, not for what she had just done with the chrome-plated .38 Smith & Wesson that her husband Jay had insisted she carry with her to the beach, but for what had almost just happened to her, what most assuredly would have happened if she had dismissed Jay's concern as paranoia.

"The beach in November? Barb, nobody else will be out there, except maybe some nut. I don't think you should go alone." Jay had been apprehensive.

"I need the solitude, Jay. With Julie's wedding plans and Kyle being at Emory, so far away from home, it makes me sad to think of it."

"What does that have to do with the beach, Barb? Can't you be sad at home or out jogging or at the library? Julie's wedding isn't until February. We've got plenty of time to worry about that."

"We?" Barbara had laughed, "Four whole months with Thanksgiving and Christmas thrown in to fill up the gaps. Oh, Jay, I wish I hadn't even mentioned it to you. I'm going, okay? I need to meditate and listen to the ocean. If you don't understand why, then just accept the fact that I do. Please."

"Take the gun. For me." Jay's request that Barbara had begrudgingly agreed to, feeling it was a covert attempt to scare her away from her retreat, resulted in this breathless corpse lying at her feet.

Homicide, justifiable surely, but homicide just the same. Barbara would tell how this man had approached her, his dark blue Ford parked 60 yards or more away. She hadn't even noticed the car when she parked her Suburban. She had no idea that she wasn't alone on the beach until she heard him coming up behind her.

Barbara was sitting ten or fifteen feet from her Suburban. The gun that she had reluctantly placed in the pocket of her parka, out of some kind of loyalty to Jay for his concern, was concealed from view. When she had turned to see this stranger approaching her, Barbara had not been suspicious or even alarmed, despite his unkempt appearance. After all, this was the beach in southeast Texas, close to the refineries of Port Arthur.

The population in the area often resembled this rough-looking character. She had expected him to smile, to say something about fishing or the gulls, or some other friendly exchange before proceeding on down the beach, leaving her to her own thoughts and reasons for coming out when the water and wind were too cold for swimming, when the tide was going out and the sky was overcast and darkening.

But he did not speak. Perhaps he thought the sand had sufficiently muffled his footsteps, and she would not turn around until he was right on top of her, responding too late to have time for any defense. Barbara had started to speak, but her words froze on her tongue in disbelief as the stranger lunged at her. His hands grabbed her neck as he began forcing her down into the sand. She heard the gulls cry overhead, and she could smell her attacker's breath as she felt the adrenaline rush pounding in her chest. Instinct. Survival. The roaring sound of waves drowned out the sound of a .38 going off somewhere, in the air, then again, and again, and into the flesh of someone who didn't seem human at all.

Barbara thought she heard him call her "bitch," but now she couldn't be sure if he had even spoken. She had pulled the hammerless .38 from her pocket and, without aiming, squeezed the trigger as she was falling backward, and then again as this madman was coming down upon her. One bullet had gone completely through his skull, exiting out the back and hitting the side mirror on her Suburban. The shattering sound had registered in her mind, but the hole in the man's forehead held her attention.

Barbara glanced up and down the beach area for another person, for help, for a witness, for confirmation that this horrible person was really dead. She was afraid he might suddenly jump up like the villains in those B movies Jay often took her to, possessing the strength of madness despite the severity of their wounds, grabbing their opponents one last time.

But he had a hole in his head—a severe wound to his brain, and Barbara marveled that she had put it there. Who was he? Had he preyed on others before her, or was this his first impulsive act of violence? Barbara stared at his face. She felt no remorse. There was nothing of the regret or disbelief or concern that she would have credited herself with if she had imagined such a scenario. Only anger. And even that was not the anger that she would have supposed.

Barbara was not angry that this barbarian had forced her to kill him, which she believed he had. Her anger was the inconvenience of it all, and this was what shocked her most about herself as she watched the blood oozing down the side of this man's nose, drifting over the cheek and into his beard. She had a wedding to get ready for, and the preparation that went with that, and Kyle's college expenses. Barbara knew that she would need a lawyer, even though this was an act of self-defense. If there was a trial, the humiliation for her family would be so unfair, both of her children at important times in their lives, having their mother's face on the front page, because of this stranger. If he was a drifter, there might not be much made of it; but if he had family in the area, or if he had no prior record of violence—well, without any witnesses—she could be accused of anything, even murder.

Barbara pictured the prosecutor asking her, "You went to the beach in November? With a gun, Mrs. Davis? You said you wanted and planned to be alone. And yet, you took a gun. You weren't planning on meeting anyone? A lover? A blackmailer?"

She thought of Jay. Even he had thought it odd that she wanted to go to the beach. Would he believe her, or would he end up questioning her story? Barbara put the gun back in her pocket as she turned, taking inventory of the damage done to the Suburban mirror. She looked back at the face in the sand. He wore an earring in his left ear, and his beard grew wild and untrimmed. The tattoo on his right forearm was a heart with "Rochelle" written in the center of it. The tattoo on his upper left arm was half concealed by the sleeve of his t-shirt, but Barbara made out what appeared to be the tail of a mermaid.

"Pirate bastard," she muttered to the corpse.

The wind blew harder, and the sky looked as if any minute it would storm. The waves were rising and the tide was going out. And still, Barbara stood there, unable to free herself from the hypnotic effect of staring down into the eyes of a man that she had killed. This felt like the most life-altering moment of her life, and at the same time, Barbara was aware that she didn't feel like the kind of person who could kill another human being. She felt no regret for taking a life. She felt absolutely nothing for this dead man.

He ("It" seemed more appropriate for the large, motionless, lump of flesh lying inches from her feet) was a nameless, ageless, and soulless mass that needed to be removed from the beach, like the refuse left by inconsiderate beachgoers whose bottles, food wrappers, and discarded or forgotten items littered the shoreline. "It" was an eyesore like the other abandoned and worthless left behind trash waiting to be disposed of.

Nothing about this stranger's behavior deserved to be labeled as human. In Barbara's encounter with him, he had displayed only animal-like aggression. In death he was a despicable reminder of all that was evil and ugly and wrong, of annoyance and inconvenience, and of wasted time, her valuable time lost and her day of retreat ruined because this piece of scum decided to come to the beach, and not just any beach, but her beach.

This had been Barbara's favorite spot, set back from the main gathering areas used in the summer when the beach was full. This was where she sat when she and Jay brought the children. Jay would take the kids out into the water, and Barbara would put down her towel in this very spot, away from the crowds that preferred the sandier beach with their stereos blasting and their coolers full of beer and their volleyballs, dragging the noise and activity of the city with them. This was the spot that Barbara had sat to read so many times while the sounds of the waves and her children laughing had blended together into one soothing song just for her.

Just for her. This man had been reaching just for her. She was his selected victim simply because she was here on this cold, November morning, and no one else was. They were strangers to one another, and yet now they were linked together in a horribly gruesome moment that could reappear like an instant replay whenever some seemingly innocent occurrence triggered her memory.

Barbara needed to start for home. It was getting late. Her attacker's car would eventually be found, but there would be no trace of her in it and nothing connecting her to him in any way. Barbara bent over and touched his skin. It was cold enough to convince her he would not spring to life like he might in some future nightmare. Stepping back from the body, Barbara quickly began to remove her clothes. When she was naked and goose bumps covered her flesh, she grabbed the man's right leg. Clutching his boot, she dragged him over the sand and into the water.

The water was freezing, and Barbara knew she could not take him out too far, but hopefully far enough. She knew he would wash up on shore eventually, but she didn't even want to think about where and when.

Barbara wondered about the man's mother. Was she alive? Would she grieve the loss of this son or would his death be some sad, yet anticipated conclusion? Was he a prodigal son, or was all his family like him? Barbara was far enough out that she could not touch the silty ocean floor. She pushed the corpse away from her and for the first time since he grabbed her, Barbara felt revulsion. She felt the heave rising from her stomach as she began to swim back. Swallowing hard, she pushed toward the shore, retching and trembling from the cold and the fear and the rage.

Barbara reached the beach and bent over at the waist, gasping and gagging with her hands gripping her stomach until she was able to stop the sensation. Then she grabbed her clothes and began to dress. In one pocket of her parka was the Smith & Wesson, in the other was her key ring. It was drizzling as Barbara unlocked the Suburban door and got inside. Turning on the heater and locking the doors, she stared out at the blank face of the sea. There was no trace of a dead man in the water. No evidence that she had done anything.

Glancing out at the spot in the gulf where she had left the corpse, Barbara put the Suburban in reverse. No one could ever know. She would not dwell on this; she must not. It was not something she did to him. It was something he did to himself. His death was his own fault and his blood was on his own hands, except for the droplets that had splattered on her parka and her jeans. Barbara would wash them the minute she got home. And she would take a hammer to the mirror and bust the rest of it out, leaving it to look like a random act of vandalism.

She would get the Suburban mirror replaced tomorrow, and she would never, not ever, tell anyone (not even Jay) about what had happened. There was a wedding to get planned. Kyle would be coming home for the holidays. And then it would be Christmas.

Barbara turned on the windshield wipers and her headlights. She took a deep breath, exhaling slowly and deliberately to calm herself as she gripped the steering wheel and headed for the paved road. From the corner of her eye, she saw a dark blue car, and she quickly checked to see if there was someone waiting in it. But it was empty. Just an abandoned, older model Ford LTD with Texas plates. Barbara would not get any nearer to it. She had seen all she needed to see.

Lightning flashed in the distance, and Barbara hoped that the coming storm was a big one that could sweep the Ford's owner so far out into the ocean that he would never be found. The empty car would be a mystery mentioned on the evening news at some point in the future, when it was discovered and attached to a missing person's report. Barbara hoped that would be how it transpired, and even more she hoped that it would be weeks or months from now, after her day at the beach had been forgotten by any who knew she had driven this way.

Moving her Suburban away from the beach in the direction of her home, Barbara pushed down on the accelerator. Deliberately, she locked her eyes on the beach road in front of her, being careful not to glance one last time at the dark blue Ford parked just off the road to her left with its windows left down in the rain.

Daniel Bartlett
Don Coyote

I'm standing on the side of the road in front of McDonald's trying to catch a ride and this truck, one of them real big eighteen wheelers, comes hauling toward me, and first I think that mother's gonna run right over me, but then he slows up and stops right in front of me and this hand waves at me, so I climb up inside.

The driver's this big fat-ass guy—I mean this guy's huge, like that big Jabba snail looking thing on *Star Wars*. His hat says "Mack," so I figure it's his name or something, but I don't say nothing about it. His face looks like a bulldog cause it's all wrinkled and his cheeks flap down and wiggle around when he moves. They got a word for dogs' cheeks like that, but hell if I know it.

So I get in, and he looks at me out the side of his eyes and pulls back out on the road and says, "Where you headed?"

"Nowhere," I tell him.

The truck smells all sweet inside like a Dunkin' Donuts I used to hang around, and sure enough there's a box of donuts next to Mack's seat. He's still watching the road, so I just reach in and take a donut from the box. Mr. Brent used to bring donuts to our class. He was always trying to be all friendly and tell us how we got to improve ourself, like I think he really gives a rat's ass. But I know he was full of it. He always had them donuts with that cream crap in the middle. That stuff makes me want to puke. But Mack's got plain donuts, so I figure he ain't all bad and maybe I ought to say something.

"I never been in one of these big trucks like this," I say.

He don't look at me, but them big cheeks kind of raise up like he's growling. Only he ain't, he's smiling a little.

Then he says, "You got a name, kid?"

"Don," I tell him. Then I remember what Mr. Brent used to call me so I also tell him, "But I ain't Don Coyote."

He cuts a look at me then turns back to the road. And he kind of laughs and them big cheeks jiggle around like he's got some of Mr. Brent's cream donuts stuffed in his face.

"Got you. Don—not Don Coyote— who's going nowhere," he says.

"Yeah," I say.

I just got to make sure Mack knows that ain't my name cause Mr. Brent used to think it was. He called me that all the time after I told him about when I got picked up for attacking this pay phone cause it kept ringing and it pissed me off, and I needed some cash anyway. But those pay phones are hell to bust open and the cops picked me up. So when I tell Mr. Brent about fighting that pay phone, he laughs and calls me Don Coyote or Cojones or some stupid shit like that. I can't remember cause it was stupid, and he was always laughing about it, and he'd always ask me if I attacked any more phones or windmills or whatever. He thought he was real damn funny, but he's a dumbass.

I used to have to put up with his crap in high school cause they sent me and a bunch of idiots to his class all day instead of real classes. But it was cool. We didn't do nothing but screw around in there and eat donuts and watch TV. We saw this show one time where there was a bunch of guys acting like old knights and talking all funny and going around looking for this magic cup or something, and they got tore up by this rabbit, and then they blew it to hell with a grenade. It was crazy. They was just going all over the place looking for this stupid cup and whacking around with swords and talking like weirdos. But it was cool cause we made some of them swords out of cardboard and whacked around with them and talked like them guys and acted like we was looking for that magic cup.

Then Mr. Brent said something about them guys was on a quest or something, and he would get all serious and tell us we had to figure out what our own quest was, and we got to get our shit straight, or we'd end up wasting our lives. He was always saying stupid stuff like that. That's when it sucked. But I ain't even lying, you got to be a real idiot to just go around all over the place looking for some stupid cup just cause that's your quest, or whatever Mr. Brent said you got to have. I figure quests are for morons, and Mr. Brent can just get bent if he thinks I'm going to go around doing something stupid like that. But I ain't got to put up with him no more, so it's nothing.

Then I see Mack's kind of looking at me, and I stop thinking about Mr. Brent, and I finish that donut and lick my fingers where they got sticky from it and wipe the rest off on my jeans.

"So Don—but not Don Coyote—why are you running the roads?" Mack says. "Out looking for work?"

"Naw, man," I say.

And he kind of laughs, and he looks even more like a bulldog with them big cheeks scrunched up and them teeth showing. Then he takes the last damn donut in the box and shoves it in his mouth and says, "So you're just out cruising around."

"Yeah, you know how it is," I say. I don't say this to Mack, but I was tired of hanging around the house hearing my momma bitch at me about something stupid like leaving a mess, or not doing some crap for her, or hanging out with Jimmy. I don't got to listen to that. I can do what the hell I want.

I hang out with Jimmy all the time. He's real stupid, but he's all right. There was this one time when me and Jimmy were hard up for some cash, and my momma wouldn't give me none, and his momma wouldn't give him none, but he knew this little meat market down the street he figured we'd hit up. So Jimmy rips off with this car, cause we ain't got one, and comes pick me up, and we roll by that little store a couple times and check things out. We figured it was clear, and we go in there with a couple pistols Jimmy had got from some guy he knew. Mine didn't work, and I don't think Jimmy's was loaded anyway, but you just got to point a gun at them kids behind the counter and they go to pissing their pants

So we go in there yelling and showing them our guns, and they give us the money, and we run out like we figured on, but that heap-of-junk car Jimmy had got us won't start up again. He was jerking with the wires and all, but it flat won't start. Course I was cussing him for getting us a piece of shit like that cause if I was going to run off with a car, I'd least get a good one. Jimmy just kicked it and told me it was dead, and I told him *we* was dead if we didn't get out of there cause right then we could hear the cops coming. So we hauled ass, but the sack they gave me had busted open, and quarters and dimes and nickels and pennies and even some dollars was falling out all over the place, and I was going in circles trying to pick it all up cause I sure as hell wasn't going to leave it. Then I seen the cops coming down the street, and I took off around back of the store, and I seen Jimmy waving at me from inside this dumpster, and I jumped in with him. Man, I want to kick Jimmy's ass every time I think about that dumpster cause it was full of blood and guts and meat and stuff from that store. I ain't even lying, that thing smelled like something died. And the cops found us anyway, and then they laughed at us when we got out of it cause we had meat and blood all over us, and we smelled like a dead dog's ass. We both got busted for that and didn't even get to keep the cash. But that's done with now and it's nothing.

I was kind of pissed that Mack took the last donut, but then I seen a bag of Cheetos between the seats, and I see Mack ain't messing with it so I grab it before he does and start in on it.

Then Mack says, "So, what's got you out wandering around? You running away from home, kid?"

"No," I tell him, "And I ain't a kid."

"Okay," he says, and he gives me another of them bulldog-face-smiles and says, "Don, I'm sure you're in a hurry to get nowhere, but I'm not going much further. Just right here to the toy store to drop off this load."

"That's cool," I tell him.

And right then he pulls into Toys R Us, and I remember there was this one time me and Jimmy got kicked out of there cause sometimes, when we didn't feel like hearing Mr. Brent tell us what we got to do, me and Jimmy would hang out in the toy store for a while and play around with the video games and balls and stuff. They had this thing with a bunch of football helmets and pads and stuff in it, and this other thing with some baseball bats in it, and me and Jimmy put all that junk on and went to acting like them guys on that old knight show when this one guy cut off this other guy's arms and legs and stuff. We was whacking each other with them bats cause we had on the pads and helmets—it was cool cause it didn't really hurt—and I was making like I had to get past Jimmy so I could find my quest or whatever, and he was telling me I had to tell him a bunch of stuff like my name and my favorite color, and I had to give him some money or something, but I wouldn't do it, so we had to fight just like on that show.

Then this rent-a-cop guy comes up to us, all like he's big and bad, and he tells us, "You kids get the hell out of here before I call the cops," and we was laughing already, but it makes him even madder, and his face is all red and he just stands there staring at us like we give a shit if he calls the cops cause it ain't like we done nothing. But he squinches his eyes all tight and points at us, and we drop all that stuff on the floor cause it was starting to suck anyway, and Jimmy says we ought to go get something to eat, and that guy tells us he'll get the police to pick us up if he ever sees us in there again, so Jimmy flips him off and we haul ass. I bet that guy's still pissed.

I had done finished all them Cheetos, and I was licking all that cheese off my fingers, and Mack stops the truck and kind of looks at me, so I wipe the rest off on my jeans, but I don't say nothing.

Then he says, "Well, here we are." And he gets out.

I was going to go in and play around, but I think about that rent-a-cop and I figure I'll just wait right where I am. While I'm waiting on Mack, I find a bag of them peanut butter cups shoved way up under his seat, and I figure he don't care if I eat them too cause he ain't said nothing about the donuts or the Cheetos, but it don't matter cause he ain't even in the truck right now, and I can hear him screwing around in the back. So I just go to eating them and watching the little kids running around in the parking lot and chasing and fighting with their new toys and stuff.

Them kids make me think of when me and Jimmy and some other kids that lived around us would all have rock wars. We'd get in teams, and me and Jimmy was always on a team cause we knew all the places to get and hide, and then we'd find rocks and throw them till the other team give up. Them other kids was always crying if you hit them too hard, cause they wasn't as big as me and Jimmy, and they got scared of us sometimes like they thought we was monsters or something and we was going to hurt them.

There was this one time when this little kid got hit right in the eye, and he was all crying and wanted to go home, but me and Jimmy told him he was being a baby, and if he didn't act cool we wasn't going to let him in our gang. You can tell little kids shit like that to make them do whatever you want, cause they're stupid and think whatever you say is for real.

And I finish them peanut butter cups right as Mack comes back and gets up in here with me, and I put the empty bag up under my seat and wipe my fingers off on my jeans cause the chocolate's all melted all over the place.

Mack kind of looks at me and shakes his head, and his big bulldog cheeks get all red like he's mad about something, so now he looks like that red dog on the beer bottle, and he's real quiet for a minute, and I figure that rent-a-cop's done pissed him off too.

Then he says, "Don, I'm just going right back the way I came."

"That's cool," I tell him, "I ain't going—"

"Yeah," he says, "I know. Nowhere."

Then he goes to put something behind the seat, and I see he's got a doll and I say, "What's that?"

89

"Nothing. Just a doll for my daughter," Mack says. Then he puts it behind the seat and starts the truck back up again.

"You got a kid?" I say, and I try to think of Mack screwing, but it ain't nothing I want to see.

"Yeah, she's been wanting one of these for a while," Mack tells me. "Supposed to be some cartoon character, I think."

When he says that about dolls and cartoons and kids, it makes me think of this one time when me and Jimmy was both doing some time cause this judge was a prick and told us, "If you kids are old enough to do the crime, you're old enough to do the time," and it was in Christmas and they called us all in the cafeteria cause they was going to hand out all the gifts people sent, and they had all this junk laid out on the tables, and they was calling us up to get our stuff. Mostly it was crap like cookies and food, and me and Jimmy was standing there waiting, and I didn't figure on getting nothing, but Jimmy said he'd split what he got with me cause his momma had said she sent something.

Then they call Jimmy up there, and all the guards was laughing, and when he gets up there they shove this Goofy doll at him, and then everybody's laughing and whistling and throwing cookies at him and calling to Jimmy saying they going to make him their doll and all that. I hauled ass before he got that thing over where I was, cause I don't want no part of it. There we was in jail and his momma sends him a damn Goofy doll. Goofy, like on TV in the cartoons. He like to got his ass kicked every day after that, and so did I just cause we was friends. They called him "Jimmy the Kid," and then they'd say, "and here comes his little friend Donnie-boy." I ain't even lying. We got tore up just cause they thought he was a kid and I was a little boy. I'm still pissed about that, but it's done with now and it's nothing, so I don't tell Mack about it.

This ain't no big city or nothing, but there's this big highway goes right through the middle of it, and that's where we been going, and right now Mack's done hauled ass out the parking lot, and he's booking down that road again, and I figure he's in a hurry to give that doll to his kid. I don't see nothing else to eat in here, so I just kind of check things out cause like I told Mack, I never been in one of these big trucks like this. I ain't even got a car at all, but I'm going to get one cause people laugh at you walking all over the place, and I'm sure as hell not riding a bike. If I had a cool ride, I'd cruise around everywhere.

Me and Jimmy was talking about that, and he says he knows some guy who's got a car we might could get, but I think it'd kick ass to get hold of a big truck like this cause then nobody could jack with us.

So I say to Mack, "How much is a truck like this?"

And Mack don't even look at me, but he says, "How much have you got?"

"Don't know," I tell him.

Then he looks at me and shakes his head, and them big cheeks jiggle around, but he don't say nothing for a while. He's just all hanging onto the wheel and looking at the road, and his mouth is all tight like he's biting something, and his eyes look all squinched up. I figure he's just trying to think how much it cost, so I stay quiet and just watch outside. I got to look straight down to see them other cars, and I know if I had a truck like this, I could smash all them cars like they was bugs, and I wouldn't let nobody but Jimmy ride up in here, not even my momma cause she won't never give me no money, and me and Jimmy would cruise around and wouldn't nobody tell us what to do.

Then Mack slows down and stops and looks at me, and I figure he's going to give one of them bulldog-face-smiles that looks like he's growling, but he don't. He just reaches over, and I think for a minute he's going to hit me, but he opens my door and he says, "Well, Don—but not Don Coyote—here you are."

And we're right back in front of McDonald's, and I figure I got to tell Jimmy what I done today, and I bet he's going to be pissed he didn't get to go too, and I tell Mack, "That's cool."

And I get down out the truck, and he takes off, and I figure I'll go fool around on the playground cause Jimmy usually comes finds me there. I ain't even lying, Jimmy's going to shit when I tell him what all I done today. But it's done with now and it's nothing.

Kyle Boudreaux
A Stuck Peanut and a Monkeys' Paw

I am a sick elephant...I am a spiteful elephant. An unattractive elephant. My trunk hurts. To be honest, I'm not altogether sure what is causing my pain, I just know that I hurt. It is a dull, throbbing, consuming pain, one which is causing the hairs on the end of my tail to fall out. My housemate, in this Houston enclosure, has begun making light of the balding tuft of my tail, saying I should maybe pluck some hairs off the llamas in the adjacent pen and make myself presentable. I considered this, but llamas are filthy creatures who spit, and I want no part of that.

I took my case to Monkey in the next cage over from mine. He was busy directing an imaginary choir with a stick he had stolen from a crying boy standing in front of his cage. He shook his hands back and forth violently, trying to rouse the choir to a fever pitch. This was a trick he had learned last fall when the zoo was visited by a high school glee club, and he used it when he wanted to get extra attention.

I called him over to the side of the cage next to my enclosure and asked him to take a look. He scampered up with his stick in hand and peered up my twin-holed appendage, scrunching his human-featured face. He scratched his nether regions in perplexity and said he could see what appeared be to a peanut, lodged deep within my trunk, it's specked shell covered with a shiny substance.

"I could take that out for you." Monkey spoke wildly with his hands, almost poking himself in the eye with his stick. "Of course, Elephant, you'll have to do me a favor in return."

He grinned, letting me gaze upon a gleaming pair of banana yellow teeth. "These," he said, showing me his paws, "Don't come cheap."

I looked at his black and white furred body, hanging from his perch by his tail. His dirty paws gripped the stick as he sniffed the underside of one arm. I didn't trust Monkey. He is surrounded by what the Haitian chickens in the aviary call *bad mojo*. Instead, I declined his offer and decided to suffer with my condition. My trunk swelled and throbbed with a fiery pain, and a hazy fog of delirium covered my eyes. The veterinarians tried to poke and prod my trunk, but I ran them out of my house, then listened to them, just on the other side of my enclosure, talked about how old I was and that I really wasn't worth wasting their time.

I am old. I've lost track of how many years I've accumulated here. They seem to have melted into a swirl of fat ladies towing dawdling children, of flashing bulbs of camera light, of a constant parade of animals coming into the zoo but none going out. Me taking peanuts just because they are offered. My head hurts.

I can see my new enclosure mate stirring in his sleep. His ears wave, creating an easy breeze which the flies surrounding him glide upon. He arrived fresh last week from a private estate in Texas in order to fill the zoo's vacancy left by the previous tenant. He was bought for a wealthy mans' son to ride. I told him he was the world's most extravagant pony. He was none too amused. He glared at me and asked if he was a mere pony, then what was I before I got here? I huffed my chest out and glared right back at him and said they had to drag me kicking out of the African wild, where I was king! I stomped my foot for effect.

This was of course a total fabrication. I actually hailed from Magnificent Mac's Monster Circus and sideshow, where I was forced to perform, of all things, a ballet. The show was complete with a three-piece orchestra, consisting of Mac, who besides owning the circus was also a frustrated cellist, Cecile, the horn playing walrus, and Thurl Weed, a retarded circus clown who played a horrible screeching violin. When this musical atrocity would begin playing, I would parade out, directed by my trainer, Willy. All across my body draped yard upon yard of shimmering pink fabric and ruffles fashioned into a horrendous tutu. My trunk still shivers at the thought of the spectacle. When the circus finally folded, I learned my fate would be a well-fed life at the Houston Zoo.

I'm too well fed. I caught a glimpse of my bulk in the reflection of the watering pond, and I don't remember ever being this big. Too many peanuts have made it into my mouth. I'm going to cut down. I have to.

The pain is searing now. This humid Texas air is making it hard to breathe. Little white spots are floating in front of my eyes, and my knees feel wobbly. I might have to do business with monkey.

I close my eyes and listen to the sounds of the zoo. It is quiet tonight and cool. No ruckuses from the nocturnals, which is unusual. I can hear the chuffing growls of the tigers, and monkey is talking in his sleep. He keeps telling someone to give him a high five, a trick the trainer taught him last week.

I feel a nudge at my side followed by a "Pisst, Pinky." I look down and see Paddy, a stray dog whom I've come to know. She sneaks into the zoo after dark and scrounges for dropped hotdogs and soggy ice cream cones. If I come across anything sufficiently malodorous, I save it for her and see if she's interested. She insists on calling me Pinky since I told her of my pirouetting past.

"I'm afraid I'm a bit under the weather today." I can see what looks to be mustard stains brightening the tip of her muzzle.

She cocks her head to one side. "Get a hold of a bad peanut?" She titters lightly as she stretches her back leg around and takes a few absent swipes at her ear.

"You might say that. I think I have one stuck in my trunk." I wince as a bolt of pain sears itself on the back of my eyes. My skin is dry and cracked from not being able to douse it with water vacuumed by my trunk. I have considered asking my enclosure mate to help me, but he isn't very cooperative.

"Wow. Really? Let me take a look." She trots around to my once proud trunk and peeks up the swollen mass, her eyes squinting as if looking at something from a great distance. "I don't see anything, must be too dark." She turns her head away, and I can feel the wetness of her nose brush against my tender flesh.

Paddy begins sniffing her way around the perimeter of the enclosure.

"You're looking in vain you know. The keepers are extraordinarily careful to not leave anything in the cages."

"Yeah, I know, but I still have to look." She skirts around my roommate, finishes her inspection, and makes her way back to my side. "That new guy giving you any hassle?" she asks lifting her nose to some hidden smell in the air.

"A bit, but not enough for concern."

"You want me to take a leak in his bale of hay? I don't mind. Not that I think it would really hurt him, but it would be wicked funny." Her tail is slapping the dust of my floor, causing little smoke signals to go up.

"Thank you, but I believe I can handle his bulk." I lean forward onto my front feet and then ease my rear haunches down onto the floor, careful not to hit my trunk on the ground.

"Well the offer's on the table," she says as she resumes her sniffing for a phantom snack.

"Must you continue that?" I flap my ears to create a breeze, hoping it will help cool my fiery trunk. "Would it be so terrible if you missed a morsel?"

"Yes it would." The moonlight bounces off her reddish coat as she dips and dives amongst the bales of hay which litter the enclosure. She pauses as she passes my left flank and turns her head towards me. "What if I missed a sandwich or something, then what?"

"Then you miss it. What is the tragedy?"

"What the hell kind of dog would I be if I missed a perfectly good sandwich laying on the ground. I couldn't live with myself." She pads up to me and says, "If I can't find any food with this baby," she taps the side of her muzzle with her paw, "then I might as well call it quits." She lies down beside me and rests her head on her front paws.

"What are you going to do about your sniffer?" she asks.

As she settles herself next to my front foot, I look down and notice how it can almost cover her entire length. I hear monkey still chattering softly in his sleep, and I am reminded of his offer. I can imagine him tucked inside the tire hanging in his cage, clutching his tattered stuffed animal, his hands opening and closing around the toy.

"Monkey offered to take the peanut out for me, but he wants something in return." I watch Paddy close for her reaction. I know she and Monkey have had a previous encounter involving her tail and Monkeys' fevered paw. She sniffed too close to his cage one night, and in a fit Monkey grabbed her tail and told her to never get that close to him again, that whatever was near his cage belonged to him. Her tail still holds a slight crimp, of which she is thoroughly embarrassed.

"You're not really thinking of doing business with that little punk, are you?" Her words have a slight growl.

"If this pain doesn't get any better then I'll be forced to do something." I struggle up from my position on the floor and walk around the enclosure, hoping the movement will jar the peanut loose.

Paddy rises up and begins to walk back toward the hole in the fence where she crawled through. Over her shoulder she says, "If I had a choice between pain and dealing with Monkey, I'd choose the pain. You can trust the pain. And by the way, if you do get that peanut out then I've got first dibs on it. I don't care what it looks like." And with that, she disappears through the hole.

When morning comes, the veterinarians are waiting for me to open my eyes. I feel sick and defeated, and in no mood to run them out of my house. All I want now is relief. When they tell me to stand, I do. I also raise my trunk obligingly, allowing them full view of my appendage. When they are done with their examination, they leave shaking their heads and muttering that I'm old anyway, and they shouldn't waste their funds on my care when a new elephant is what the zoo really needs. I feel disheartened by their diagnosis and begin to fear my fate may be that of my last enclosure mate, who when escorted out was a lot stiffer than when he came in.

The zoo's normal bustling sounds are slowly replaced by a steady throbbing sound of expiration deep within my skull. I loathe this place and everything in it. I want to leave, to take an excursion through the fence like Paddy and sniff my way to someplace else. I want to live off of the hotdogs the land provides and not have to kowtow to a child holding a bag of roasted nuts.

Throughout the day, people parade by my enclosure, never stopping to look at me, as if sensing I am something to be ignored, something that will soon be gone. No children look and point at my trunk, which should be waving in the air but instead lies limply on the ground. No one throws peanuts my direction. They all prefer to harass the polar bears in the pen directly across from mine. I am grateful to be left alone with my misery.

My body has betrayed me by being so big. I should have been a mouse.

My housemate manages to give me hourly reminders of his health. He keeps his posterior to me, swinging his tail with arrogant waves, showing me his beautiful bottle brush mop of hair on the end. He vacuums gallons upon gallons of water from the drinking pond and into his massive trunk, spraying himself with liberal spurts. The water looks soothing, and I wonder how it would feel on my parchment-thin hide. I again consider asking him to douse me, but after each display he looks over at me in my misery and gives a little wink. Damned showoff. If I ever get over this pain, I'll speak to the Haitian chickens about placing a voodoo curse on him to shrivel his trunk to the size of Monkey's tail.

The day passes slowly, and I am anxious for night to come, for everyone to leave so I might talk to Monkey.

Once everyone is gone, the zoo quiets to a low hum. I can see Monkey out of the corner of my eye looking at me. He is gripping the side of his cage with his hands, and his eyes are bright and glittering. He is humming something to himself, and his tail is swishing from side to side.

"Poor trunk hasn't gotten any better has it?" He asks in mock pity.

"No." I sigh through my mouth and settle back on my haunches.

Monkey loosens himself from his perch and scampers around his cage twice. He hoots and raises his arms into the air, then kicks and beats on a tire in his cage.

He shouts over to me, "All you have to do is ask and I'll take that peanut out. You know I can do it. I have hands. It would only take me a second, then," he raises his hand, holding an imaginary object toward the sky, "I would have it." He runs around his cage bouncing off the bars and hooting.

"What do you want?" I cast my eyes downward, and I can feel my dry skin is crawling, begging me to soak it with water. It cracks with each shift of my weight.

"We'll talk payback after the work's done."

He is picking his fur clean with his nails. I dread the idea of those monkey hands ranging on my snout, filling me with all manner of infestations. I notice how he is constantly scratching and sometimes loses patches of his hair. He is filthy, and I distrust him. I think about how strong my trunk used to be, how easily I could knock about anything I wanted. I think about how handsome my tail used to be and how easily I could dismiss the flies. I decide I'm not ready to die.

I raise my bulk and lumber over to him. "Ok then, take it out."

He jumps up and down, flashing a huge grin. "Ok, ok, then raise your trunk and repeat after me."

"Why? I'm not going to pledge allegiance to you."

He continues bouncing while saying, "No allegiance, just an oath to make sure you don't try to skip out on payment."

My eyes widen. "Monkey, I promise you I'm a pachyderm of my word. If I say I'll honor something—"

"Yeah, yeah, just repeat after me. 'I, Elephant, promise'."

My shoulders slump as I feel myself sinking to an unutterable low. I feel betrayed by my body, and I hate myself, and this place, for making me do this. My pride is bigger than my bulk. "I, Elephant, promise."

"Not to screw over Monkey." He begins rocking back and forth on the bars.

I sigh, "Not to screw over Monkey. There, I have said it. Can we get on with the procedure?"

He waves me in close with his hand, and I step up to his cage, putting my pitiful trunk through the warm metal bars. I can feel his breath on my throbbing and parched skin. His eyes seem to glow in the little bit of light the moon is providing, and I can almost taste the stink off his cage fermenting in the humid air.

He softly pats my lower trunk until he finds a spot of interest. I wince with each pat, my tender flesh resonating pain. Monkey keeps his hand on the spot while licking the fingers of his other hand. He uses his disgusting moistened hand to paint a crude sticky bulls-eye around the place he has marked. Then with a sudden deft movement, he raises his hand high into the air, and it comes crashing down on my pitiful skin, causing white dots of light to dance before my eyes. Blinded with pain, I stumble back away from his cage, knocking my trunk against the bars, and fall on my haunches. The dots clear just in time for me to see the smashed remnants of a slimy peanut slide out of the end of my trunk.

A cool breeze of air flows up my inflamed trunk, and I stare at Monkey with disbelief. "You actually did it," I say, my eyes wide.

He is busy with a victory dance on top of the tire. It is spinning and swinging, and he is on top performing his conducting routine, waving his stick about wildly, causing his black and white hide to jitter back and forth. He hops off the tire and back onto the bars of his cage. I can see drops of feces falling from his feet onto the bottom of his cage.

"Was there any doubt?"

"Yes," I say.

"I'll collect my payment tomorrow! I'll collect my payment tomorrow!" he sings as he begins dancing in a dark stained patch on the bottom of his cage.

Tomorrow, I think.

I pretend to sleep as long as I can, and when monkey starts calling my name, shouting for me to wake up, I still pretend to not hear him. I just barely crack my eye and watch him running quick circles around his cage, taking time to beat and kick the tire every time he passes it.

"Elephant, Elephant, Elephant," he calls. "Get up, you promised. You promised." He begins throwing feces at my posterior, which is turned towards him.

Finally in disgust I answer him, "Okay, Monkey. I can hear you. What do you want?" I rise up and feel just the slightest bit of soreness in my trunk. I stretch out my stiff legs and think about how good my skin will feel when I douse it down with water from the watering pond. The smashed peanut is still on the ground by Monkey's cage, the mucus around it having dried during the night. I lumber over to it and tuck it into a corner, making a point to remember to show Paddy when she comes scrounging.

Monkey is on the side of his cage, next to my enclosure. He is leering at me and smiling, and for the first time I realize that I am bound to do what he wants. I had promised. The fuzzy haze of sleep dissolves into complete awareness of the black and white thing in front of me. He waves his arm in a circular manner, motioning for me to turn around. I hesitate for a minute, then, remembering my promise not to cheat him, I go ahead and turn my backside to him.

"Back up to the bars, Elephant," he says, waving me on.

I lower my head and ease my bulk backwards until I can feel the metal bars pressing into me. I can feel Monkey's paws dancing back there, making my skin crawl. His paws are grasping and pulling at my tail, when suddenly, the sting of Monkey plucking out one of the hairs on my tail makes me cry out. One after another he plucks out the few remaining hairs on my tail until I am bald. I turn around and look at Monkey and watch as he fashions the hairs from my tail into a crude sort of wig, which he places on top of his head. He stands there looking proud in his new wig, holding a stick in one hand and a bright red rag he stole from the trainer in the other.

"Is that the payment? Are we equal?" My head is lowered.

"No, just one more thing, one more." He hops on top of the tire so he can look me in the eye. "I want a pony ride. I want to swing from your trunk and ride on your back, so I can show off my wig," he says, taking his paws and fluffing it up. "That's what I want. That's what I want." He jumps off the tire and runs full speed around his cage, with a hand on top of his head to hold his wig in place.

I stand by Monkey's cage and watch him run so fast that the black and white of his hide seem to melt together. In my mind, I can see the spectacle that will unfold. I can see him perched on my back, leading the crowds' cheers with his stick, bouncing up and down and waving the red rag, his wig glued firmly on his head with some sticky feces from the bottom of his cage. The crowd will be huge, shunning the polar bears in favor of seeing the fabulous Monkey ride his fool elephant with a bald tail. And they will take more pictures than I have ever seen them take. And mothers will not have to drag their children along, for they will come running. And they will throw more peanuts than I have ever borne witness to. And I will eat them. And I will hate myself.

Danielle Jackson
Honeymoon on the Beach

"You want a what?" she had asked.

Rebecca's eyes got big as she stared back in disbelief at the statement he had just made. Her fork had paused in midair halfway between her plate and her mouth. Everything seemed to have to come to a dead stop until a grain of rice fell off her fork onto the table. She blinked at the food on her plate and then looked straight back at the man across from her and repeated the question.

"I'm sorry. What did you say?"

"You heard me. I want an annulment," he replied.

"You're not even Catholic. You don't even know what an annulment is."

"I know that if being married to you is going to be like this, then I want out."

"We've only been married four days," she pleaded as the tears started to gather in her eyes.

"Yeah, and it fucking sucks," he shouted.

The rest of the restaurant got quiet. The waiter quickly hurried over to the table to make sure everything was okay. He was trying to keep a scene from being made, but it was too late. It had already started. She put her head down, wishing she were anywhere but here on her honeymoon.

"Is everything to your liking, sir?" the innocent waiter asked.

Chris eyed the waiter, looking him up and down. He seemed surprised at first to see someone standing there, then a smile crept slowly onto his face.

"As a matter of fact, no, everything is not to my liking. You see these rolls here?" he said as he took one out and pounded it on the table, "They're hard. They fucking suck."

His voice crescendoed on his last statement as he threw the roll across the room. It made a thud as it hit the back wall and fell to the ground.

She glanced at the waiter sideways as he picked up the basket of rolls as quickly as possible and tripped over his own feet while backing away from the table.

She looked back down at her plate of food. She had lost her appetite. Funny, she had so been looking forward to eating a good meal.

So far, she had been sick the entire trip. There was no such thing as morning sickness. It was more like morning, noon, and night. This evening had been the first time her stomach felt settled enough to accept some decent food.

The rest of the evening was somewhat of a blur. She had pleaded with Chris to stay calm. Whatever it was, they could talk about it later in their room at the hotel. However, the more she pleaded, the louder and the meaner he got.

What sticks out most in my mind is the spitting. He was spitting Skoal everywhere but in his cup. Brown grainy spots were all over the booth.

To me, each ugly spot represented something ugly he had said that night. Oh yes, it is me in this story. It's just that that time in my life, that night seems so surreal, so unbelievable that it is easier to remember it happening to some other person, like you remember a scene from a movie or a character in a book. I know in the back of my mind that it is me, but then again it's not, because I'm nothing like that girl that night on her honeymoon. I'm nothing like her anymore.

Anyway, back to the story.

When it was all over with, Rebecca was left standing outside of the restaurant by herself. He was gone, and it was as if that whole horrible scene had not happened. At least that is what she wanted to believe. Then reality set in.

She had no money or I.D. She was stranded at a restaurant about two miles down the road from her resort on the tiny little island of Aruba. She was four weeks pregnant and also known to have asthma attacks at the most inopportune times. This would be one of those times since she did not have an inhaler.

After standing there for a few moments considering her options, she did the only thing she could—she began to walk. The moon was bright and the air warm and balmy. The mood in the air was festive because once the sun went down on the island, it was a party until the sun came back up.

A cab offered her a ride, but she had to shake her head no. Then a group of drunk guys offered their services, but she kept on walking. Of course, she was still in shock. She had no idea what she was walking back to. She just knew she had to go.

In the end, she ended up in a lawn chair on the beach, set slightly away from the party that was going on. The limbo contest was just getting started, and laughter and music filled the air. She took her shoes off, dug her toes in the sand, leaned back, and considered what in hell she was supposed to do now.

The night clerk, who barely spoke English, would not give her a key to the room. She had nothing on her to prove she belonged in the hotel, so she really did not blame him. There had been no answer to her knocking on their door, so that meant A) he was not there, B) he refused to answer, or C) he was passed out from the non-stop drinking he had done since they had landed Sunday afternoon.

The best bet was on C. The travel agent said an all-inclusive resort was the way to go, but that was before she knew her husband would try to pickle himself with an incessant flow of alcohol. That was before she knew her husband would decide to back out after only four days of being married.

Closing her eyes, she took a deep breath. Exhaling slowly, she stared straight up into the stars.

I remember doing that when I was a little girl. I would lie on my back on the trampoline in our backyard and gaze away. The slight breeze would rustle the leaves of the two trees back there. The crickets would sing their song, and a soft glow would come from the lights on in my house.

One light would be from the kitchen, where my mother would be cleaning the dishes from supper and getting lunches ready for the next day. The next light would be from the den, where my dad would be drinking his coke, smoking his cigarette, and going over his legal briefs. My younger brother would be set square in front of the television watching *The Dukes of Hazard* and playing with his latest toy.

I would stay out there until one of my parents insisted I come in, or until the mosquitoes did the job for them. They would always ask me what I was doing out there, and my reply was always the same, "Just thinking."

I would think about what every little girl thinks of—my future. I had the perfect family at that time, and I knew I would grow up to live the perfect life. Even though I wanted Prince Charming to come along and sweep me off my feet, no other man in my life could ever equal my father.

Of course, fast-forward a couple of years from the nights on the trampoline, and my parents divorced. I realized my father was not perfect but human. The idea of the perfect life was then adjusted to becoming an independent lady who relied on no one or nothing but herself. This was a role that both my parents supported and encouraged, so I went with it because they hardly agreed on anything anymore.

So how did I end up in this situation? That is something I am still not sure about.

A tap on Rebecca's shoulder startled her. She thought maybe it was Chris coming down to apologize and bring this whole nightmare to an end. Instead, when she looked back she realized it was only a waiter.

"Something to drink, Miss," he asked in his Aruban accent.

She thought about it for a moment and decided a coke would taste good right about then, so she ordered one.

The waiter brought the drink back just a few moments later along with a tiny table he set up next to her chair. He handed her the slip, and she signed it still using her maiden name, putting her room number at the end.

Just right, she thought. She couldn't get a key to her room, but she could get a drink. She chuckled as she handed the slip back to him. Taking a sip of her coke, she thought about the name she had signed.

Most brides looked forward to becoming Mrs. So-and-So, but that was the one thing that had not appealed to her about marriage. For one, she liked her name. It represented the person she had worked hard to become. Second, he had a horrible last name—Lamb. Who wants to be Mrs. Lamb and have sheep sounds made at you all the time?

His last name was the only thing that had nagged her about him. Everything else about him seemed pretty near perfect. You put all his assets down on paper, and he was the Prince Charming for her, or at least he had seemed so until now.

She spent the rest of the night making plans and drinking the many cokes the waiter brought. She figured that he had to come out of the room sometime, and she would get her airline ticket and passport.

She would immediately change her ticket to the first flight off the island. The wedding presents would all have to be sent back. He had not moved any of his stuff into her house, so that was good, she guessed. She would have to talk to her dad to find out legally what the fastest and best way was to get out of this. Then she would have to talk to her mother. Her mom would help her figure out the rest.

The baby was still Rebecca's secret for many reasons, and she would keep it that way for now. They had been engaged for a year, so the pregnancy was not the reason for their marriage. However, in the small town she was from it was still better not to say anything until after the wedding.

As she was making plans, she assumed that if he did not want to be married then he did not want to be a father either. Resting her elbows on her knees, she put her head in her hands and shuddered at this thought. Raising her head slowly, she looked around and realized the last of the partiers were straggling in to their rooms to get some sleep. She was still in shock, but she felt better because at least now she had a plan.

Then she saw him. He came from the direction of the lobby and was walking up to the bar by the pool. Actually, it was more like staggering. He was ordering another beer.

Taking a deep breath, she got up from her chair on the beach and began to walk towards him. She knew she must look a mess. Her hair was tangled and matted from the wind and the sand. Her make-up had worn off a long time ago. Her sundress was wrinkled from sitting, and she was holding her shoes. Looking good, however, given her life and her plan, no longer mattered anymore.

She walked up right behind him. Clearing her throat, she asked, "What have you been doing?"

Chris turned his head and stared hard at her with bloodshot eyes for a good ten seconds. They both heard the clink of the beer being put down in front of him, and he turned his head back to his beer and the bartender without answering her.

She waited until he was through and then asked again, "What have you been doing?"

Taking a swig out of his beer, he faced her and finally answered, "I've been sleeping."

"Well, I have been sitting in that chair over there all night. I couldn't get in our room."

Chris shrugged his shoulders and took another gulp of beer.

"Don't you have anything to say?" He shook his head.

"You said you wanted out of this marriage, and then you left me stranded all night, and you don't have anything to say?"

Her voice was starting to get hysterical, and hot tears were starting to form in the back of her eyes.

"It was just an argument," he stated and then turned and walked away.

She lost it then. She tried to say everything that came to her mind all at the same time. Her sentences were getting jumbled, and she knew none of it was making sense. Still, he continued to walk.

She was shouting after him now, begging, pleading, demanding, and still she got nothing. Finally, she ran after him. When she caught up to him, he stopped and faced her.

"Look it was just an argument. They were just words. It did not mean a thing."

"But how..."

"I just said it."

"But did..."

"Look, chalk it up to our first argument," he said. Stepping back, he looked straight at her, put his hands on her shoulders and said, "I love you." Then he gave her a kiss on the cheek and a long hug.

After the night I had just had, it actually felt good to be hugged. He rocked me from side to side, still holding me as my mind went back and forth between my plans and my emotions.

Breaking the hug, he stepped back again saying, "Now I am going back to the room. Are you coming with me?"

Rebecca stared back at him and nodded her head yes. She walked behind him the rest of the way. When they got to the room, he headed for the shower. She immediately crawled into bed. As she drifted off to sleep, it hit her. He had never once said, "I'm sorry." By then it was too late anyway. Like I said earlier, she was different than I am now.

Daniella DeLarue
Maple Sanctuary

I never understood why my grandma sang those old songs. They didn't make much sense to me when I was young—she was always changing the lyrics to them. She would sing a lot of them during the Christmas holidays. Most of them sounded so sad. My parents would close their eyes and sway to the rhythms. My mother would hum with Grandma, and my father would slowly tap his foot in time. I, on the other hand, was constantly told to stop making noise with the wrapping paper while the adults sat in a circle with my grandma and listened to her songs.

I had my own way of listening to things. One of my relatives long ago had decided that he wanted a tree in the back of our property so he could sit under it and read. He ended up planting the tree near a small pond. I don't think there were ever any fish in it, but there were enough frogs to have their own choir. I would sit under the tree myself, listening to the leaves fall from the tree, and wonder what my dead relatives thought about when they sat here before me.

"Gigi! GIGI!! Get your tail in this house right now!" I picked up my bony knees as fast as I could and ran across the field to my grandma's house. I got to the back door and walked up the stone steps. I could smell food. Grandma was cooking supper, and we hadn't eaten lunch yet.

"Gi, go wash up and come back and peel these garlic for me." I was standing by the table near the back door, and she set a bowl down with five bulbs of garlic. I sighed, relieved I wasn't in trouble, but agitated I had to stink up my hands for a supper I wouldn't appreciate until I tried to imitate it for my own family.

I went to the bathroom and rubbed soap over my face and hands up to my elbows. I wondered what my brothers were doing back in Florida. I missed waking up on Saturday mornings and riding my bike down to the beach. While my brothers collected bottles and cans for candy money back home, I was stuck all by myself with my grandma every single summer.

As I peeled the thin layers of the garlic cloves, I watched my grandma cook. She didn't use measuring cups or spoons. She just took a handful of this or a dash of that, and it always came out right. Now, she wasn't neat about it. I know because I had to wash up and put everything away to dry in the oven. I would clean everything because Grandma would have flour all over the stove and grease splatters on the cupboards. My momma complained whenever she'd see me at the end of the summer cause all my clothes were stained with bleach, but I couldn't help it. The mop was taller than I was, and sometimes it was just too sloppy and wet to control.

Grandma was tough too. She chewed tobacco and could hold her drink better than her sons, I've been told. I never saw it, but I believed it. I once saw her smash a cockroach with her bare hand. And it wasn't like the small ones we got in Juno Beach. This one was long and black, with big, hairy legs and horns sticking out of its head. It had crawled right over my toes one night in the kitchen. I screamed so loud I hurt my own ears. Grandma ran into the kitchen, flicked on the light, and popped the roach with her open palm before it could do anymore damage. I had already dropped my sandwich and wet my panties, so the damage was done. My bill from the exterminator reminds me yearly.

I would hand over some of the cloves to her, and as she would smash them with the flat end of a knife, she would start singing. It was a low hum that would start deep in her chest, then rise higher with each clove she smashed. She looked up sometimes, and I'd hear, "Thank you Jesus," and she'd start singing again.

She sounded so unhappy with the words, but they came out so beautiful. Some words were quiet like a whisper, and others would shake her cheeks. She would sing about how she would rise up and see Grandpa again. Then she would turn to me and tell me, "One day, you'll know. You'll know all about it. Then you'll sing too." I rubbed my eye with my hand and started crying. That garlic stung worse than it stank.

My crazy Uncle Ronny lived in a small shack behind my grandma's house. I had to go knock on his screen door with a plate of food every night. There were only two rooms in there: his bedroom with a radio and his bathroom. Sometimes he would tell me to leave it on the steps outside because he was in the bathroom, but I had to wait right next to it so the dogs wouldn't eat it. I only ever stepped in there once because he didn't answer the door right away. I saw more magazines than I knew existed. There were some old model airplanes on a shelf near the radio and about twenty-something glass bottles like from a laboratory by some chemistry books. There was an eighty pound bag that had wasted all over the floor in the corner, and above the bag on a shelf were small rice plants growing near a lamp. It was dark in the room since there was only the one light and no window. It smelled of old leather, man sweat, and smoke. Uncle Ronny had heard his screen door and hopped out of the bathroom with his drawers down to his ankles, yelling at me to get out of his business. I dropped his supper and ran back to Grandma's, hiding and hoping I wouldn't get in trouble for dropping his food and getting into his business. I found out years later that he was trying to find a way to grow a grain of rice to the size of a potato. He thought he might end world hunger, but he never did. All of his work is still in notebooks, which my daughter has because she's continuing his research.

Grandma had a small patch of garden behind her house, on the side of Uncle Ronny's shack. She didn't grow much, just some tomatoes, peppers, and cabbages. She'd bend down and pick through the rotten ones, throwing the bad ones behind her back and gathering the good ones for supper in a dish towel. She'd stand up, take a deep breath, and stretch her back. I saw her one time, turning around to face the back of her house, looking up at the roof. It was covered in dead leaves and rotten magnolia flowers. I'd crouched behind the tree, hoping the tall weeds would hide me. She put the dish towel with the vegetables on the ground and walked to the back corner of the house near her two fig trees. She rubbed her wrinkled hand up and down the dull corner. Then she turned around to face the garden patch and Uncle Ronny's shack. She put her hands on her hips and smiled. "Mhmm." She stooped over to pick up the dishtowel with the tomatoes and walked to the back door. I heard her humming on her way in.

I ran across the field with my back bent over so no one would see me. I felt the weeds whip past my already scratched knees. I ran past the garden patch to the corner on the back of the house. I saw green paint pieces on the dirt below where Grandma had put her hand. I touched the bare wood underneath, wondering what was so important, what had captured my grandma's attention.

My summers were predictable: lazy, unrushed, and full of my grandma's cooking, stitching, and singing. She'd sing when she combed my hair or hung our clothes out to dry in the sun. She would especially sing when we would go to bed at night, telling me all kinds of stories about heroes and their adventures. I had them all memorized by heart. My Uncle Ronny would venture into the house from time to time. He rarely left his shack except to pick up a few things for Grandma in town. I would be peeling garlic at the kitchen table, and he would walk in the back door smelling of garlic, fertilizer, and stale clothes. He'd put Grandma's groceries on the kitchen table, pull out a lemon, and start peeling it. He noticed me eyeballing him one time.

"You want some?"

I shook my head no.

"You should eat lemon. Keeps you cool when it's hot outside. Here." He tore off a slice and pierced the middle of it with his thumb. I could see the cloudy liquid seeping from the flesh. I put the garlic bulb down on the table and wiped my hands on my shorts. I took the half torn slice in both my hands and held it to my nose. It smelled bitter.

"Go on. Just put it between your teeth and bite down hard." I did as he said as the sour juices moved past my teeth to my tongue.

"Now, move your jaw side to side and break open the rest of that skin." I felt juice flow over my back teeth, and I gagged when it hit the back of my throat. I coughed out the piece of lemon into my hands and felt my eyes tear up. The lemon juice was clinging to the back of my throat. My grandma shook her head at the stove and ran some water from the faucet and gave it to me in a mason jar.

"Ooo, Ronny! Leave that child alone! You know she don't like none of that stuff like you."

"Ah, Maw, you know I'm just playing with her. It ain't gonna hurt her."

She had her back to him while stirring something on the stove. "Boy, I done told you leave that child alone. Go back outside with them lemons stinking up in here. Go on."

Uncle Ronny snickered and grabbed his three lemons from the paper bag and reached for the door handle. He brushed past me as he said, "You'll be alright, Gi. One day you'll be able to take it." He smiled and stepped out the back door. I heard the screen door on his shack slam a few seconds later. My grandma had one hand on her hip and the other stirring some cabbage.

"Damn fool. Always messin' with stuff he ain't got no business with." I finished the water and picked up the garlic bulb to start peeling again.

In the late summers I would eat figs from the two trees on the side of my grandma's house. She would cut hers into squares and pour sugar over them. We'd sit by the fig trees after lunch sometimes and eat until we were full.

"Come on child," she'd say. "Let's go eat some toast so our stomachs don't go sour." I hated eating that burnt bread, but she said we had eaten more than our fill, and we'd pay for it if we didn't take care of it now. I'd take my dark brown toast and promise to eat all of it if I went to my tree on the side of the pond. I played with the dark crust, rubbing it over my lips to make it soft enough to eat. I watched a few yellow leaves fall from the tree and float in the ripples of the water. I thought about pirates in the ocean and the adventures they might have had. Grandma had told me stories of when they came to America, and how they took our ancestors from their homeland and brought them here. She had showed me some dark, rusted chains one time and said they were put around her great grandfather when he was sold to a man to work for him. Then she started singing. She sang words and spoke in between some of them. She had tears running down her cheeks as she told me how that very man that bought her great grandfather lived on her property. Everyone from her family had come from this property. Many years later, another man had bought the land for a church and some nuns lived here. My grandma worked for those Irish nuns, and when the last one died, she gave the property to my grandma and signed papers that it would remain in her family until my grandma sold it to someone else.

I smelled trash burning and turned my head towards my grandma's. I got up and followed the smell to the other side of my Uncle Ronny's shack. He was behind his old car, burning trash in the rumble seat. He was poking the pile with a long tree limb. He looked up and saw me and smiled.

"Come see Gi. It ain't gonna hurt you. Come see." He waved his hand over for me to come, so I walked towards him and covered my nose with my arm.

"I seen you looking at the side of the house the other day. You know why this house is so important to Grandma?"

"She said she got it from some nuns. They said it was hers until she gave it to somebody else." I felt proud answering my uncle with little effort, knowing the answer without even thinking.

"Well, that's part right. You know that old brick building with the boards up around the windows, the one on the corner of the street?" I knew which one he meant. I was never allowed to go there when I was playing in the yard. It didn't look like anything important, just some two story building with a bunch of broken glass around the edges of it and rust coloring the door hinges.

"You know, your grandfather used to work there. My father. It was a mattress factory years ago, before you were born, and I was smaller than you now." He poked at the fire and pieces of black ash rose into the sky.

"The man who owned it liked your grandfather. He said he would help with anything if he needed it. So your grandfather asked if he could help him build a house for those same nuns Grandma told you about. They needed an extra place for when travelers came through and needed a place to stay for the night. You know, them nuns never did live in that house. Your grandfather and grandma hadn't been married but a few months and were already expecting a baby. They kept your grandma while your grandfather built that house with his bare hands. His boss, the one from the factory, gave him spare lumber so he could make a good, strong frame for the house." I slapped a mosquito on my leg and scratched where it had bitten me. My uncle continued on, speaking out the side of his mouth with his cigar.

"Mhmm, your grandfather built a mighty fine house. Painted it and even planted a few trees for those nuns." The trees caught my attention. My ears went up.

"Were they good climbing trees, Uncle Ronny? Like my maple tree across the field there?" I pointed with my finger towards the tree.

He bent over real close to my ear and whispered, "You tell me." I followed his eyes and he was staring at the two fig trees on the side of Grandma's house.

My eyes flashed as I thought about my grandpa planting those trees when they were small and green. Now they were taller than the house, with figs hanging on every branch. I turned back to my uncle. He stood up and threw his poking stick into the burning pile. He looked down at me, waiting for me to say something. He held his cigar in his fingers.

"So, Grandpa built Grandma's house? How did she get it? Did the nuns give it to her with the land? Did any travelers stay here? Did you ever see any of them?"

He chuckled and then coughed a dry cough. "You sure ask a lot of questions. That's good. Grandpa did build Grandma's house. But what he didn't know was that when he finished the house, the nuns wanted him and Grandma to have it so they gave it to them. They told 'em it was their wedding gift. They were the nicest people your grandparents ever met.

They told Grandma that her family would always be in their prayers, and they would ask God to keep special watch over them." I looked over at the house in awe. I thought about the inside door frames and the front porch with the rocking chairs on it. The kitchen floor leaned enough you could put a ball on it, and the ball would roll away on its own without a push. I could see the back steps from where we were and the hand rail that Grandma used. I turned my head back to my uncle.

"Not everyone was so nice though. That man from the mattress factory, the boss who helped your grandfather, well, he found out about that house. He thought your grandfather had lied to him about using the lumber for the nuns. He called him a thief. Embarrassed him in front of everyone. Your grandfather tried to tell him what happened, but the man wouldn't listen. He fired your grandfather right there for what he had done."

I had never met my grandfather. He died before I was born. I had seen two pictures of him in my grandma's house. He looked like my dad, only taller. He had black, black hair and wide eyes. In both pictures he had a smile on his face.

"Then what happened? What did Grandpa do?"

"Well, that man from the factory tried to take the house back. He said it didn't belong to your grandfather because he had stolen the materials to build it. But the nuns claimed it was for them, and they could do with it as they wished, so they let Grandma and Grandpa stay there. That man tried to get papers saying that the house was his, but the state said that it belonged to the church and they couldn't touch it."

"So they got to stay there, for free. And what about the nuns?" I asked, getting deeper into the story.

"They stayed next door for a while. Some left and a few stayed. That empty lot next to the house is where the nuns used to live. They left and the place just fell down. Your grandparents lived here for free and took care of everything for the nuns. Your grandfather never worked a paying job again, but he did all kinds of work for those nuns, and so did your grandma. That was how they got along. That last nun Grandma took care of in the house; she died in there. That's when she gave her those papers she was telling you about. The house and the land are ours forever. Nobody can touch it. Ever."

The fire was dying down, and my uncle adjusted his loose pants. He looked down at me, his small eyes searching my face.

"You like that story?"

I nodded my head yes.

"Okay. You know that shelf of books in your Grandma's guest room?"

I nodded my head again.

"I want you to start reading those. Take 'em under your tree and read 'em. All the way through. No skipping parts. You do that and I'll tell you about the—"

"Ronny! You crazy fool! What you doin' burnin' that trash in the back of that car for?" My grandma came down the steps, throwing a dish towel over her shoulder.

"Come on here, Gi. Go wash up and get me some garlic peeled." She grabbed my face and looked at my forehead. "And get those cheeks good. They're filthy."

I walked to the back door from my uncle and grandma and watched them from the inside the back porch.

"How many times I told you not to be burnin' trash in that car? Huh? You want it to explode? There's still gas in there."

"Maw, it's too dry to burn it on the ground. I don't want to burn the place down."

"Oh, so you'd rather blow yourself up? Put this mess out." He grabbed a bucket nearby and threw it on the rest of the ashy pile. It popped and sizzled when the water hit the embers. He dropped the bucket off to the side and looked at Grandma.

"Boy, you get on my damn nerves with this shit. And you stay away from Gi with them crazy stories. She don't need to hear that."

"Maw, it ain't like it's a secret. The rest of the family knows. She'll find out anyway."

"Boy, she ain't ready yet, you hear? She'll know when she's ready to know."

"What the hell is that supposed to mean? She's twelve years old. Soon she won't be coming here for the summers cause she'll have to work back home."

My grandma stepped up close to Uncle Ronny, causing him to step back. I wondered if she could smell his lemon sweat.

"Now, you listen. It ain't up to us when she's ready. That's up to Him." She pointed towards the sky. My uncle rolled his eyes and grunted out a breath.

"Until then, we just supposed to look after her. She's special. Not like her crazy-assed brothers. She'll be the next one in the family to look after everyone. She'll do what the rest of you didn't want to do."

"Alright Maw. If you say so. I'm going back to my room." He walked around her, and she turned to watch him walk away.

"That's right, go on back to your hole. Write your notes and grow your plants. What good will it do anyone? Just go on back!" Grandma swatted at a fly with her towel and started for the back door. I ran to the sink in the kitchen and splashed some water on my face and rubbed my cheeks on my sleeve. I grabbed a bowl from the cupboard and two bulbs from the hanging basket. I sat down and tore as many pieces as I could before Grandma came through the back door. She was puffing. She walked past me to the baking trays next to the flour jar. She started to grease one with some bacon fat.

"Only one bulb tonight, Gi. It'll just be the two of us."

* * *

My grandma died on a Thursday. My Uncle Ronny said she didn't want any doctors there. He brought me into her room, and I saw her there on the bed. Her mouth was closed, holding a handkerchief to her chest. There was a candle burning on her dresser and some magnolias in a wide glass vase. I could smell sugar cookies in the room. We had made some the day before and the smell mixed with talcum powder made the room have sweet smell. Grandma liked having her back powdered. Her powder puff was next to the vase on her dresser. I walked over to touch her arm, but my uncle tightened his grip on my shoulders. I looked at him and frowned. I wriggled my shoulders loose and went to the side of her bed. We had slept in this bed for years. I got the hiccups one time, and I every time I hiccupped the whole bed would shake. Grandma got so mad at me because she couldn't sleep with the bed shaking. I put my hand out to touch her. Her arm was cool. I grabbed her hand, and it was warm underneath. I took a deep breath and backed away. I didn't look at my uncle as I ran through the house and out the back door.

I ran as hard as I could with my eyes closed. I knew my tree was close. I could hear the water. I stopped at the base of the tree and grabbed the lowest limb to climb. I wrapped my legs around the trunk and pulled myself up. I felt my scarred knees rub against the bark and scrape my bony legs. I reached for one limb and then another until I saw one of the dead yellow leaves on a branch. I strained to reach it, scratching my chin on one of the main limbs. I grabbed it, perfect in its shape, yellow veins reaching to the ends. Then I grabbed a green leaf, a smaller one from one of the smaller branches. I hopped down and ran back to the house. I was out of breath as I walked back into my grandma's room with my uncle following me. I put the two leaves by her magnolias. I grabbed my uncle's hand behind me, and he led me out of the room.

That night, under my tree, I cried and hugged my knees. I snuck out after my uncle had drunk too much and was asleep on the couch. My knees were ashy, and my tears made dark lines down my legs. My nose ran. I had a pain right by my heart, high in my chest that I had never had before. I couldn't hear my grandma's voice in my head. I cried some more.

By the time my folks got there it was Saturday night. The funeral was that next morning. When we showed up, everyone looked so dressed up. My mother even made me wear a dress, which I hated. My cousins and aunts held each other as they cried. My brothers looked at everyone with their eyebrows high and their nostrils flared. I think they wanted to cry, but not in front of everyone.

The preacher spoke about Grandma's life and how hard she had worked. My father kept his arm around my mother's waist while she squeezed my hand. She dabbed her eyes with a handkerchief. Everyone was sobbing and shouting *amen* when the preacher would talk about what a wonderful person Grandma was and how now she was in heaven with Grandpa. After the ceremony, we walked over to the burial site at the back of Grandma's land. She had wanted to be buried there, so Uncle Ronny chose a spot on the other side of the pond, far enough away you had to squint to see it from my tree. When the men lowered the casket, I pulled on my mother's dress.

"I feel sad but I don't feel like crying. Is that bad?" My mother blew her nose.

"No honey. That's okay. You do what *you* feel is right. You don't have to cry because everyone else is. We all grieve in our own way. God knows what we feel inside. Grandma does too."

My father was looking at the casket and nodded his head. His eyes were red, but there were no tears.

A few people picked up some dirt and threw it on the casket. My parents threw some too, but I just stood there. As the crowd grew smaller and the talking increased the further away they walked, I sat down beside the open earth, with my knees under my chin, rocking myself. I smelled the fresh unearthed soil and the wet grass. I saw the pale wood of the casket with the dark clumps of dirt broken on top. I started humming. It was three simple notes, the next one lower than the one before. I did it over and over in my chest. I sang two more notes. I felt the melody vibrating below my jaw. I opened my mouth and hit my tongue against the roof of my mouth. I closed my eyes and swayed with the sounds. I started making words from the sounds and lifted my head up towards the sun. I raised my voice louder and louder until I couldn't hear the birds anymore. My parents stopped and turned around. My uncle dropped his cigar. I stopped long enough to hear more footsteps coming to me.

People walked back and formed a circle around me. I opened my eyes to see them all with a hand on each other or leaning on another's shoulder. Everyone had their eyes closed. I would sing my few notes and they would all answer. I peeked at my mother and father on my right. She was smiling with tears running down her face. My father had pulled his lips in and tapped his foot. My uncle stood back behind everyone, with his clothes hanging loose on him. He smiled as he got out his lighter and another cigar. He lit it, puffed a few times, and turned to walk away.

Mary Baswell
Glory Glory Hallelujah

The temperature had dropped fifteen degrees in the last two hours, and the sky was a weird gray darkened with black thunder clouds. I could feel my lips chapping, and I licked them in spite of it. I pulled my jacket collar up over my nose and reached in the front pocket and dug around for my Walkman. I fast-forwarded the tape and cranked up the volume. "November Rain" seemed appropriate on this day.

I looked up at the sky one more time, and knowing the rain would be here sooner than later, I hunched my back against the gusting wind and decided to book it the rest of the way to the house.

Not that I was in a hurry to get home. Most kids have moms waiting for them at home with plates of warm straight-from-the-oven cookies and glasses of icy cold milk. The only thing I had waiting at home was Chuck. In fact, if it weren't for the rain, I'd be headed in the opposite direction.

I jogged the rest of the three blocks from school to the corner of Hall and Oates. I rounded the corner just as I thought my lungs would collapse. As leaves crunched under my shoes, I remembered every autumn since I was ten. Chuck had made me rake up all the leaves in our yard. I wanted to make big piles of them to jump in, but Chuck made me bag them up immediately.

Slash was just finishing up his guitar solo as I stopped the tape and pulled off my headphones to look for my house key. I stood in front of my house, staring at the eaves and shutters that were a disgusting olive green. I noticed the glare from the TV through the front window and could hear a little girl's peal, "Its Shake and Bake, and I hay-elped!" I rolled my eyes and looked around to make sure no one was watching me hesitate at my own door.

I glanced at the house directly next to ours. The house had been empty for several years, ever since Ted moved with his family to North Dakota. It looked abandoned and sad, and I wondered if I ever looked that way to people. A roll of thunder sounded in the distance. I took a deep breath and turned the key in the doorknob.

The stench of cigarettes and the old space heater filled my nose as soon as I opened the door. I listened as I stepped through the front hallway and heard the pop of a can opening somewhere out of view in the living room. The rhythmic squeak of Chuck's decrepit rocking chair assured me I had time to duck through the kitchen and avoid any contact with him. I slunk past the crusty old pictures and purple and gold medals in grimy cases that hung in the hallway and made my way to the kitchen. I threw my backpack into one of the padded vinyl chairs sitting at the dinette. I crept past the table to my room.

I shut my door without a sound and walked to my bed. I freefell backward onto my shitty little mattress. I saw Pam Anderson staring back at me from her place on the ceiling with her tiny red bathing suit and hard nipples. I had focused on her blond hair and pink lips many a night, locked in my room with the covers up to my ears and a tube sock in my pants. I sat up, shrugged my jacket off, and headed back to the kitchen, stomach growling.

I could hear Chuck mumbling and flicking his Bic as I opened up the cabinets. I found a half a loaf of bread, some dusty cans of tuna and Spam, a jar of Jif, and some Raman noodles. I went to the fridge and examined a few takeout boxes before grabbing the butter and reaching for a slice of cheese I could see hiding behind the six beers that were left of Chuck's 12-pack. I took it, the butter, and the loaf of bread to the counter and began my search for a pan. As I bent down, I could hear a man's lilting voice in the living room announcing the next show, the eerie melody of Taps warbling in the background. A clap of thunder shook the windows of our old house, and a flash of lightning lit up the dark sky.

I stood rooted to the dirty linoleum floor, careful not to move or make a sound. I could hear the explosions and gunfire on the television, but I was listening for Chuck. Though I couldn't see him, I could hear his labored breathing as it came faster. He started to wheeze, and I could hear him gasping for air as if he were being choked. I tip-toed to the doorway of the den and watched the back of the old man's head as he stared at the TV. His head flipped back, whipping the greasy gray strands back from his face.

"Damn gooks! Goddamn you bastards!" yelled Chuck, suddenly coming alive, jumping up off his chair, shaking a fist at the TV. I knew better than to try to calm him down, and I absently fingered the scar on my chin given to me as a reminder.

Chuck hit the floor, belly down, in his sweat-stained wife beater and gray sweatpants, barefoot, toes clinched. He pointed an imaginary gun, closing one eye, aiming to kill. "I'll kill you all, you goddamn gooks!

Run, Tommy, run! I'll kill those sons of bitches, run!" He looked back for his comrade that was not there. He motioned to the end table, seeing his friend instead of a piece of furniture. I wanted to laugh at the sight, but the weight of the situation kept me from doing so.

He was crawling on his belly, using his knees and elbows, trying to make it to other side of the room. Another explosion on the TV, and Chuck's eyes went wide, foam starting to form at the corners of his mouth. He flew to the other side of the sofa, knocking over the end table and taking out his beer and the ashtray that had been sitting on it. Beer splashed on his face, and the ashes stuck to the beer and sweat on his forehead.

"Man down, man down! Someone help me over here, goddammit, man down!" he kept repeating, his voice cracking and losing volume. He hugged a sofa cushion that had fallen to the floor, whispering to it, wrapping his arms protectively around it. He was drooling now, his eyes foggy with tears and confusion. His eyes stared past the stained shag carpet and into Vietnam. After a few moments, Chuck had quieted, and I stepped over him and turned off the TV. I studied Chuck's face as he slept fitfully.

I hated that I looked so much like him; our noses had the same crooked bridge; our eyes were the same muddy green. I hated him for these episodes, and I hated him for driving my mother away. I picked up the old Indian-style afghan off the sofa and threw it over Chuck's body. It landed, half covering his face, and I didn't bother to adjust it. I picked up the spilled beer can and ashtray, righted the end table, and plopped the ashtray back on it. I took the beer can to the garbage and tossed it in. I returned the butter and cheese to the fridge, put up the loaf of bread, and turned the light off in the kitchen.

I returned to my room, turned off my light, climbed into bed, and allowed my eyes to adjust to the dark. I turned on my side to face the nightstand that held my alarm clock and a small gold picture frame. The photo inside was tattered and old. It was the only photo I had of her. My hair was the color of hers, and I had her smile. She held a chubby baby in her arms, their faces pressed together, cheeks touching. I didn't remember the photo being taken, but I knew the baby was me. She wore an old Army issue jacket, green with pockets spattered on the front. She loved that jacket. Chuck had sent it her while he was deployed and she was pregnant with me. He had told me that once, when he was more sober than usual.

I fell asleep clutching the picture against my chest, the sound of fat, angry raindrops pelting my window.

* * *

I had stared down the clock on Ms. Thompson's wall for the last hour and a half. It was Friday, and I was ready to get the hell out of there. At exactly 3:32 pm the last bell rang. I ran to my locker and shoved my books in while getting my Walkman out. I slammed my locker and headed out the main door. I looked both ways and ran for the street lined with cars.

Banana yellow school buses lined the front of the campus. The diesel fumes choked me, and I could hear the bus drivers yelling at the kids to sit down and shut up. I made my way through the school yard, bumping into a group of girls as I scanned the area for dickheads. The girls screamed at me to watch out, but I had spotted Troy and Jake. I had to make it past the buses and across the street before they saw me, and I didn't have much time.

Too late. Jake had heard the girl's screams and jabbed his elbow into Troy's side and pointed in my direction. They both started to run, and so did I, knowing what would happen if they caught up to me. I could hear the two morons behind me yelling for me to stop, as if their saying it would make it happen. I flipped them off while still running and never looking back.

I had just rounded the corner of my street when I felt a hand on my jacket, whipping me around, almost ripping my collar.

"Watch the jacket, douche bag," I said, trying to sound unafraid.

"Why, did your mommy make it for you?" Troy teased in a baby voice. "Is it your favorite wittle jacket, Donnie?"

"He wears that damn jacket every day," chimed in Jake, "Are you poor, or are you just a retard?" They both snickered as if they had made an incredibly funny joke.

"Why don't you leave me the hell alone?" I said, and I turned to walk away, my knees knocking through my Levis.

"Not so fast, Army boy, why don't you drop and give me twenty," Troy said as he grabbed my shoulder to stop me from leaving.

"Fuck off," I threw my elbow up to shake his hand off.

"Wait a minute, Army boy, you ain't going nowhere." Jake said and threw a punch that landed smack dab on my nose. Blood spurted from my nostrils Mortal Kombat style, and I could feel myself falling to the ground.

"I don't think he liked the mommy comment, Troy," Jake said, standing over me. "It's because he doesn't have a mother. She ran away when he was born because he was so butt ugly." The two boys laughed again and high-fived each other.

I picked up my backpack, and holding my bloody nose with a sleeved arm, turned to walk away again. I silently calculated the distance from my house and tried to block out the two jerks behind me. I was almost home.

"I know why he wears that jacket every day, Jake, it's because his Daddy was in Vietnam. Fried his brains out there with Agent Orange. I hear he's a freak now, with no job and no brains. How's it feel to have a freak for a dad, Army boy? Like father, like son!"

My eyes were stinging with tears, and my nose was throbbing, but I kept on walking.

I was whirled around a third time, this time with a boy at each side. One pushed me over to the other while chanting, "Freak, freak!" Then from out of nowhere, a voice piped up.

"What the hell is wrong with you two? Leave the kid alone!" A small wisp of a girl ran up to the three of us. She bowed up to the bigger boys. "Get your hands off him, or I'll knock both of you into next week." She put up a fist to prove it. "Get on, now, get!" Whether surprised or really intimidated, the two boys loosened their grip. I immediately jerked myself out of their reach and stared at the girl next to me in amazement.

"What you gonna do about it?" Jake taunted, lowering his face to hers. She couldn't have been over five feet tall standing on her tip toes. Without hesitation, she clocked him in the left eye. Jake fell to the ground.

"You bitch! You really hit me!" Jake growled, getting up quickly and dusting the gravel off his pants. Troy was holding his gut laughing. Jake looked from Troy to the girl, his eye starting to swell. She stared him down, and started to walk toward him, fists up and ready for round two.

"L-Let's just get out of here, Jake," Troy said. "Screw her and that freak." Jake looked from her to me to his buddy. He was embarrassed that a girl had gotten a shot in on him. With a huff, the two boys turned and ran down the street, looking back to throw me warning glares. "Just wait 'til your girlfriend ain't around, Army boy!"

"You ok?" the girl asked.

I was still holding my bloody nose with my jacket sleeve, and I was trying to put my backpack back on. I lifted my eyes from my dirty Converses to look at the girl who had saved my life. She was wearing a Beastie Boys t-shirt and pink denim jeans. She was olive-skinned, with jet black hair down to her shoulders and straight as a pin, and she had almond shaped eyes the color of coffee. Her lips were full and caramel brown. She had pulled a tube of lip balm from her pocket and was slathering her lips with it. I caught a whiff of strawberries.

"You've got to fight back when people push you around, you can't just sit there and take that shit." She looked down the road at the two boy's figures growing smaller in the distance. "Dipshits," she mumbled, turning back to me. "Let me see that nose, it looks pretty nasty." She made a move to touch my face, and I flinched. "Oh, stop, let me see," she fussed, and grabbed my arm from my face before I could object. "You're going to need some ice, and you're going to have to look up to stop the bleeding." She tipped my head back with her fingertips, then looped her arm through mine. "Where do you live?" she asked me.

"Two houses down, that brown and green one," I replied, pointing to my house.

"Really? I live in the house right next door, just moved in last week." She pointed to Ted's old house. The once black windows now glowed with the light from a lamp somewhere inside. "Looks like we're neighbors. Is this a rough neighborhood? I don't want live here if I'm going to have to fight thugs off every day," she rambled while still holding my head back and guiding me to my front door. My cheeks burned, and I was glad that I was bleeding so she couldn't see my embarrassment. We were at my front door.

"Oh, wait, I have to get my key," I said, reaching into my shirt and pulling out the key tied to a string around my neck. I turned the key, and we stepped into the house. There were no lights on, and the house was dark and still. Chuck must be sleeping, I remembered suddenly. In my excitement, I had forgotten about Chuck. I could have kicked myself for letting this girl walk into my house without so much as a thought as to what he might be doing.

"We have to be quiet," I whispered to the girl, and she put a finger to her lips in agreement. We tiptoed through the hall to the kitchen. The girl immediately sat me down at the table and motioned quietly for ice and sandwich bags. I obediently pointed to the drawer by the sink, and she filled the baggy with ice from the freezer. She came back to the table, studied my wound for a moment, and put the pack on the bridge of my nose. I was in pain, but at the same time, I was nervous and suddenly aware of our arms touching ever so slightly.

"The ice will keep the swelling down, but you're going to have two huge shiners!" She smiled at me over the baggy and plopped down in the chair next to mine. "Are you going to make it?" she whispered, tilting her head to look at me. All I could manage to squeak out was a yeah. My face was pounding and I felt like throwing up.

"Good thing I was there to save you ... Donnie, is it?" she joked as she slapped my hand away from my face to keep me from removing the ice pack. "I'm Glory, nice to meet you."

I suddenly spit out a laugh. "Like Glory Glory Hallelujah?" I asked. The old hymn Chuck used to hum came to mind.

"I have no idea what you're talking about. That hit must have gone straight to your head," Glory giggled, her dimples deepening.

"Well, thanks anyway, but I was just about to punch their lights out when you showed up," I stammered, lying and hoping she would buy it.

"I'm sure you were," she replied, covering her mouth with one hand to stifle her laughter, "I'm sure you were. So, what grade are you in anyway?"

"I'm a junior. Eleventh grade. What grade are you in?"

Glory rolled her eyes. "Oh, I'm not in school, I dropped out when I was fifteen. Hated it. I would always skip and go smoke cigarettes behind the gym. I got suspended, so I just never went back." She was putting on the lip balm again.

I studied her as she applied the goo to her lips. She pursed her lips and slowly circled her mouth with the tube. She smacked her lips together as she put the cap back on. I must have been staring because she looked up at me, surprised.

"Keep your head back, silly. You're going to start bleeding again." She stood and pushed my head back and leaned on the table right next to me. I was eye level with her chest, and though they weren't big, I was impressed with the outline of them underneath her shirt. I could feel an erection growing, and I had to shift my position. She examined her cuticles on one hand while holding the ice pack on my nose with the other.

"Well, you are the only person I know here, so try not to get yourself killed, okay?"

I nodded and smiled.

* * *

It was afternoon but seemed much later, and Glory and I were holed up in my room. She had met me at the end of the sidewalk after school as she had for the past several weeks, jumping up and down to keep warm, hands buried in her hoodie, cheeks bright pink from the frozen wind.

We escaped to my room and turned on my tiny old TV. Layers of clothes came off as we got more comfortable and our bodies warmed. I was sipping hot chocolate while sitting against the headboard, Glory turned opposite, facing me against the footboard, our legs stretched out to each other's waists.

"So, how did your mom come up with the name Glory? Not that it's not a great name. I mean it's just... different." I regretted the remark as soon as it came out of my mouth. It seemed like I said a lot of stupid things to Glory. I felt like an idiot around her most of the time, but it seemed like she either didn't notice or didn't care, and I was grateful for that.

"It's short for Gloria, if you must know. It was my great aunt's name and my mother's middle name. I always thought it sounded like an old lady, so I changed it to Glory in the eighth grade. My mom still calls me Gloria, but everyone else knows me as Glory. Well, no one really knows me anymore." She paused, licking her lips. "I mean, I don't really know anyone here yet."

"You know me," I said.

"You're right, I do." She smiled at me from across our legs and wiggled her toes at me.

We made eye contact, and I smiled and looked away, blushing.

"Is that your mom in the picture?"

I hadn't mentioned my mother to Glory, and she had never asked, until today. I winced at the question, and I knew she meant the picture on my nightstand. I had never thought about her seeing it, and I wasn't quite sure I wanted to talk about it.

"Yeah, that's her," I said, not looking at Glory or the picture.

"She's pretty," she said reaching past me and grabbing the picture off the stand. I wanted to stop her and yank it back, but I stayed where I was. Glory studied the photo. "She looks like she loves you. You can tell," she whispered in a softer tone, her eyes fixed on the image of the woman and baby. "What's she like?" She was looking at me now.

"Er... I don't really know. She left when I was three." I focused on the mug in my hand.

"Oh, sorry, Donnie, I had no idea." Glory's face fell, and I actually felt sorrier for her than for myself.

"No, it's okay. I-I just don't talk about it much." But it was easy to talk to her, and I found myself telling her the whole story. "I don't remember much about her, except for a few fuzzy images from when I was a baby. Like I remember her hair. I remember seeing her flipping her hair and it shining in the sun like gold or something." I trailed off, thinking I may have sounded stupid again. "And you see the jacket she's wearing? Chuck had sent it to her while he was deployed; she loved it. At least that's what he says."

"That's why you wear that coat every day! I knew it looked familiar." Glory snapped her fingers and looked up at me.

"Yeah," I said.

We sat in silence with MTV playing a Dr. Dre video in the background. I had never listened to rap song until a week ago when Glory insisted I listen to one of her mixed tapes. I didn't really like it, but I lied and told her I did.

"So, what about your mom?" I asked her, glad to be changing the subject. "Doesn't she hate that you're over here every day?"

She hopped up from her spot on the bed and started rummaging through her purse on the floor. "My mom's not the supper cooking type," she said. "She's never even home in the evenings. She goes on dates or out to clubs."

"She knows people here already?" I asked.

"It doesn't take my mom long to find a man. Or for them to find her," she said matter-of-factly, standing up and returning to the bed with a baggie and square packet of cigarette papers. "You wanna burn?" She changed the subject this time, knowing what my answer would be.

I hated any kind of smoke. Chuck chain-smoked cigarettes, and I had despised the smell since I was young. And besides, weed was illegal, and frankly, I didn't feel like getting arrested, and I told Glory so. She offered it every day, and every day I would turn her down, feeling like a dork.

She was fingering the buds and smoothing a paper to roll a joint. Her tiny brown hands moved expertly over the book she was balancing on her lap. My eyes darted over her body. Her purple sweater fit snugly over her chest, and her jeans had holes at the knee. Her toes were painted a deep red, and somehow this turned me on. I had never touched a girl's toes before, and I wondered how they would feel between my fingertips. I adjusted my legs and the crotch of my pants. She looked up and saw me watching her. She smiled while narrowing her eyes at me.

"Were you looking at my tits?" she asked. She was finished rolling and stood up to walk to the window. She slid the window up and a rush of frigid air immediately cooled the room. She cupped her hand over the lighter to keep the wind from blowing it out. Glancing out the window and exhaling, she said, "Dudes are such perverts. But some are ass men, some like tits. I guess you're a tits kind of guy?" Her small mouth was dirty, and I was a little uncomfortable discussing this with a girl who actually used the word *tits*. I snorted but didn't respond. She took another pull as she looked warily at me.

"How old are you again? Sixteen?"

"Almost seventeen, in two months," I interjected a little too quickly.

She paused. "Don't tell me," she said a little faster and more hushed. "Are you still a *virgin*?" The question was hanging in the air along with the haze. She was giggling. "You *are* a virgin! Of course, why didn't I realize that before? That explains some things."

"What things?" I asked her, my voice cracking.

"Oh, nothing. I'm sorry, I didn't mean to embarrass you." She could see my face burning. "That's cool, being a virgin is an awesome choice. You should be proud of yourself," she said, trying to make me feel better. She took one last pull and dropped the remnants into a rusty Altoids can. She stepped over and dropped the can into her purse while pulling out her box of Kools. She returned to her perch at the window and lit up a cigarette. She looked sideways at me. "You ever had a girlfriend? I mean, other than Pam," she said, pointing her finger at the poster on the ceiling over my bed.

"Yeah." I offered no details. There were no details to offer.

"Mm-hmm." She didn't buy it. "What was her name?"

"Um, Stacy." It came out as more of a question which didn't sound too convincing.

She flicked her butt out into the snow and slid the window back down. She returned to the bed, her eyes keeping contact with mine as she came nearer.

"A-Are you a virgin?" I asked her, my eyes locked on hers.

"Nope." She replied, closing the gap between our faces. She hesitated only a second before closing her lips over mine. They were soft and warm and smelled like an ashtray. She moved her tongue past her lips and over mine, and I could hardly breathe. Her mouth was wonderful and awful at the same time. She didn't realize she tasted like cigarettes, but as long as she kept kissing me like that, I would never say a word.

* * *

Glory had become a permanent fixture at my house and had even started to cook for Chuck and me in the evenings, using what little we had in the cupboards and bringing over what we lacked. She wasn't the best cook, but it beat grilled cheese and scrambled eggs with ketchup. One night, she even made barbequed Spam for Chuck.

I had tried to keep her from Chuck as much as possible, but with her coming over as much as she did and the fact that he never left the house, they were bound to run into each other eventually. On Spam night, he offered her a beer, assuming she would turn her nose up at it, but she popped the top and nearly finished it in one long swig. This impressed Chuck to no end.

"You're one woman who can hold your liquor, little lady," Chuck snorted.

"The name's Glory, not little lady," Glory feigned offense.

Chuck looked puzzled for a minute. "Like Glory Glory Hallelujah?" He begun to hum the only song I had ever heard him sing.

"What is it about that song and you two?" Glory giggled and put her chin in her palm and listened to Chuck sing the song.

I was relieved that Glory was not embarrassed by Chuck, but I was jealous of their new bond. They smoked cigarettes together in the kitchen, their ashes missing the ashtray and ending up all over the kitchen table. They glanced over at me: Chuck spitefully, Glory apologetically.

"Oh, you hate the smoke smell, don't you, Donnie?" Glory asked, waving the smoke away with her hand. She ran to the window over the sink and slid it up. The cold air did little to push the smoke out, and it lingered in a cloud above Chuck's head.

"Close that damn window, it's freezing out there!" Chuck roared.

"Oh, hush it up, you!" Glory shushed him. "Donnie doesn't like the smoke, and it's only fair to open a window if we are going to smoke around him." Chuck crossed his arms and glared at her but kept silent. Glory was removing the Spam from the oven and began to make plates for each of us.

Chuck dove into his plate, barely bothering to chew.

"You know," he said between mouthfuls of meat and sauce, "We ate nothing but Spam for two whole months over in 'Nam. Spam and beans, yes ma'am. We'd be eating beans one minute and the next we were being bombed."

Glory looked wide-eyed at Chuck. "No shit?" She sat and listened intently as Chuck recounted every 'Nam story I had ever heard him mention as we ate. She asked questions and acted truly enthralled by his war stories. He came to life talking to her about his teenage years and being drafted into the war. She had opened up a side of my father I had never bothered to uncover myself.

* * *

I was sitting in Mr. Townsend's third period Geography class, and the last thing on my mind was the rivers of South America. While the class learned about the Amazon River, I thought about Glory and me. We made out every night, but she had never tried to sleep with me. Why? Did she think I was just a dumb kid who had never had sex before? I was beginning to get nervous.

As soon as the last bell rang that afternoon, I jumped up and ran out the front entrance of school. I didn't go to my locker, and I didn't bother to see if Troy and Jake were following me. I had to see Glory. She would be waiting for me on the sidewalk, and she would smile and kiss me, and everything would be okay.

I rounded the corner of our street, expecting to see Glory hopping up and down and waving to me. But I saw nothing but mailboxes. I checked my watch to make sure of the time. Yep, it was 3:40. Where was she? Maybe her mother was actually home for once and they were having an early dinner, I rationalized to myself as I walked down the sidewalk to my house. I pulled the key from its place around my neck and glanced at Glory's house one last time, disappointed that she had not come bounding out to greet me.

I walked through the door and listened for Chuck. Nothing. He must be sleeping. I walked into the den to double check that the TV wasn't on since I hadn't heard it. Glory's head snapped around as I entered the room, and she gasped. She was sitting on the couch with Chuck's head in her lap. He was out cold, and there was blood trickling from his temple. Glory's eyes were puffy from crying, and she looked scared.

"I didn't know what to do. He started freaking out, screaming and cursing. Then he came at me! He tripped over the afghan on the floor and hit his head on the end table. He's out. I tried to wake him, but he won't budge." She looked from him to me and back again. She looked helpless and scared, but I was seething.

"What the hell were you doing here?" I asked her.

"W-well, I-I came over earlier than usual. My mom didn't come home last night, and I was lonely, so I thought I'd come bum a smoke from Chuck." Her voice trailed off, and her words were slightly slurred, something I didn't notice at first.

"Are you *drunk*?! Have you been drinking?" I asked, my voice becoming higher.

"Me and Chuck had a beer... then we found some tequila way back in the cabinet, so we did a shot... or two." Glory averted her eyes from mine. "I went to the kitchen to grab some beers, and all of a sudden I heard Chuck. It sounded like he was choking. I ran into the living room to see what was going on, and there he was, screaming at the TV. I asked him what the hell was wrong, but he just looked at me and screamed 'you gook bitch' and lunged for me. That's when he tripped over the blanket."

I was so mad I couldn't see straight.

"Sometimes the TV makes him have flashbacks of Vietnam." I spit out. "He gets crazy, then usually passes out for an hour or two. Longer if he's been drinking, and it looks like you've taken care of that." I snapped at Glory, my words causing her to wince. I walked out of the living room to my room. I slammed the door and lay on my bed. Glory crept in and shut the door. She lay down next to me and put her head on my chest, her hand under my jacket and over my heart. The smell of alcohol was strong.

"I'm sorry if I did something wrong. There was another reason I came over early today." Glory whispered into my shirt.

"Oh, yeah, what's that?" I asked, my anger still fresh.

"I wanted to be lying naked on your bed when you got home from school," she purred, the tequila slurring her speech.

"Yeah, right, Chuck would have walked in." I shot down the idea.

"I didn't think about that," she replied nonchalantly. She got up and went to her purse to find her pack of smokes. She nearly fell over while bending down, and she clumsily made her way to the window and slid it open. She looked out into the dark and exhaled. I looked her up and down, taking in her full lips and round butt. I was hard, but I was still angry with her for what she had done.

"Do you think I'm sexy, Donnie," she asked me, still looking out the window.

"Of course, you are the sexiest woman I've ever seen." I stumbled over each word. She was the only woman I had ever seen naked that was not in a magazine.

She slid the window down, went through her gigantic denim purse again, and pulled out a cassette tape. She put it in the tape player, pressed play, then turned off the light.

"Too dark," she decided, and I could hear her bumping into the wall and over our shoes on the floor. She turned on the closet light, leaving the door half open, creating a sliver of light that stretched from the closet to the bed. "Mood lighting," she said softly. The tape had begun to play and rap music was blaring from the boom box. "You like Kriss Kross? I just got it," she asked, crawling like a cat over to my side of the bed. I didn't like it, but I didn't have a chance to respond. She climbed onto my lap, straddling my legs and facing me. "Is this really going to be your first time?" she asked.

"M-my first time?" I stuttered, my heart beating faster under my jacket.

She pulled her shirt over her head and tossed it to the floor. I was sweating. She pulled my jacket off and threw it over the picture of my mother on the nightstand.

By the light of my closet, I watched her undress herself and I touched her. The cassette tape was too loud in the small room, and I got distracted.

"You don't like my body?" Glory asked, looking down. I had shriveled up, and I wanted to crawl under the bed. "You're just nervous, I'll fix it," she said as she slid her face down over my stomach. And she did. She was so good at fixing it; in fact exactly three minutes later, I was done.

Done. Not even started and done! I had thought in my stupid virgin mind that she and I would make love for hours and collapse on the bed sweaty and satisfied. Instead, I was just... done. The song on the tape had lasted longer than I had. And I was still technically a virgin.

"Well, at least we didn't have to open a rubber!" She tried to play off my embarrassment, but I was inconsolable. I quickly got dressed and threw her clothes at her.

"It's really okay, Donnie, we can start over. I can go slower, really." But I was not about to try it again, not tonight, not after what had happened today and not while she was drunk and I was humiliated. I couldn't even look her in the eyes, and I wanted her out of my room.

She lit up another cigarette and gathered her shoes and purse. She hesitated in the darkened room and bent down to kiss me. This time her mouth was nothing more than an ashtray, and I pulled away.

"Goodnight, Glory." I turned over, my back to her. I heard the door close softly behind me.

* * *

It was early March, and I was on my way home to surprise Glory. It was her nineteenth birthday, and I had left school early to go to Walgreen's to buy her flowers and perfume.

I had no idea what kind of perfume she wore or what kind of flowers she liked. I had walked around the store for an hour while old ladies looked nervously at me as if I might stick something in my pockets. I finally got up the nerve to ask one of the ladies at the counter to open up the perfume case for me. I made my selection, grabbed a bouquet of white and yellow daisies, and headed home. I practiced my happy birthday speech on my way home; I wanted it to be perfect.

We had gotten over that first night in my room almost two months ago. We had done it six times since then, and I was beginning to get the hang of it. Each time we had to listen to some damn rap tape, but I learned to tune it out and concentrate on Glory and her body. I was in love with her; I was sure of it, and I was about to give her the first present I had ever bought for a girl.

I expected to see her waiting for me as I walked down our street, but I remembered that it was not even noon yet. I wondered if I should knock on her door or go to her window. At the last minute, I thought I would go put on a clean shirt and comb my hair before going to her house. I tucked the perfume into one jacket pocket, trotting past her house and into mine.

I could hear screams coming from the kitchen. Actually, it was more like moaning. I dropped the bag containing the flowers and made my way to the kitchen.

Chuck was standing facing away from the doorway. He was naked from the waist down except for socks, his hairy ass clinched. His wife beater was still on and he was slightly bent over the table, grunting. I could see two small legs on either side of his, and my stomach turned. Two small feet with deep red toenails wrapped themselves around Chuck's waist. I could see jet black hair swaying with the rhythm of Chuck's butt, and they were both breathing hard. Glory's slim arms were holding her weight on the kitchen table, and she threw her head back.

The world had stopped, and there was nothing but these two bodies writhing on the kitchen table, and me. They didn't see me, and they didn't stop. She started to moan and growl deep in her throat—a sound she had never made with me. I could hear Chuck whispering something in her ear that sounded like "Glory Glory Hallelujah."

I calmly reached into my jacket pocket and pulled my Walkman out. I put the headphones on, pressing the play button. "November Rain" began to fill my ears. I reached in the other jacket pocket and pulled out the perfume bottle. I held it over my head and let it drop. It crashed at my feet, liquid and glass spraying the floor and my shoes. I heard no sound but my tape player, but I could see the looks of astonishment on their faces as I turned to leave.

I stepped outside into the cold daylight. The sun was bright, and there were no clouds in the sky. I shoved my hands in my jacket pockets and began to walk.

Stacey Vickers
The Professional

In a dimly lit restaurant, David sat in a corner booth, absently stirring a glass of vodka with his finger. He drummed on the table with his other hand. He needed a cigarette, and he began to search in his pockets for one. The green ribbon on his finger caught his eye, and he remembered for the first time today that he'd quit smoking. He stopped searching for a minute, but then he remembered he'd already had three today, so one more couldn't hurt. David couldn't figure out why his mother had thought tying a ribbon around his finger would help; it just made him look as pathetic as he felt. He still smoked at least five cigarettes every day. He took out his Camel Filtered Lights and his lighter and set them on the ornately tiled table. Looking at the ugly green ribbon, David figured that it wasn't as bad as the white band that his wedding ring left. Over the two years since Sheila left, it still hadn't faded.

Today had to have been the worst day of his entire teaching career. He showed the first part of *Gettysburg* to his U.S. History classes. From his desk at the back of the room, he could barely hear the sound over the snoring and whispering. David didn't know why he expected anything different. After class, Carrie, a pretty blonde cheerleader with freckles who sat in the front center row, asked him why all the men were wearing such bad beards. "Tom Berenger is too cute to be wearing such an ugly beard." This was the same girl the guys asked to pick up their pens repeatedly on game day. While she bent over, they all craned to get a glimpse of firm ass and white underwear barely concealed by her white cheerleader bloomers. And after two months of this routine, she never caught on. He almost felt sorry for her. On days like today, he found it hard to remember why he'd become a teacher.

Sheila always helped him forget days like today. She'd smile and tell him tomorrow would be better. Then they'd cook dinner together, drink a bottle of wine with dinner, and take another one to the bedroom. Sometimes David could still feel her warm body curled up next to him at night. Her long brown hair would brush across his face when she would move in her sleep. Two years ago it used to bug the hell out of him, but now he'd give anything to feel her hair on his cheek.

An anorexic looking waitress with stringy blonde hair and too much red lipstick walked by every now and then to check and see if he needed anything. When he said no, she smiled and walked away, swinging bony hips. David tried not to watch; she looked only slightly older than his students.

The restaurant was crowded tonight. Usually, he was the only one who came in on week nights. Tonight, two couples sat in secluded benches savoring the dimly lit atmosphere. Little Roma's was always dimly lit, even in the middle of the afternoon. On the few occasions David came here during the day, walking in reminded him of walking into a cave. Silk flowers and vinyl ferns decorated the dining room. On each table, a candle sat in a worn wine bottle covered with wax from a variety of colored candles. When they were lit, the familiar smell of crayons filled the air, mixing with the sweet smell of tomato sauce and pasta. The mixture made for an aroma he had yet to find in any other restaurant. David heard soft mandolin music drifting from the tiny speaker on the wall over his booth. It was barely concealed by a plastic ivy in a clay pot suspended from the ceiling with rusting chains. He'd been here since six. It was now nine.

Just as he got up to walk out, the door opened, and a woman stepped into the dark candle lit restaurant. She whispered something to the hostess, and David sat back down. When the young girl pointed in his direction, she turned and walked toward his booth. She had neatly twisted her hair and secured it with a jade comb. Her silk Oriental-style dress showed well-proportioned curves. It was long and black with slits on each side. Her hips swayed when she walked. Not like the waitress's, but with a natural rhythm that made him ache.

When she stood in front of his booth, David realized how young she was. Not much over twenty. Standing there staring at him, her mouth was pressed into a hard line. David felt an uncomfortable tightness in his khaki slacks. She stared back at him coolly. It occurred to David that she was waiting for something. Quickly, he stood and motioned with his hand for her to sit. He smelled lilacs as she leaned to take the seat across from him.

The sickly blonde came back to take her drink order: chardonnay, very tasteful. She sat and waited for the girl to bring her drink. He didn't like the silence. He shifted in his seat and looked down at his rumpled red plaid shirt. Lamely trying to smooth out the wrinkles, he suddenly felt that he should have gone home and showered. He ran his fingers through his hair and wondered if any of his any cowlicks were making his hair stand up. He hated having curly hair; it tended to look lumpy if it wasn't combed. She stared at him. Her look was unreadable.

"So, Mr. McCormick," she said finally with a hint of a Texan drawl, "Do you know what you want?"

"I get to choose?" he asked too quickly and too loudly for his taste. Then he looked around to see if anyone was paying attention.

"Of course. We aim to please." She smiled coolly, tasting her wine. She made a face. The wine must have been too dry for her. She calmly pushed the glass to the edge of the table.

"Um, well," he cleared his throat, "I never really thought about that. Didn't really think it would matter." He looked into his watered down vodka.

"Take your time. We'll just sit here and drink until you know for sure." She looked toward the bar for the waitress, circling the rim of her wineglass with her finger. It made an almost inaudible ringing noise. Her red nails matched the red of her lipstick. They were neatly trimmed, but not sculptured like most women. David finally got the attention of the waitress, who walked over and took away her wineglass. She ordered a beer instead.

"I don't know. I just don't know," he said, and then leaning in closer. "See, I've never done anything like this before." He ran his fingers through his hair and began to drum them on the table again.

"I know. I spoke to Mr. Mears, and he explained your situation." She stared down at his fingers, smiling almost pleasantly. He saw her staring at the ribbon.

"I just quit smoking two weeks ago. My mother thought it would help me remember." She glanced at the pack of cigarettes on the table and then up at him. She was smiling. He laughed.

"Yeah, well it evidently isn't working too well." She turned away to look for the waitress. He caught himself staring at her. A strand of red hair had escaped her twist and curled in front of her ear. Her ears were pierced three times, and she wore a diamond stud in each hole.

The waitress brought her a Corona long neck with a slice of lime on top. He ordered another vodka. She brought it quickly and took away his first drink, untouched. His companion squeezed the lime's juice into her beer. Then she pushed the battered lime down the long glass neck. Placing her thumb over the opening, she tilted the full beer upside down. David stared as the lime piece slowly floated to the bottom of the bottle. She took a long drink and smiled. "That's much better." She licked the excess beer from her thumb. Then she must have remembered why she was there because her smile faded. "Have you decided?"

David liked it better when she smiled at him, but he didn't say so. "How's it done? You know..."

"You tell me what you like. I make a phone call and go about getting it for you. It's very simple really." She smiled that cool smile she'd worn when she came into the restaurant. Her eyes changed though. On the surface they were still cold, but underneath there was a kindness that he hadn't seen before. She cleared her throat. "You didn't answer my question. Have you decided?"

He liked the way her voice sounded: deep and a little raspy—like Lauren Bacall with a hint of Texas drawl. "Are you from around here?" Her agitation grew. He took out a cigarette and lit it, inhaling deeply.

"What difference does it make? Mr. McCormick, this is not a social call. I thought Mr. Mears explained things to you." She drank her beer. Her lipstick left a greasy red ring around the top of the bottle. David stared at it and exhaled, thinking about Jack, the chubby balding accounting teacher who talked him into this. It figured that he'd be into this kind of thing.

"Please, call me David. I get called Mr. McCormick all day long."

"I don't think so."

"Please. I'd prefer it that way." He smiled and took another drag, looking down at her arm resting on the table. As he blew a cloud of smoke over her shoulder, he asked, "The smoke doesn't bother you does it?"

"No."

"Good." He inhaled again. Smoking always relaxed him. "You know my name, but I don't know yours. What should I call you?"

"Didn't the card Mr. Mears gave you have my name on it?"

"Yes, well, it said Ms. Austen, but.."

"Well, that's my name."

"Oh, come on. You know as well as I do that it's not really that. What's your first name? Jane?" She shifted in her seat. Her lips pressed into a thin line again. "Please, why don't you tell me your first name? I would feel more comfortable if you did."

She sat for a minute. He saw the tension slowly leaving her body. She shrugged. "I don't know why it matters. It's Samantha. Now, could you please tell me what you want?" She looked annoyed.

"Um, well okay." He took another drag to give himself time to think. The perfect Bogart move—if you don't know what to say, just sit there and smoke until something comes to you. He almost asked for someone with brown hair, blue eyes, about 5'4", slim build. Without realizing it, he had described Sheila. He didn't want to think about her. She was somewhere in France finding herself again. David had no idea what the hell that was supposed to mean. He exhaled slowly, sat up straighter and cleared his throat. "How about someone like you?"

She straightened her back and stared at him wide-eyed for a minute. "I don't make personal calls." After a quick glare, she smiled, trying to hide her anger, David winced. He drained his drink. It was watered down. Pulling out a small cellular phone, she pressed some numbers and began speaking in low tones to someone named Celine.

When she hung up, she placed the phone back into her large navy leather purse and faced him again. "Celine should do nicely. She needs about an hour to get ready and get to the hotel. You stay here for about thirty minutes after I've left, and then go to the Red Dragon Inn. Here's the key. Room 1236." She pulled a key card from her purse and placed it on the table in front of him. "You pay her up front and don't get rowdy. All my girls carry mace. It's three fifty. Okay, any questions?"

"How will she get in?"

"I'm gonna go over now to give her a key. She doesn't live far from here." She finished her beer and got up. Picking up her purse, she reached in and pulled out a black business card. Tapping the edge against her chin a few times, she placed it on the table in front of his hand. She briefly grazed his hand with hers. "If we can be of any service in the future, please, let us know." She turned and walked out of the restaurant, hips swaying rhythmically. He watched her. When she was gone, he ordered another vodka.

He waited his half-hour and two more vodkas, then got up, paid his tab, and left. He wasn't too drunk to drive, but he did feel the vodka. Finding the hotel was no problem. He smoked a cigarette outside and went in to find his room.

The room was nice. It had a queen-size bed, and the bathroom was larger than most hotels he'd been in. The usuals were provided: shampoo, a sewing kit, coffee and soap shaped like a dragon's head. Turning out the light in the bathroom, David walked to the bed and sat down. He took off his loafers and sat back against the pillows. His head started to feel heavy. He closed his eyes.

They shot open when he heard the door open. Quickly he swung his legs over the side of the bed and sat waiting for the woman to come in the door. She walked in, but stopped short with wide eyes. She wore blue jeans and a short pink sweater with white Nike hightops. She had her strawberry blonde hair pulled up into a ponytail. It swung back and forth as she walked. "Oh, you're here already. It must've taken me longer than I thought to take a shower. Were you waiting long?"

"No, I just got here myself. I'm probably early." He smiled at her. She smiled back. She had light red-brown freckles across her nose and cheeks. Her smile betrayed her age. She couldn't have been over twenty. She could have been one of his students. "Celine, isn't it? How old are you?"

"Nineteen. Why, is there a problem?" Her smile faltered. She looked nervous.

"No, no. No problem at all. I was just curious."

"If you don't mind waiting a little while longer, I'll go change. You can set the money on the bedside table." She went into the bathroom and shut the door. David hadn't noticed any bags; she must have been carrying a large purse. Pulling out his wallet, he placed three hundred fifty dollars on the table next to the ceramic lamp.

"Get comfortable, if you want," she said from behind the door, "Or I could help you when I come out."

David unbuttoned the three buttons of his shirt and pulled it over his head. Then he pulled off his socks. There was nothing worse than being seen naked with your socks on. He threw both his shirt and socks across the room. They landed somewhere around an overstuffed plaid armchair. He lay back against the fluffed pillows and waited for Celine to come out of the bathroom.

She opened the bathroom door and turned off the light. She wore a black satin and lace teddy with black garters and black thigh high hose. Her hair brushed over the tops of her shoulders. She had on black stiletto heels. Her freckles were hidden behind make-up. She didn't look nineteen anymore. Smiling, she began to walk toward the bed. She stood at the foot of the bed and smiled at him. She licked her lips, making her red lipstick even glossier. "You're nothing like the usual clients. I like your curly black hair. It's real cute. So," she said, her eyes traveling the length of his body, "What do you want?"

"Why don't you surprise me."

"On or off?" She waited for a response.

"I'm sorry?"

"My shoes. On or off?"

"Whatever makes you comfortable," he said, his voice almost a whisper. She slipped out of her shoes and knelt on the bed, straddling his feet. Catlike, she crawled toward him. When she got close to his chest, she ran her hands from his stomach to his shoulders, dragging her fingernails lightly over his skin. He closed his eyes. He felt her breath next to his ear, feather-light against his skin.

"Let's take these off." David heard her unzip his pants. He opened his eyes and saw her face was next to his. She was smiling. He realized that he was holding his breath. Up close David could still see her freckles; they reminded him of Carrie, in his third period class. He slowly exhaled, rested his head against the pillows, and closed his eyes again.

* * *

The cold water shot out of the showerhead. David gasped, but he didn't turn on the hot water. Back in her jeans and hightops, she'd smiled at him and told him to call for her again sometime. The last thing he saw was her blonde ponytail swinging as she walked out of the room. He quickly bathed and dressed. He'd had trouble finding his socks. He had overshot the chair, and they had fallen behind it.

The minute he was out of the hotel, he pulled his cigarettes out and lit one, his hands shaking. He smoked it quickly, hoping it would calm his nerves. One didn't work, so he lit another. He got into his car and drove home to get some sleep. He finished the pack before he got there. Unlocking the door to his apartment, he heard Archie's welcome meow. Once he was inside, the cat curled his lithe black body around his legs.

"Okay, I guess you're hungry. I'll feed you. Then I get to go to bed. Alone, again."

After he poured some of the dry cat food in Archie's glass dish, he left him to devour his dinner in the hall and walked back a few steps to the kitchen. He got a glass out of the cabinet over the sink and pulled out a bottle of Sutter Home Chablis from the refrigerator. He made quick work of the cork and filled his glass. This wine was always Sheila's favorite. She liked the way it was not quite dry but wasn't very sweet either. David took a long drink. Its chilled tartness felt good going down. Grabbing the bottle, David rounded the corner into his living room and sat on the navy and white-striped sofa on the back wall.

His bedroom was on the other side of that wall. He should be in there trying to sleep, but thinking about Sheila staring at him from her picture on his bedside table kept David on the couch. He barely noticed the slight vinegary taste. Old wine sometimes did turn to vinegar. Somehow David thought it would take a little longer than two years. He couldn't help asking himself what Sheila would think if she knew what he'd done tonight. What would she care, he thought, she's probably "found herself" with some French bastard. She's probably fucking his brains out right now, he thought. He drained his glass and refilled it. He needed a cigarette. He searched his pants pocket for them and found his lighter. He was about to search his shirt pocket when he remembered that he'd finished his pack on the way home.

"Great. Just great," he said out loud. Archie came into the room and leapt onto the glass coffee table and then into his lap. He stared at him with his head tilted sideways for a moment, then curled up into a tight black ball on his lap and went to sleep, purring. "If only it was that easy." David rested his head against the back of the sofa and closed his eyes.

* * *

A week later, David found Samantha's card while doing some laundry. It took him two days to finally sit in his office, the third bedroom of his apartment that he and Sheila had redecorated, and dial the numbers. It rang for a while, and he heard her voice on the other end just as he was about to hang up.

"Hello."

"Samantha, this is David McCormick. You do remember me, don't you?"

"Mr. McCormick, yes, of course. How can I help you?"

"I was wondering if we could set up another meeting. When are you available?"

"Well, I can meet you in, say, two hours. Is that okay?"

"Yeah, that's perfect. We'll meet at Little Roma's, you remember where it is don't you?"

"Yes, I think I can find it just fine."

"Great, see you then."

She didn't say goodbye; she just hung up. David showered and changed. He put on some black Levi's and his red Polo shirt. He left food and water for Archie and sprayed on some Eternity cologne. Cologne was always an afterthought, which was why the bottle was always on the small glass top table by the door, supposedly reserved for his keys.

He got to the restaurant about an hour early. At six o'clock, he was the only customer there. He sat in a corner booth and ordered a Corona beer. The same mandolin song was playing over the speaker. The owners must not have an extensive collection of romantic music, one of those compilation jobs you could order off TV at three in the morning. The waitress, the sickly girl who waited on them last time, brought his beer. He didn't like lime so he set it aside and began to drink. His palms began to sweat while he sat there waiting,.

Three beers and four cigarettes later, she came in. She looked around and spotted him. She walked quickly over and sat down. He noticed that she was dressed casually. Her red hair was twisted and pulled up in a clip. She wore a short wrap skirt made from floral silk, a white V-neck tee shirt, and brown sandals. David watched her legs as she walked over. They were muscular and very pale, not tanned like most people in the area. When she sat down, the faint smell of lilacs reached his nose, just as the whisper of silk reached his ears. She carried a backpack instead of her purse.

"Hello, Mr. McCormick."

"Samantha. How are you? You look different from the last time we met." He stood and waited for her to sit.

"I had class this evening. I don't usually do business tonight unless it's a very important client, but I made an exception. Now, what can I do for you?"

"You can start by calling me David. I believe we settled that last time. I like it better that way."

"David. Of course, I'd forgotten. Now, would you like to spend another evening with Celine? She was very complimentary when she spoke of you."

"Celine? Uh, no, I don't think ..."

"Why, was she rude to you, or just not your style?"

"No, she's just...um....too young for me."

"Oh, I see. Okay, you tell me what age you'd prefer."

The waitress came by with a beer for David and asked Samantha for her drink order. She ordered the same but with lime. When the girl left, David stared at Samantha and smiled. "So, I didn't know you were in school. What are you going for?"

"I'm working on my masters. Now, about your age preference..."

"That's pretty impressive. I always thought about getting my masters, but in history of course." He smiled and took a sip of his beer. "I like this place. Don't you? I mean I know it's a bit on the cheesy side, but it's always quiet and dark. I'm practically the only one ever in here. I worry that I'd miss it if they close." He pulled out another cigarette. He lit it and inhaled; he was nervous and talking way too much.

"Give up on quitting?" She eyed the green ribbon he still wore.

"Yeah, just about. Mom'll be disappointed, but smoking is the only thing that relaxes me anymore." David turned his head and exhaled. The skinny waitress brought her beer. She squeezed her lime and stuffed it in the bottle. He watched as she did her trick with the lime.

"Celine didn't relax you?" she asked, while licking her thumb.

"No, just smoking."

"Smoking is a bad habit. It'll kill you someday. My dad smoked. He died a few years ago of lung cancer. Not a pretty way to go." She sipped her beer and left her greasy red ring around the top of the bottle.

"Where are you from?"

"Amarillo. Why?" She shifted in her seat.

"Just curious." He smiled at her.

"I've never had a client ask so many questions. You sure you're not a cop?"

"I'm a teacher. We like asking questions, too." He finished his beer.

"So, you never said what age you want."

"What? Oh, yeah... uh, well, I'm not sure." He signaled the waitress for another beer. "I'm hungry. Have you eaten yet?"

"You keep changing the subject." She stared at him coolly. "Cut the crap, okay? You didn't call me out here to talk business, did you Mr. McCormick?" Her lips were pressed tightly together again.

"Well, no."

"This is not a date. I am a business woman."

"Business women need to eat too," he said. She grabbed her backpack, threw a five-dollar bill on the table and walked out of the restaurant. When she was gone, he slammed his fist against the table's cold hard tile.

When the waitress came back with another beer, he sent it back and ordered a double vodka.

* * *

David was kicking himself the next day—and a few days after that—for that evening. After Samantha left, he got entirely too drunk. By closing time, that skinny waitress looked pretty damn good. She drove him home. Sissy even cooked him breakfast, much to his hung over chagrin. He could not believe that he'd said what he did to Samantha or did what he did with Sissy. But when David thought about it, he guessed it was better than wasting another three hundred and fifty dollars on getting what he got from Sissy for free. God, he hoped that was her name.

When the phone rang on Thursday evening, a week after the incident, and he heard Samantha on the other end, David almost fainted. "Hey, I thought I would never hear from you. Listen, I'm sorry about what I said to you. I'd had a few too many beers." That was a lie, but it sounded good.

"It's all right. I need to talk to you. It's kind of.... It's urgent. Can we meet? Say, Little Roma's in half an hour?"

"Sure, that's fine." He barely got the words out when she hung up the phone. He showered and changed again. This time he wore jeans, a navy Polo shirt, his Astros baseball cap, and vowed not to drink a drop.

She was waiting for him when he got there, sitting in the same booth he usually did and sipping on an Italian margarita. He walked over to her, smiled, and sat down. He could smell lilacs mixed in with the usual Little Roma's aroma. David closed his eyes and inhaled. He loved the way she smelled.

"Hi."

"Hi. Did you know that there was such a thing as an Italian Margarita?"

"Yeah, I've had a few. They're pretty good."

"I like them." She smiled at him, licking her lips. Both her eyes and her smile were warmer than he had ever seen them. She'd evidently had a few.

"How long have you been here?"

"I was here when I called you. I said half an hour so you could shower if you wanted, or whatever, you know." Her words were a little slurred.

"What was it you needed to see me about?" He looked at her clothes for the first time since he'd come in. Her hair was in a ponytail, and she wore a Green Polo shirt much like his. He couldn't see, but he guessed she was wearing jeans or shorts.

"I don't remember. Have a drink with me while I try to remember." She motioned for the waitress. She came over; it was Sissy. She looked even more emaciated than when he'd last seen her. She recognized him. He couldn't quite meet her eyes when she asked what he wanted to drink. David could swear that he heard amusement in her voice. He quickly mumbled that he wanted to see a menu. If Samantha noticed that he shifted uncomfortably in his seat, she didn't let on.

"I'm hungry. How about some food?"

"Yes, that would be nice. What's good?"

"Oh, I always eat the spaghetti. I figure you can't mess that up."

"Sounds like a plan. Let's have some shall we?" When Sissy came back, he ordered for them. Samantha tried to order another margarita, but he convinced her that she wanted water instead. She smiled at him. "I had the worst day today. Professor Winston gave me a 'C' on my paper about Hemingway. He said that I should have spent more time on it. I tried, but with work and all...." She shrugged.

"Why do you have to do this...the girls, I mean?"

"When I applied to grad school, I tried to get a teaching assistant's position. I didn't get one, and I had no other way to pay for grad school, not to mention all the loans I got to go for my Bachelor's degree. Work pays the bills and for anything else I want. But lately I don't have time for school. Business is booming and very profitable, not to mention more interesting." She gave a short laugh.

They were the only people in the restaurant as usual, so Sissy brought the food quickly. They both ate in silence. It made David nervous, but he figured that the food would take the edge off Samantha's buzz. He finished before her and waited, trying not to watch her eat.

When she was done, she sat for a while and didn't speak. Gaining Sissy's attention, she had her refill her water glass. She took a long drink, then said quietly, "I am so sorry. I can't believe I just acted that way. I don't really even know why I called you. I guess it was because you were so nice. And you were flirting with me; it's been forever since anyone's done that."

"How'd you get my number?" He looked at her. She seemed to be turning paler by the minute.

"Easy. I called every David and D. McCormick in the book. You were number six of eight. Now, can I ask you something?" She waited until he nodded slightly and then, "Why didn't you want Celine again? She evidently enjoyed your company. All she could talk about is your black curly hair and green eyes. Sounds like *she* should have paid *you*."

"Celine deserved the money. I'm satisfied. I just learned that your services are not for me. She was just too young." He smoothed a hand through his hair. Sheila always liked his curly hair, but he always thought it was a little girly. He used to keep it as short as possible, but it had been a while since his last haircut.

She looked confused. "I don't understand. You don't look like the usual type to call. Why did you?"

"Just lonely, I guess. But it looks like I'll have to go about finding women the old fashioned way."

"They say that my profession is the oldest one." She smiled

"That's not what I meant." David blushed.

"I know, I was just making an effort at flirting with you. I guess I'm pretty rusty." Samantha smiled at him sweetly. "So much for subtlety. I've got a room at the Red Dragon, if you'd care to join me."

"Now, I' m the one who doesn't understand. I thought..."

"Don't think, don't talk. Just pay the bill and let's go."

Speechless, he motioned for Sissy and paid the tab. She got up and they walked out. He carried her backpack out to his '65 Mustang. He opened the door and let her get in. "I'm not taking you there."

"Then where?"

He didn't answer her. He got in his car and headed toward home.

* * *

David woke slowly, but didn't open his eyes. For a second he thought he was still dreaming. He felt the warmth of a woman curled against his back. Her hair was tickling his ear and nose, but it didn't bother him. He smiled to himself at first. Something was wrong. He smelled lilacs and the night came flooding back to him. He felt her move. She rolled away from him, and he felt her sit up and get out of bed. Rolling over, David watched Samantha fasten her bra and slide her silk underwear up her legs. Her hair was hanging in a rumpled, knotted mess around her shoulders. She must not have noticed him watching her because she didn't speak. She pulled her green Polo shirt over her head and walked the few steps into his bathroom. He heard the water in the sink running and rolled onto his back and stared at the peeling plaster on the ceiling.

When she came out of the bathroom, he turned his head to the right to face her. She had neatly rolled her hair into a bun. She looked at him with no expression on her face. "I didn't know you were awake."

"Yeah, well, I just woke up." David didn't know why he lied. It just seemed easier. "Where're you headed?"

"Home. I'll probably miss my first class, but I need to get to my second one." She looked serious. She didn't even have that "just had sex glow" that women got. Sheila always had it. He hadn't seen it in a while. David liked her better drunk. She was sober now, and she was waiting for him to say something. He didn't know what to say.

"Do you want me to call you a cab?" Somehow he knew offering to drive her was futile. He could see it in the uncomfortable look etched on her face.

"No, I'll do it."

"Okay, well, I guess I'll go get changed for work." He didn't wait for an answer. He knew there wouldn't be one. Throwing the rumpled navy sheets back, David rolled onto the side she had recently occupied—it was still warm—and got up to take a shower. He took a long hot shower. When he opened the door to the bathroom, he knew she was gone.

* * *

David sat in the back of his darkened classroom. He was showing the movie version of *The Red Badge of Courage*. Today he finished the unit on the civil war. The movie flashed on the talking and sleeping faces of his students. In high school, he'd slept through this boring antique of a movie too. He looked down at his watch: five more minutes. Then he could go out into the parking lot and smoke. The white line on his ring finger glared at him in the movie's flashing light. He sighed and got up, moving down the center aisle to the VCR at the front of the room, tapping a few of his sleeping beauties on the head as he went. He pressed the stop button and asked Kevin, who sat in the back corner, to turn on the light.

"Well, there you have it. The best example of fighting in the Civil War era..." The shrill ringing of the bell interrupted him. Above the rustling of paper and books, he finished, "I'll give extra credit to anyone who writes a short essay comparing and contrasting this movie and *Gettysburg*, which we saw a few weeks ago. The one with the bad beards, for those of you who didn't remember. See you tomorrow."

David straightened the desks. They always left in such a hurry, he thought. In the front desk of the middle row he found a pink folder. Carrie had left it behind. The folder had flowers and hearts drawn all over it. The words "I Love" were written in her familiar, bubbly handwriting. Beneath them, several unlucky boys' names had been scratched out with bold, black marker. One of them must have been fairly recently crossed out: the noxious smell of permanent marker reached his nose and made his eyes water. Obviously she got a lot out of the movie. That was ok though. David knew that there were just some things you can't fight. Smiling, he set the folder on the ledge of the chalkboard and walked out the door and toward the parking lot for his cigarette.

Ashlyn Ivy
Grass Hearts

I've never been much of a worker. That's not to say that I'm one of those lazy bums that hang out at the Lonely Hearts Tavern all night and day. No, I've got my hobbies to keep me busy. I like to build things. Yeah, I can build pretty much any kind of chair or table from pine, even maple if you like the grain better.

A few summers ago, before my wife died, I made about twenty of them swings and even carved little hearts into the armrests on account of my wife's nagging.

"No, Al," she said to me, "they need more heart. Maybe they need some kind of decoration to make them look more like swings."

Well, I didn't really see nothing wrong with them being plain old wood, but I figured she might know better than me about such things, so I added the little hearts. Have you ever noticed how, when you're on a swing, swinging, things look closer, then farther away?

Eva was real smart. She studied books and things, and she always knew how to say words that I could barely read. The swings came out real nice, sold well. People liked the hearts, and I was pretty proud of each of them, up until she died.

Strangest thing happened after that, I couldn't look at a single one of those swings without feeling something awful all through my body. They made me queasy all over. I tried to sit on the one strung up on my own front porch, but the little hearts and the motion of swinging nearly drove me batty. I decided that day never to swing again.

I just couldn't understand it. I mean, I'd always loved to swing, but it just didn't seem right without my wife balancing it out on the other end, talking silly about poets and nature. She liked to talk about the grass, said she loved it. When I would get done mowing, she'd come out in her apron, the red one with the tiny heart on the pocket, and bring me a glass of water. Sometimes she would sit right on the lawn and breathe in her "favorite smell in the world." She said she felt close to it because of some book about it being one with everything. Later on, after she died, I read that book for myself and even memorized a few lines from it. The author, I think his name was Walt. Yeah, Walt, I remember it now because it seemed such an honest name, a name I might have given my own son, if I'd ever had one.

Well, I can't even bear to take that swing down. Every time I try, that thing in my stomach starts up again. Yep, that swing still sways with the breeze as it's supposed to, I guess. Eva used to call those soft breezes "the breath of angels." But, hot as hell as it has been all summer, I think that their halos must be slipping a little.

After the swing hobby ended, I decided to switch things up a bit. I started making these little helicopters out of coke cans. I got pretty good at it too. I got one up in the attic that the mayor himself wanted to buy. Came right up on the front porch, he did, and offered me twenty dollars for it. He took a seat on the swing and rubbed his fingers right over the little heart I carved while complimenting me on everything.

"I can't say I've seen such an exquisite attention to detail," the mayor said as he rubbed the sweat from his brow. I nodded and continued to paint a small pilot onto the side of the aluminum can. "Yes sir," he said, "this plane here is perhaps the best of the lot." He then went on to tell me how much he wished he could have a hobby like mine.

As he talked, I couldn't help but feel a little funny, seeing him on that swing. There he was, right up close one second, then farther away the next. I noticed a bead of sweat roll off his neck and land on the little heart I'd carved. Anyhow, after seeing how much he wanted the darn helicopter I made, I realized that it might be in my best interest to keep it. I thought there must be something special in the plane, if he wanted it so badly. I don't know; he'd just shown a little too much interest. I guess that's where the trouble started.

I didn't like the mayor, never did. My wife once described him as a man who would "kiss the devil on his tongue right before patting the head of every baby in our town." Don't think harshly of my wife on account of that. She hardly said a thing about anyone, unless there was a lot of truth to be told in what she said. What she said about the mayor was true.

Not selling that helicopter was the beginning of my troubles. You see, every year in my hometown we throw a little festival. We call it the Groves Pecan Festival, being that the pecans fall around this time, and every citizen kind of takes pride in the whole thing. Last year Mr. Hoffman, who lives to the right of Mrs. Palmer, donated a couple of thousand dollars to the park grounds in order to build a covered pavilion for the entertainers. My wife always liked Mr. Hoffman because of his nice kept yard and well-tended garden. We would watch him from the porch sometimes, his white calves beaming in the sun, as he went after weeds and whatnot. When his roses were in bloom, he would let my wife pick a few to put on the windowsill. After Eva died, I couldn't bear Mr. Hoffman any longer, and I especially couldn't stand his perfect roses. One night, after a particularly scary dream, I snuck over across the street and uprooted every single one of them. His face the next morning was redder than any rose he'd ever grown.

With the Pecan Festival, there usually comes an awful nice parade that rolls down Main Street. A couple of years ago, my wife helped some kids decorate their float and then decorated my old red Mustang and threw out candy while I drove. She was always up for that kind of thing. She said she did it for "the spirit of the children."

Me and my wife used to spend weeks sweating and preparing for the festival. She would make about ten pecan pies and batches of pralines to sell, and she would make a special tag for each one that had the price circled with a tiny red heart. I would also gather up my favorite pieces I had whittled and carved, and we'd set ourselves up a spot at the Pecan Festival. It was a real joy to see people admiring and buying the things we'd made, their faces sticky with candied apples.

One year, we made our tent look like a circus. Eva painted thick red and white stripes up and down our tent, and I made the animals out of wood. We had horses, giraffes, elephants, and tigers all around us. Eva looked beautiful, even all dressed up head to toe like a clown. She had even painted a tiny tear shape under her left eye. The children loved it. They seemed grateful for the handfuls of candy she passed out, and I wasn't even the least bit upset when she made me wear one of those silly red noses. I remember the mayor walking by and tweaking it between his fingers as he passed our tent laughing. It didn't bother me at all.

This year, things were different. The pecans that fell this year were rotten before they even hit the ground. First time in years we'd had a rotten batch. I pillaged the backyard for a while trying to find at least one I could crack open and eat, but all of the ones I found were black and filled with worms. So, I gathered up all those rotten pecans in an old bucket and sat in my favorite lawn chair in the backyard, waiting for something to move. I emptied that whole bucket, aiming at squirrels, my neighbor's greenhouse, and the occasional roaming cat. I felt better after throwing a few of those pecans, but I've always had such an awful aim.

Due to the rotten pecans, most people seemed a little less enthusiastic about the whole festival. Mrs. Palmer, who lives between me and Mr. Hoffman and is the only neighbor I can stand, said she wished the "rest of the town would shrivel up and die along with the pecans." Mrs. Palmer was still a little upset that her children had grown up and left her in a town she hated. I could couldn't help but agree with her about the pecans.

This year at the festival, I decided to set up my spot as usual, next to Donny Freeman, the old hippie who sold incense and tobacco pipes from behind tie-dyed curtains. I hated all the smoke and every punk kid that hung around the place, but I couldn't bear to leave the shade of an old elm that stood above us. I swallowed my disgust as young hooligans with metal pierced all through their faces, looked over my goods. I just don't understand it. Metal in their eyebrows, nostrils, ears, chins, and God knows where else.

"How much is this?" One such fellow asked, handling a jar of sea glass my wife had collected.

"What's next," I asked, "your eyeballs?"

"Excuse me," he said, looking confused.

"I said," pointing to some ring in his lip, "Are your eyeballs next?"

"Oh," he laughed, realizing what I was talking about, "Maybe one day," he joked.

I thought of chasing him around with a nail gun, but he left before I had a chance. He didn't even buy anything.

This year, I realized I hadn't made as many pieces as I thought. I decided, instead of just putting out my helicopters and my wood pieces, I would put out a few things that had been crowding the house up. I found a few pots, a couple of dusty records, and an old coffee table me and Eva had been meaning to get rid of. As I was putting up the sign I'd just finished making from pine, displaying the prices for my pieces, the mayor walked up.

"So, Al, it looks like your grass is getting a little long," he said while looking over my pieces, probably hunting for the darn helicopter.

"I suppose it is, Dean. I hadn't really taken much notice. Been real busy lately," I said back to him without even looking up. I knew this would get to him because I didn't add "Mayor" to the beginning of his name. People in high places like to know they are up there for some reason.

"Pretty soon I'm going to have to send the city workers to cut it," he said, "and I'm sorry to say they'll charge you around fifty bucks to do a job like that, Al." I hated his shined up shoes and his thick whiskers. I knew he'd probably kissed the devil right before coming up to talk to me.

"Well, Dean," I said. "you do what you have to, but if someone trespasses in my yard, I'm going to start shooting." I said it without blinking, and this made me kind of sad because I knew how much my wife hated guns. What the mayor didn't know was that my wife had buried my gun before she died. I'm sure it must be somewhere in her flowerbed. "I just need a little time is all, Dean. You know it's only been a year since my wife died, and I just haven't gotten around to it." It was the truth I was telling him this time. I guess I hadn't taken notice to my yard all year. I mean, I remember my rake and tools disappearing underneath all that green, but I guess I forgot to trim it down.

"Well, it makes the whole neighborhood look tacky, and people are starting to complain about it, Al."

"Tacky?" I asked. "To me it seems to be like the un-cut hair of graves growing," I said knowing how smart I must've sounded to the old fool. I could tell by his expression that he had never known an honest man like Walt.

"Whatever, Al, just cut your grass and stop dumping your trash in the bin at the police station. Everybody knows it's you," and with that he walked off. Mrs. Palmer was right about those pecans. The rest of the day was a daze. I don't think I sold anything, and I might have even left everything there.

When I got home, I realized right away that things did seem a little overgrown. In fact, the flowerbed my wife had tended was overgrown with weeds. The sidewalk was barely visible, and an old car that I had been meaning to fix was hidden in the brush. Yeah, time to clear it out, I thought. And sure enough, that's what I did.

I don't know what came over me exactly. I first dusted off my old riding mower from the shed in the back. It took a while to get it started from all the time it spent just sitting there. I started on the front yard, working in a small pattern. The air felt good on my cheeks as I went. The big stuff was hard to get around, but once I got going, I was breezing around corners and hedges. I hooked a sharp left to avoid the azalea bush my wife planted, and finished my yard, in what seemed only a few minutes. But, then, something odd happened.

I just kept going. I finished my yard, which is on a corner lot, and then moved right on to Mrs. Palmer's yard. She waved at me from her front porch while her cats brushed up against her ankles. I'm not sure if I waved back, but I know she watched me the whole time.

Mr. Hoffman's yard didn't really need trimming because his grandson had done it the day before, but I just couldn't stop. I kept to the pattern, veering only to miss his Doberman.

I then breezed through the Elmore's acre. The Elmore's live next to Mr. Hoffman. I used the pattern again, but had to circle once around one of the Elmore's grandchildren playing in the yard. She had a scared look on her face as my old John Deere hummed next to her dainty little pink shoes. It went on like this all day and into the night. I worked all the way down my street then back up again. I don't remember stopping for gas, but I must have because I finished every yard. There was a perfect heart-shaped pattern in every yard on the block.

I'm not sure who all came out to watch me. I noticed them, but only in a dreamy kind of way. They called out to me, and some even tried jumping in front of me. I think I might have even run over the Mayor's foot with a wheel. Every once in a while I'd recognize a face or a voice, but I'd never stop to talk or listen. I just kept going.

I thought of my wife and Walt and everything else that meant anything to me; my legs went numb. At one point, I think I cried. I might have cried the whole time; I don't remember. All I know is that now I'm sitting here on this swing, and I can't stop. I can smell freshly cut grass, and I think I can feel the breath of angels, and maybe Walt is sitting here next to me, but I can't stop swinging, and the world is closer then farther away, closer then farther away.

Eric Gunter
Sparagmos: The Colored Boy

Tim wiped the sweat out of his eyes and lit another cigarette butt. It was hotter than hell, even in the shade. It was the middle of a sticky summer day, and Tim had a good collection of butts hidden under his Indian style lap. He sat in one of the apartment stairwells, half way up. That's where there's a platform, and the steps turn around and go the other way. The boxed-in stairwells each had a window a ways up, a little higher than Tim was tall when standing tiptoe on the platform railing. Tim wasn't short, but he wasn't exactly tall neither.

The stairwells were on the ends of each building. Some smelled bad, and some were busier than others. This one didn't stink too bad and didn't have hardly any people. He had tried them all; he knew the good ones. The stairwells kept him cooler than the sun did, not by much though. No wind blew, but at least he had some shade. Not many people used the stairs at this time of day. And no one really used this staircase anyway. All the morning hustling about had stopped. It was after lunchtime, and most of the people had gone to work. The people who didn't work had already walked to the corner store—gotten their cigarettes, milk, beer, and other junk—and were probably sitting at home staring at TV and smoking their brand, usually the cheap kind.

Tim had an interest in cigarette brands; there were so many kinds. He smoked the leftover butts off the ground. Cigarettes butts were everywhere, but Tim had a hard time getting his hands on the good ones. He always ended up with the leftovers, the ones left by the other kids who smoked. He got stuck with the ones that got flicked into the wet grass or the dirt—the ones with little brown spots on them, the ones that made his cheeks itch and made his stomach sink. But they worked all right. They felt good, made him cough, and made his head spin.

He also had some bread with him today, just a couple of stale pieces really, but his dog would be happy—dogs love white bread. He wasn't sure exactly when he started calling the dog his, but he had, and he stuck to it. The dog wasn't anyone else's, so claiming him wouldn't bother anybody. He named him Lucky Strike, not a very original or cool name for a boy dog, but it fit. He had been smoking a Lucky Strike at the time, and he really liked Lucky Strikes—all tobacco, no butt. Smokes with filters were just a tease; part of the cigarette couldn't be smoked. Eventually the name got shortened to Lucky. It was just easier to say. Small and wiry and a yellowish color—Lucky was old, or so Tim thought. He acted old at least. He always moped around alone, digging his nose in stuff.

The first time Tim saw him, Lucky had his whole head buried deep inside a ripped garbage bag left out on the road. Tim crept up from behind to pet him and got real close before Lucky noticed him. Lucky flinched, but Tim grabbed him right in time. Lucky squirmed and almost broke free, but Tim gripped him tighter to his chest and petted him and talked to him until he calmed down. The dog smelled, smelled bad. But Tim rubbed and scratched him anyway; he figured someone needed to.

Tim put Lucky down and watched him run off across the street behind the metal recycling place. He didn't see Lucky again that day, but later on, when Tim saw him, Lucky wouldn't come, but he wouldn't run either. He would stay put and wait for Tim. He always looked like he was ready to run out of there if he had to. But after a couple belly rubs and some small bits of bread and stuff, Lucky would find Tim. He usually found Tim every day. But some days he didn't come around at all, and Tim wondered where he was. He'd gotten used to seeing Lucky every day.

By this time of day, Lucky had usually come around, sniffing and stinking up everything. Not today though. Tim even brought a nice treat for him, and still no Lucky.

Tim took out his rusty lock-blade deer knife, hunched over, and started to pick the black dirt out from under his fingernails. He always had two things with him—matches and the knife. A while back, he had found it under some rocks by the railroad tracks and had it with him ever since. He had never seen or heard a train go by in the daytime, but he would hear them at night. Once, he sat on the tracks all day and nothing.

Tim took out his box of matches, struck one, and lit another cigarette butt. Putting the match as close to his eyes as he could, he watched the flame hiss and crackle through the rest of the match. He put his head back against the brick wall below the window and blew smoke. The sunlight turned visible when the smoke gave it shape. The smoke swirled around in the light and made funny shapes. The outline of the light took shape again every time Tim blew more smoke. He took long, deep drags just to see how good he could make the sunrays fit into a nice little smoky box the shape of the window.

The voices of people from the corner store parking lot came into the stairwell through the window, and Tim listened. The alley behind the corner store was one floor down out the window. A couple of air conditioner units in the alley whirred pretty loud, but Tim could still catch voices from the front parking lot. He mostly caught voices that yelled and hollered.

But this was different, closer. Tim heard a rough bark and a whimper. He twisted his head up towards the window and scrapped out his cigarette on the concrete. He stood up, trying to be quiet. He balanced on his toes, grabbed the window ledge, and peeked down into the alley. He saw two black kids facing the wall below him. Their knees bent a little, and they took small steps toward the wall, their elbows bent and their arms out.

"Come here, you little bastard. I'm gonna eat you, you little shit."

Tim tried real hard to see down straight below him against the wall. His arms shook, but he managed to pick his body up and stick his head all the way out the window. There was Lucky right below him, pressed sideways against the wall, looking at the two kids. He was cornered real tight. He seemed like he had tried to escape a couple of times and wanted to plead mercy and give up.

The short, fat kid was Big Dog. At least that's what the kids called him. Big Dog wanted it that way, and nobody ever called him anything else. His real name was something like Lawrence. He kinda looked like a dog really, with his fat cheeks and his wide nose, almost like a bulldog. His hair was frizzy, grew on his neck, and poofed out over his ears. He sweated a lot, but even in the heat, he always wore football jerseys that were really big. And he usually had a big toothy grin on his face. He was thirteen, and his voice cracked and barked when he talked. He had a little black hairs growing here and there on his lip and on his cheeks, sort of like whiskers.

His buddy's name was Jimbo. He probably wasn't as old as Big Dog but not as young as Tim either. Jimbo was skinnier and a little bit taller, his hair a little bit neater. His clothes fit better, but the colors were faded. He stayed pretty quiet most of the time. He was really the only kid who hung around Big Dog. The other kids around the apartments must have thought Big Dog was too cool for them. Maybe Big Dog thought he was too cool for the other kids. Either way, it worked out because maybe he had room for Tim. He had been hoping for a long time to get in good with Big Dog.

"I got you now, you little shitter!" Big Dog threw an empty coke can at Lucky, and it looked like it hit him on the back. Lucky yelped a little and flinched like he wanted to run. Jimbo was right there to stop him though.

"You better not let that dog get away, Jimbo. It's your ass if you do." Big Dog kept his face pointed toward Lucky when he said it.

"No way," assured Jimbo.

"Watch him, Jimbo, watch him." Big Dog warned. Jimbo and Big Dog pushed closer and closer to Lucky. Tim couldn't seem to quit staring at the soggy mud between Big Dog and Lucky. Tim stared and didn't blink. He wanted to do something but knew he wouldn't. They really did have Lucky cornered. They must've had a good reason for being mad. They were going to hurt him.

"Hey, stop!"

Big Dog and Jimbo both suddenly looked up at Tim. Lucky took his chance and limped off along the wall and around the corner. Big Dog looked down to where Lucky had been pushed against the wall, stared for a second, and looked back up to the empty window.

"That you, Crayon?" Big Dog's yell flew through the window. The kids around the apartment always called him that. He was one of the only white kids in the apartment and the only one with red hair, green eyes, and yellow eyebrows and eye lashes. All the black kids had fuzzy black hair and brown eyes. The slanty-eyed kids and the kids who spoke Spanish all had straight black hair and brown eyes. But his hair was red. Red, red.

Even the other white kids picked at him because he was covered in red and green and yellow. The other white kids mostly had different sorts of brownish hair, but their hair was still different. Some of them had lighter or darker hair. Some had wavy hair, some had straight hair, and others had curls like springs. Tim used to see one kid around that had blue-eyes like the sky, but he hadn't seen him for a long time. The white kids never stuck together anyway. They mostly stuck to themselves, probably because they all looked different.

He thought nobody liked him because he stuttered, but then they started calling him Crayon because of all the colors. He stood out. He had never even seen another kid with green eyes like his. They were ugly, the color of thick snot when you're sick or the color of a lime—both things that make your eyes squint to think about.

"You hear me up there, Crayon?" Big Dog sounded serious.

Tim squatted just below the window in the shadows, just below the ray of light. He was stuck to that spot. His feet stuck like they were nailed to the concrete, and his head started to spin. He had yelled at Big Dog. He didn't mean too, but it didn't matter now. He dug his fingernails under the scabs on his arm. His arms were sweating, and his fingers and his palms and his face and eyes were sweating. His nose burned, and his eyes stung. As Tim pulled at the scabs on his arms, he figured out that he had no idea what to do next. His mouth tasted like glue.

"Come on, Crayon. We know it's you. What's up, man? Come down here and talk to us, huh?" Big Dog spoke a little nicer this time.

Tim knew he had no way out really, so he forced himself up, poked the top of his head out the window, and looked down at Big Dog and Jimbo. Both still stared at the window.

"Hey, Big Dog. What's up? Hey, Jimbo." Tim stuttered out just loud enough so they could hear him over the humming of the air conditioner units. He didn't always stutter, just at the wrong times and places.

"Hey, Crayon?" spoke Big Dog.

"Yeah?" Tim forced out.

"Come down here and talk to us."

"What's up, Big Dog?"

"Just get your colored ass down here," Big Dog said, frustrated. He looked at Jimbo, and the pudgy rolls on his face scrunched up. "I said..." Big Dog started as he turned back to window. Tim wasn't there. He was already headed down the stairwell, each step shaking and rattling the concrete and metal.

He took it slow; he needed time to think on what he was going to say. He had yelled at Big Dog. Jimbo was really the only one who talked to Big Dog from what Tim saw, and that didn't happen much, either. But he would be extra cool and smart, and they would like him for sure. They would want to hang out with him, no doubt. Should he be friendly? Tough? Funny? Friendly was for wimps, and tough could get him into trouble. He'd bet on funny.

Tim rounded the corner and felt kinda dizzy. He ended up right in the same spot that Lucky had been: in the mud, backed up against a brick wall, and a little scared and shaky. Big Dog took one big step, pinching Tim hard against the wall. Tim took two small steps backward, and his back scrapped the rough brick. Big Dog cocked his head a little to the side and sniffed at Tim. Then he pulled his head back and puffed out his chest.

"Jimbo, you smell something?" Big Dog asked without taking his eyes away from Tim's. Big Dog didn't blink. His mouth hung half open.

Jimbo followed quickly, "What you smell, Big Dog?"

"I don't know Jimbo, smells like wax or something."

"Like wax?" Jimbo said, playing along.

"Yeah, like a crayon, a pimply orange crayon."

Jimbo let loose a small laugh, nothing that shook his shoulders or anything. But Big Dog just stared at Tim and smiled. Tim smiled and looked at Jimbo and then back to Big Dog. Tim forced a small laugh. The air conditioners were louder down in the alley between the store and the apartment building. Tim needed to speak up to be heard. He wanted to sound confident but not too much. He needed something funny.

"Hey Big Dog, you kinda look like a real dog." Tim managed to only stutter a little. The air conditioner units shut down right when he said "real dog." What he said didn't come out like he expected. His words sounded real loud down in the alley without the air conditioners humming, and well, they just didn't come out right.

"What'd you say?" Big Dog's eyebrows sunk lower on his forehead. So did Jimbo's. They moved a little closer, only some inches away. Tim could smell Big Dog's breath. It smelled like real dog breath, like dog food and cigarettes and butt and wet fur. Their noses almost touched. Jimbo stood behind Big Dog, keeping watch.

"You know. Tough like. Tough, like one of those big mean guard dogs. That's what I meant." The stuttering made him nervous so that he stuttered more and began to pinch his scabs. Because Big Dog's face almost rubbed his, Tim held his mouth tight to not lose spit when he talked.

"Whatever," growled Big Dog, a little calmer. He stepped back. So did Jimbo. Big Dog's face loosened up a bit, and some of the rolls and muscles eased up and looked less mean. His eyebrows rose up to their full height and perched in the middle. Big Dog lowered his head to the mud at his feet and stared, thinking. Then, suddenly and with a jerk, his head popped back and looked at Tim again. "Oh, you mean tough like that little mutt that just ran out of here?"

"No, not like that." Tim said, starting to feel itchy, his eyes searching back and forth to both sides. "That dog? No, he's only a little mutt. I meant like a real cool guard dog. You know, like tough and mean and doesn't take any sort of crap from no one." His stuttering bounced his words around. When Tim's stuttering got real bad, Big Dog cocked his head, gritted his teeth, and squinted one eye more than the other.

"You let that dog get away, Crayon."

"No, I didn't."

"You said, 'hey stop.' We looked around, and it took off. That was you, wasn't it? That yelled 'hey stop' and let the dog get away?" Big Dog was calm and sounded curious.

"Yeah, Big Dog. I'm sorry about that. I was lighting a cigarette butt, and one got away from my pile and started rolling down the crack and under the stairs, so I yelled out 'hey stop,' you know, with reflexes." Tim scored big with that answer. It sounded real and not fake at all. He only stuttered a bit, too. He knew he'd have to give up his smokes now though.

Big Dog turned his head and peeked at Jimbo. "He talks to cigarettes, Jimbo."

Jimbo smiled and stared at Tim. Jimbo kept staring, and he kept smiling. His teeth had chunks of food stuck in them. Tim, with his mouth open, stared at Jimbo. His stomach sank. Big Dog turned back toward Tim, and Tim hurried his look to Big Dog and put his smile back on. Tim needed to say something now, right now.

"Why don't y'all take these smokes? I can find plenty more," is what he came up with. Tim held out his hand full of butts for Big Dog to take. They liked him now for sure. Big Dog held his hand palm-up next to Tim's and told Tim to drop the smokes in his hand. Big Dog didn't want to touch Tim's hand, didn't want to grow red hair on his ass. That's what he said, something like that.

Tim dropped the cigarettes in Big Dog's hand. Big Dog handed them to Jimbo. Tim started to feel more comfortable and less shaky. He was tired for some reason, like he had run to China or around the apartments fifty-hundred times.

The air conditioners started up again. They seemed louder now.

"Well," Tim stuttered over the air conditioners, "I'm going to go look for my dog. I ain't seen him yet today."

"What's he look like, Crayon?" asked Big Dog, extra friendly like. "Maybe, we can help you find him."

He shouldn't have said anything. He was tired and didn't catch his words as well as he should have. "Never mind, I got to go do something else. Don't worry about the dog, thanks anyway. I really got to go." Big Dog looked down at the mud while Jimbo kept his eyes on Tim. Tim was shocked and relieved when they didn't press him more.

He didn't know how to leave, but he figured now was as good a time as any. "See you, later," Tim said. He began to walk off nervously like when his dad would come home from work. They might chase him. They might ignore him. He could run if he made it around the corner. The whole conversation had gone wrong from the beginning.

Rounding the corner and just out of view of Big Dog and Jimbo, Tim froze.

"Hey, Crayon!" Jimbo was behind him. Tim almost started to run, but Jimbo was too close. So Tim turned around and waited. He wasn't sure what he was waiting for, but it probably wouldn't be good.

"Hey, Jimbo, wait up a minute, man. I..."

"Shut up, Crayon. Big Dog told me to tell you to come hang out with us later."

"Big Dog wants to hang out? That's cool with me." Tim had to restrain himself. He was feeling cooler every second.

"Meet us in the park before dark."

"Sure, okay." Tim watched Jimbo round the corner back behind the alley. He stared a little longer and then realized that everything had come out perfect after all. Sweat dripped into his eyes and the sun made his hair hot and burned his head. He needed cigarettes. He had a headache, a big one. He was hungry. He hadn't eaten anything all day. The sweat made the scabs on his arms sting real bad. He couldn't believe Big Dog wanted to hang out with him. He smiled and ran home to get cleaned up, jumping as high as he could over every crack and curb.

* * *

As Tim balanced himself in the sewage, he noticed for the first time, really noticed, just how rotten the air stank this far down the canal. A mixture of dead fish and soured milk pushed into his nose and mouth. In front of him, Jimbo splashed along in the shallow water. Tim could feel Big Dog behind him keeping an eye on his sweating back. Tim wore his faded plain black shirt. Sweat and dirt glued it to his back and stomach. It was his best shirt. The sticky collar squeezed his neck. He tugged on it to keep it from his throat. The smelly air made his eyes sting every time he rubbed them and kept his greasy hair stuck flat against the zits on his forehead. Even this late in the day, the heat smothered most bugs, not the mosquitoes though. He slapped one that was sucking on his arm. The legs and blood smeared on his skinny white arms and caught his attention, slowing him down in the inch-deep water.

"Hurry up, Crayon," Tim heard Big Dog shout from behind him.

He let his arms hang more natural like and hurried up. The wet balls of dirt that held his neck to his collar, no matter how used to it he got, still bothered him. He fingered the knife in his pocket. He wanted a cigarette.

On either side of the canal grew a wall of trees. They showed where the neighborhood of apartments and corner stores ended and the refinery began. They might've tried to kinda hide the refineries from the roads and apartments, but that didn't work.

Coming closer now to the woods, he started getting nervous. His stomach and chest hurt and ached. He swallowed a large load of sticky spit, and a little bit came back up. It tasted like hot pennies, and he quickly gulped it back down.

"So guys, what we gonna do out here?" Tim sputtered out. He looked back over his shoulder and faked a grin. He wasn't so happy to be along anymore.

"You always trying to hang out with us, right Crayon? Now you ask *why* we want you to hang out with us. What the hell's your problem?" Big Dog snarled and stared at Tim. Tim hurried up and turned around and looked down. Tim knew that look meant shut up, and he did.

His dad gave him that look. His dad always had that look, especially when he came home from work late smelling like something awful. Maybe Tim just bothered him and got in his way. He learned not to do that. Guess his dad had reasons for being mad—most people do.

The canal had been used to dump the trash of the apartments for a long time. It was stuffed with used condoms, different sorts of broken glass tubes used for different sorts of things, old doctor needles, emptied paint cans, the occasional bullet shell, rusted tricycles and bikes, used diapers, all kinds of faded plastic stuff, and other nasty junk. And over and under all this grew a brownish slime, thick and slippery.

The trees grew taller as he came closer, and through his burning eyes, Tim could see in front of him, past Jimbo, at the bottom of the canal straight ahead, a younger kid's rust flaked Red Flyer wagon.

As Tim kept walking, the smell of gasoline mixed with the air. Tim no longer smelled the stink; it licked his skin and tickled his bones. He could feel the heat in his lungs, and it hurt to breathe. His head began to flash hot and tingle. He panted to not throw up.

Coming up close to the Red Flyer wagon, Tim felt a hard shove from behind. He tripped and found himself on his hands and knees in the water. Big Dog walked around to join Jimbo. Big Dog stared hard at Tim and looked like he wanted to drool.

A small way from Tim's face, lying on his side in the bed of the Red Flyer wagon, in a thin puddle of gasoline, with his hind and fore legs wrapped together in thin metal wire, his mouth duck taped tightly shut, was Lucky. The scared dog barely even moved. The wire had cut into Lucky's skin, and the dried blood in his hair blended in with the crusty bits of slime and dirt that had always stuck to the dog. With Lucky's hair greased with gasoline, the fleas and ticks were all dead, but they still clung and clotted in his matted hair.

Tim heard from a distance Big Dog call to him. "Get up you colored piece of shit Crayon motherfucker. You wanted to hang out with us? Here." Tim eyes began to fill with tears; dirt and sweat began to dribble out. He wanted to puke his guts up. He forced his wobbling legs to push his body up as high as it would go. He looked slowly from Lucky and then quickly to Big Dog's hand, he knew what he wanted him to do. Big Dog held out a used pack of paper matches.

"Here," urged Big Dog.

Tim felt real bad for the dog.

"Stupid dog," Tim muttered, shaking his head, gritting his teeth. He almost cried. His eyes hurt too much. Forever, he had felt sorry for that damn dog. He hated it now.

His faced itched and burned as he looked at the pack of matches. His muscles wanted to rip out of his skin they hurt so bad. Tim looked at his worn out shoes and his legs and his skinny white arms, and he hated himself. Then, he stared face to face with Big Dog and saw the biggest smile he had ever seen on anybody ever.

"Here damn it, take 'em." Big Dog's grin got bigger the longer Tim waited.

Staring at the boys, Tim felt into his pocket and pulled out his knife. Both the boys took a step back, flitting sideways glances at each other. Big Dog dropped his outstretched hand and watching the knife closely, hoarsely sputtered out, "What the hell you think you gonna do with that?"

Tim ignored him, turned, and moved with one steady motion toward the dog. He looked into the mutt's eyes and nodded. He began to cry real loud then drove the dull, rusted blade deep into the dog's throat. Tim felt the dog's quick whimper in his jaws and then the warm trickle on his hands. He kept thinking of how much his eyes hurt. How much his throat and chest and head hurt.

The dog went quiet. As meat gave way to bone, Tim felt shiver bumps running up his arms. The bone cracked and snapped as he finished sawing with one last grunt.

Tim let the warm, sticky knife dangle in his right hand. In his left hand, a tongue and chunks of blood drizzled through his fingers as he offered the small head to Big Dog.

"Here," Tim forced the words from his gut. "Take it."

Big Dog stared at Tim. Jimbo couldn't seem to tell who to look at, Tim or Big Dog.

"Here," Tim tried again, louder this time.

Big Dog squinted at Tim and pushed his lips together. Greasy wrinkles grew out around his eyes and nose. Then he looked at the bloody head, then toward the dull knife, then back into Tim's red face. "Fuck you," Big Dog managed to stutter at Tim.

"Here!" Tim screamed and spit.

The head got heavier. He hated himself.

Big Dog's dark brown eyes covered themselves with a thick puddle; snot leaked into his shaky lips. Jimbo watched Big Dog's face.

"Fuck you!" Big Dog's voice cracked as he screamed at Tim.

Everything left Tim at once. He felt a sudden release of the muscles in his back and shoulders. The muscles in his face went soft and flat. He dropped Lucky's head at Big Dog's feet, and it didn't even splash. It only made a soft thud.

Tim looked to the water and at the lump by his feet, and then he shot a short look past the boys, turned into the last dark-blue light of the day, and wiped his crusted hands on his faded black shirt. He turned and began trudging back through the slimy concrete canal, alone. The flames from the refineries sent weird moving shadows into the canal and brought life to things that weren't alive. They hissed and roared and lit up the canal in front of him. Everything was red. Dim and shadowy and red.

He watched his shadow flicker and twitch along with the other shadows and stretch far out in front of him. Soon, his hands stopped shaking, and for a second, he wished he were in his room. Then, he wished he were dead—maybe lying on some railroad tracks, hearing the loud horn blowing, staring at the stars, feeling the ground rumbling beneath his body, and just waiting there. Or maybe, he wished, he could just wait for the train and hop on—grab a whole pack of smokes and hop on. Maybe, they would even let him ride. Just for a little while.

Alaina Bray
Dust

Lilith froze. She turned back to consider the town for a moment. She stood on a hill just within its borders, the only break in the flattened landscape. Elevated, she saw the lamps and lanterns of Charming flicker out as it put itself to sleep—electricity a fad that had not yet reached the town. Only a few windows still glowed; most of Charming's residents were long asleep, preparing for another day of farming the cotton that would not grow except in small, bedraggled patches like the spots of fur left on a dog with mange.

She turned her back to the city once again and lifted her foot to take her next step. She stopped, left the foot poised in the air, feeling as though there was something sacred and forbidden in the step—that this dirt, though only a single step farther than the dirt she had trod before, was what her father had always warned her about. This was dirt walked upon by the immoral and the reprobate whom her father said awaited her outside of Charming. Charming abided no such wickedness. The outsiders, the ones not to be trusted who robbed banks with tommy-guns and refused to remove their hats when meeting a lady, behaved this way.

Lilith brought her foot down to rest next to the other—in Charming. She sighed. Her father would smirk if he had been watching her, proud to know his warnings had chipped their way into her skull and burrowed through to the center of her brain, where, like ear-wigs, they snuggled in her mind, laying eggs and occasionally out of sheer boredom raising their pincers to sting pieces of the soft, pink mass.

But her father, of course, did not know she was here, so he could not share his satisfied smirk. He was resting within the wooden walls of their home, a home that stood alone among acres of empty cotton fields. He lay peacefully underneath his tin roof and faded quilt in a bed next to Lilith's faded mother.

His teeth were like millstones in Lilith's presence, grinding together and eroding like the Oklahoma topsoil he could not keep from blowing away. Lilith's mother could sometimes hear the scraping as they sat in church where Lilith, lacking the proper air of seriousness, smiled in such a way that her nose crinkled while she sang along with the congregation to the slow cadence of the hymns.

Once, with the last chords of "I'll Fly Away" still resting in the air, Lilith had sung on, unnoticed at first by all except her father, whose teeth had been grinding furiously between stanzas of his own singing. It took several moments for the echoes to fade from the whitewashed walls and for the rest of the congregation to realize not everyone had stopped singing. It was a realization that came slowly, people turning their heads to see what their neighbors were looking at, starting with the families sitting around Lilith and rippling from this center to the edges of the church until each dusty face was turned towards the girl who had not gone silent with the music.

Lilith stood with her eyes closed and her palms upturned, swaying peacefully to the sound of her own humming. The corners of her lips turned up into a brief smile as the words "Fly Away" came out in a half-breathed whisper and rounded with the murmur of "O Glory...I'll fly away." The other words were swallowed by a hum that emanated from her throat like the sound of distant train horns at night.

Those sitting closest could make out the words. Others felt only the hum and its weight, but they were enough to keep them enraptured in the thin, blonde spectacle. Men stood stony faced, some clenching straw hats in the leather of their hands. Women fidgeted next to their husbands, looking at the wood floors when the men glanced toward them and then, with a swallow, quickly back to Lilith. Those Lilith's age appraised her, running their eyes from the curls tied back messily with a ribbon to the bare feet that poked out beneath her faded floral print dress and the cracked leather shoes lying next to them. Many mimicked the expressions of their fathers, and the rest found themselves humming secretly, inaudibly along with her. The children, amused, watched with the same attention and affection they'd have given a stray dog doing tricks in the street.

Lilith's eyes squeezed tighter, as if in pain, as she half-hummed half-sang the last words, "Hallelujah by and by. I'll fly away." Then she opened her eyes and lowered her palms back to her sides. Blood pooled pink in her cheeks, but she made no other acknowledgment of her audience other than a raise of her chin and a slow sweep of eyes across those who stared. Folding her body into the wooden pew, she started a ripple much like the last one, and those nearest to her sat down first with the rest following, sitting uneasily in the hard seats and hard silence.

It was then that Lilith's father chipped his tooth: the bottom left molar, second farthest from the back. His wife heard the crack and turned. Lilith looked resolutely forward as the preacher shuffled to the pulpit in his wilted suit and cleared his throat, unsure whether to begin. Drops of sweat were already beading on his pink, spotted forehead. Lilith's father spat out the fragment as he would a sip of sour milk and caught it in his hand. He looked at it, at Lilith, and back again and curled his lips in disgust at one of the two.

When the preacher had decided to speak, he began uneasily, quite aware that the congregation was still occupied with the sway and the hum of a farmer's daughter. But the farmer himself looked not at Lilith nor the preacher but at the fragment of tooth in his hand and rolled it steadily between the calluses of his thumb and forefinger until the service ended and the people filed out, heads down in eager whispers.

The tooth's ivory interior contrasted with its surface, yellowed with the well water and the food the man had been too tired to brush away after nights of plowing, sowing, and reaping under the Oklahoma sky. He came in only when dusk had begun to claim the plains and the Mexican free-tails joined him on the fields, gliding by his head and through the rows of cotton like dancers. He was fond of the bats many years ago, knowing they hunted the flies and mosquitoes that plagued him as he worked. He called them "My own personal farm hands," and when Lilith was a toddler, he would carry her outside, just after her mother had bathed her and dressed her for bed, pulling his reluctant wife too along by the hand.

"Jasper, you're going to get her dirty," she'd say.

He would smile—his teeth so white, so charming then. "We have to see the bats, Lila Beth. The girl wants to play." He waited for the toddler's affirmation—a giggle or an eager tug on the straps of his overalls—and turned back to his wife. "Have a heart."

"Your food will get cold."

He would sit at their table and place Lilith on his lap. He made a game of seeing how fast he could eat the food, much to his daughter's delight. He grabbed handfuls of whatever Lila Beth had made him that night—chicken, beans, even steak on the best of nights— and shoved them into his mouth.

Lila Beth turned away so he wouldn't see her lips turning up at the corners. "Jasper, look at yourself! She is never going to have manners if you behave like that."

He looked to Lilith and pretended to snarl with his mouth full. She shrieked with laughter at his growls. "Pa is a bear!" she would announce to her mother who was still turned away, the edges of her frown twitching and threatening to lift.

"Hear that, Jasper? You're a bear."

He chewed and swallowed as quickly as he could manage and rose, setting Lilith on the floor to go wipe his hands if the dinner had been messy that night. "Makes her laugh though. Doesn't it Lila?"

"Suppose it does." He scooped up his daughter again and wrapped a hand around Lila Beth's slender wrist to lead the pair outside.

There in the fields, Lila Beth already abandoning her pretense of crossness, they would wait for the bats to dance by their heads. "Shhh," the father prompted, his daughter trying to stifle her giggles. Then after moments of smiling anticipation, one of the creatures would pirouette by. Lilith would answer with a shriek of laughter, and her father would fake shock each time.

"You sound like a bat! Are you a bat?"

"Yes!"

"You're a bat? You're a bat!" He would lift her above his head, ignoring the soreness in his arms, and run with her through the rows of the then thriving cotton. She spread out her arms, flapped, and shrieked. Lila Beth chased them, but never quite fast enough. She caught her breath between strides and laughs.

"Jasper! Jasper, slow down! I'm not wearing shoes."

Jasper's soreness was less easily ignored later when the cotton came less easily and the top soil and the wind began to run away together like forbidden lovers—and when they found Lila Beth would have no more children. He grew too tired to do anything after his day in the sun and wind except come in and kiss the heads of his wife and daughter. And later, he grew too tired even for this. Their twilight dances with the bats became a memory for the father and a ghost of a memory for his daughter.

Lilith barely remembered the origin of her unusual habit years later when she continued with it and her father had long abandoned it. At twelve, she no longer shrieked and ran with the bats but waited with her arms out until they twirled around her as casually as if she were a tree. She watched them spin and open their mouths to emit the sounds that gave them sight. She liked to think they were singing.

Sometimes, her father would stare from where he worked in the field, but she learned to ignore him as he had done to her. He had once looked like his daughter, both of them fair-skinned and light-haired. But his pale skin had been tanned and leathered with the sun and wind, and his head of thick, yellow hair had thinned like the crops, a little more each season.

Then the storms began to carry away the soil like charmers carry away young daughters. The farmers began to wear Charming's dust in their hair and on their shoulders. Later still, in their eyes and in the hollow echoes of their laughs.

During one of the first storms, Lilith was sitting at the small wooden table in their kitchen, absorbed in sixth grade arithmetic homework. Her mother sat next to her, peeling potatoes and occasionally looking at the school work she could not understand.

"You understand that, Lilith?"

"Yes ma'am, Mamma." Her mother nodded and smiled slightly as she looked back to her potatoes. Lilith's father, driven in early by the wind and dust, opened the front door and walked without a word towards the biscuits and beans waiting for him at the opposite end of the table.

Then he noticed the Mexican free-tail that had flown in behind him, it too seeking shelter from the storm. The three of them stared at the bat while it flew in panicked circles, realizing it preferred the storm to being trapped within the house. It shrieked and flapped its wings near the wall, hoping the sound would show it an escape. Slowly, Jasper turned away from the plate and followed the bat with his eyes. He walked with heavy steps toward the wall and extended his arm, waiting for the bat to come near. He swatted for it with an open hand when it flew within his reach.

"Jasper?" his wife whispered. She swallowed as he followed the bat into the middle of the room when it flew away from the wall. "Jasper, what are you doing?"

Lilith, misunderstanding, pushed back from the table and left her seat to join him, believing they were dancing like they had in her memory-ghosts. She stood by his side and held her arms out as he did, waiting for the bat to come near. She answered the bat's shrieks with laughter and began to twirl around Jasper, mimicking the circles the bat flew around his head, and, for a moment, she almost remembered that they had once looked alike.

When the bat came near his face, he grabbed it by the corner of its wing and spun to the floor. Before it could rise, he stomped it twice with the hard bottom of his boot.

"No!" Lilith dived towards him. He stopped her, his large hand catching her at the chest, and turned to face her. His lips curled, and she was silent. The dust settled in the creases of his face made him look so much older. Dust from his boots powdered the bat's fur. Its ribcage was crushed. Its bottom jaw hung limp and sideways, and its small tongue poked out from the side. The membrane of its left wing had been torn as it was hurled to the ground.

Jasper took a deep breath through his nose. Then he kicked the kitchen wall and made his way back to his bedroom and slammed the door. Lilith knelt in silence over the small, broken form, and her mother, after a swallow and a sniffle, turned back to her potatoes.

The storms in those days were smaller and did not last as long. And when the wind and dirt had stopped swirling outside, Lilith's father emerged from his room. Wordlessly he scooped up the crumpled body that lay next to his daughter and carried it outside.

She remained on her knees for a moment, fingering the spot of blood where the bat had been, then rose to follow him.

"Lilith, maybe you shouldn't—" her mother started softly. Her words were lost as the screen door slapped shut.

It took her several moments to find in him in the dying light. She spotted his hunched over form in one of the clusters of cotton that remained in the field, shaking in sobs. He held the body of the bat, running his thumbs over the dust and blood that matted the fur on its chest.

"Pa..."

Jasper gasped and rose quickly. He wiped his face, smearing it with dirt and traces of blood. He lifted his arm above his head and cast the bat's crumpled form into the shadows. Lilith followed its arc and watched it land, more crumpled now, in a small cloud of dust.

Jasper turned to face his daughter with a steel in his eyes.

"Lilith, you won't be going back to school tomorrow. You're going to start helping me in the fields."

"Pa..."

"Don't talk back, Lilith."

"Pa, please no." Her voice fell to a whisper. "I can't do that. I can't do that, Pa."

He stared at her for a moment and then turned for the house.

"Pa!" She followed after him, his steps quickening. "Pa!" He was already locked in his bedroom when she entered the house. She kicked the same spot on the wall he had, three times, bruising the tips of her bare toes. "Pa! Pa! Pa!" The word emphasized each kick. A sob swelled in Lilith's throat. She dug her fingernails into her palms and swung once at the air.

"Lilith? Lilith, what's happened?" Her mother's voice startled her. She had forgotten she was still in the kitchen.

"I'm not going back to school." She hated the sound of the words. "I'll be working in the fields."

Lila Beth looked down at the open arithmetic book and ran her hand over it, and a tear glistened at the corner of her eye as she closed it. She rose and put away the potatoes before walking to Lilith. Cupping her daughter's chin in her hand, she ran her thumb over her cheekbone with a sigh. "I'm sorry, Lilith." She kissed her on the forehead and turned for her bedroom.

Lilith paced the floors and dug her fingernails deeper into her hands. Bile rose in her throat when she glanced at the closed book. Her tooth dug into her lip until it tore the soft tissue, and she detected the metallic taste of blood. She spat on the floor and hoped her father would step in it in the morning. Then she thought of her mother cleaning it up and turned to get a towel. Leaning down to wipe the blood-speckled froth, she noticed drops of the bat's blood on the floor next to her own. Without thinking, she ran her finger over the drops, smearing them into her saliva and blood. She paused and looked at the crimson on her finger and on the floor. She stared at the mixture for a moment before wiping it up, then rose.

Her feet carried her towards the door, into the dark, and to the bat. One wing was completely broken now, twisted behind its head. She dug its shallow grave with her hands, dirt caking under her fingernails, and twisted a small cross out of twigs. Gently lifting the bat, she set to work picking mats of blood out of its fur and spat in her hand to clean off the powder of dust. She folded the creature's wings until they looked right again, careful not to tear them further. The bat stared back at her with glassy eyes and mouth hanging open, as if she had hypnotized it. Lilith shuddered at the sight, closed its eyes and straightened its jaw, carefully putting the small tongue back in place. Then she gently kissed its head, placed it in the grave, and covered it with dust.

It felt wrong to leave, but she could think of no words, no eulogy to utter over it. She sat for a few minutes, then began to sing the only song that seemed to fit. Her voice was unlike a child's in the night's warm air, as if her twelve-year-old body housed the voice of a woman.

"I'll fly away, O Glory...I'll fly away. When I die—Hallelujah by and by. I'll fly away."

The Mexican free-tails accompanied her song, dancing near her and shrieking to the background melody of the cricket chirps. Lilith did not want to go back into the house.

Each day for six years—except for the days of the storms that had begun to grow larger, blacker, carrying more and more of Charming's soil away— she rose and worked in the fields that grew more bare each season. The steel she saw in her father's eyes and the dust in the creases of his face never went away. And though her skin never leathered the way his had, she grew leaner, thinner from the work and the meals that were also growing smaller.

On Lilith's eighteenth birthday, a week after her father had chipped his tooth, the family sat at the wooden table, eating dinner together. A storm had driven Lilith and Jasper in early. Lila Beth had given her own portion of rice and beans to Lilith as a birthday present. Her mother said little, as had become her habit.

Lilith looked at the empty plate in front of her mother.

"Pa." He looked up from his plate. "We can go to California. Like the others are doing."

He sighed and looked again to his food.

"Pa."

"We are not talking about this, Lilith."

She shook her head, pleading. "No!"

Jasper's worn hands dropped the fork, and it clinked against the plate. "Lilith, do you know what kind of people are in California?"

She met his gaze, and her eyes narrowed. "Do you?"

"No!" His voice cracked as he pushed himself back from the table and stood. "I don't. This," he motioned with his left arm. "*This*," he stomped the floor, "is what I know."

Lilith too rose, picked up her mother's empty plate, and threw it before his feet. "It is *killing* us."

He stared at the broken pieces, and his body almost shook the way it had the night with the bat. He blinked slowly. Then, kicking the wall on his way out, he stepped out of the kitchen and away from his daughter.

A daughter who now stood filled with resolve after the fight, both feet together on the border of Charming, considering the difference between its dust and the dust she was too afraid to place her feet upon.

She squatted to better see it, letting the hems of her cream-colored cotton dress touch the ground, kiss it. She sniffed the night air and then extended her neck, which seemed to glow in the fullness of the moon, over the forbidden dirt and drew another cold breath through her nose, hoping to discover a difference between the air of Charming and not-Charming. She liked to think she had detected one—that the air over the forbidden dust hinted faintly at the smell of fruit that had just become overripe.

Then, her neck still extended over not-Charming, she lowered her back and brought her head closer the ground. The tips of her blonde curls touch its dust. Lilith swallowed. She lifted her left hand and let it hover in the air of not-Charming, paused, and felt for a difference. This air was perhaps thicker, filled with the pollen of the forest she faced and with a hint of the smoke of the city beyond it. Her hand drifted down gently and touched the dust with the tip of its middle finger. It felt different. She brought the other four fingers down, each landing softly on the dust like the lips of a mother on a newborn child. She drew the fingers slowly back toward her body and Charming, letting them trace patterns in the wonderful new dust, and then forward again. The new dust stuck to the tips of her fingers, coloring them with its lovely red-brown.

Then she fell to her knees, unconcerned about staining the cotton of her dress. The dirt made it seem even lovelier. She brought her other hand, without hesitation this time, to meet the dust and brought it down with the full force her palm. She curled her fingers and scraped the ground of not-Charming, collecting as much of it as she could under her fingernails. A staggered breath emanated from the bottom of her ribs. She was sure this dust was different. She leaned over it, resting her weight on her shins and curling her spine to bring her face close to the ground. She clenched her eyes shut, let out another shaky breath, and gasped for the thick, lovelier air. Lilith sobbed, guttural noises rising from the back of her throat. Her ribcage was wracked with each sound, and she pulled her lips back over her teeth, baring them slightly. She was not sure for whom she cried. Perhaps for her mother who would wake up tomorrow alone with her father. Or for herself, the daughter of the man who needed a son. Perhaps for the dying lights of Charming.

Digging her hands into the ground, Lilith collected handfuls of the foreign dirt and stood. She turned once again to face the town, her face stained, knuckles clenched white over the dirt, and mouth in a snarl. She waited for the wind to come and then with one last sob, threw the dust towards her town, hoping it would reach the window of her father and that he would know this was not the dust of Charming. That he would smell her own scent mixed with that of the dust and know that she no longer belonged to him.

Satisfied with the gesture, she sighed and brought her dirty hands up to wipe her face. A Mexican free-tail flew by, and the small breeze from its wings kissed her face. She did not think one had come that close since she was a child. She stooped to pick up the small satchel that held her spare dress and the biscuits she would eat tomorrow morning when she reached the smoky city beyond the thicket. Lilith stepped forward, without pausing this time, across the border and into the trees. Behind her, the last light of Charming flickered out.

Grace Megnet
Effects

Those low-heel pumps—the catalog said "Jenny Pumps" when she ordered them, but you did not know that—had caught your eye before, burned into your cornea, and danced over the polished surface of your imagination. The little skirt, mauve—she liked mauve—skipped just above her knees, her Botticelli knees. She put the memo on your desk, her arms announcing victory, her lipsticked lips triumphantly pursed, her gaze hanging on your face an instant too long. Then you watched her dance through the doorframe again, the pull of her zipper bouncing up and down, up and down.

It was spring, and you did not think of the summer's heat, the winter's freeze. The world looked rosy as it always does through your pink glasses, when her alizarin lips whispered innocent words into innocent space, her fingers dainty, accidentally touching your hand, making your blood ripple. A game you could control, you thought, a pleasure you deserved like a cupcake, eaten in secret in the car, wrapper tossed out the window, evidence destroyed, hidden from the watchful eyes of Sally. You felt guilty at first, surreptitiously guilty, when you sat in the pew on Sunday next to Sally contemplating your socks, but it was so exciting. Finally there was action, real action. Well-behaved Henry turned into *Die Nadel*, scouring legal documents by day, scanning crimson lips at twilight before returning home to your recliner and the smell of chicken broth. You knew you walked on slippery ground, but you were smart, smarter than Adam. You would not be chased out of paradise—you held a juris doctorate. All was well, you whistled when you came home, smiled when you pecked Sally's cheek, when you flung your coat on the hook. ("How was your day, honey?"—"Great.") You had figured it out. You could make it happen. You were the man, until Sally found the wrapper.

To hire Sally was a mistake—nepotism, people whispered between filing cabinets—but sometimes you have to do what you have to do: house note, car notes, kids in college. She screamed into the phone, a thunderbolt in late afternoon. "Sally, be reasonable," you pleaded. She dropped the receiver, the call, walked out of her office—the pumps were not even at work that day—out of her job, out of her marriage, out of your life. She could have waited until five and spared you the humiliation, but no. "Did you hear?—"What?"—"Sally left. Took the canary and left." Now what, mister? No chicken cacciatore when you came home. The fridge was empty except for a bottle of crusted French mustard and a jar with three pickles swimming in cloudy muck. You ordered pizza, gave the delivery boy a five-dollar tip. It tasted like the box. You almost missed Sally, flipping through the channels. You called her cell phone, texted "Come back." No answer. You almost missed the nagging—almost. She had taken the hairdryer, and the bed linen, and the photographs of the kids. "Damn it." You spent a lonely night twisting on the mattress cover, remembering the zipper, up and down, up and down. In the morning you discovered that your razor and your toothbrush were missing—"Damn it"—and when you put on your shoes to dash to Wal-Mart and make amends, you realized that your shoelaces were missing too. Already late, you opened the closet, and all your ties were cut midway, all except one with a Christmas theme. Rudolph, the red nosed reindeer. "Damn it. Damn it, damn it." When you finally arrived in the office, shaved, laced and toothbrushed, your whole existence announced: bad mood. Lupe, your secretary, rolled her eyes. "Leave me alone," you said when the Jenny pumps walked through the door. She turned around, and you noticed her zipper. Up and down. You had to call her and apologize. Later you pressed her against the wall and ate her face like a starving wolf. She wore a very short dress that day with a flower print. "Honey."

"Don't talk," you said, a spit of land awash in exploding waves. "We have to be careful," you said. She put a polished nail on your lips and whispered currents of pleasure down your spine; then you ambled back past Lupe's desk to your computer screen, your desk stacked with legal documents. The firm prohibits …You called her later. She left Jerry and moved into an apartment. You had hired Jerry too; he was your friend. You smiled and kept your cool ("How are you today, buddy?") counting on Jerry's dull-wit and love for Jesus Christ.

Your divorce from Sally was drawn-out and vicious—Sally did not have a degree, but Sally was smart: she hired your nemesis, took half of your assets and the summer home. Of course, you deserved something sweet, a consolation prize. You called her more often, entrusting hushed words to the receiver: "Tonight." Her truck claimed its spot next to your Chrysler in the double-garage, her pumps under Sally's vanity coveting the Chinese rug with the dragon. You flew to Aruba for a week on different planes, wore flip-flops, drank coconut water, and wore hats and dark glasses.

"We have to stop," you pleaded over a plate of stuffed turnovers. She laughed.

"You don't love me?" she asked, poking with her fork into flaky crust.

"It is too dangerous. If they discover us..."

"Nobody will know. You are too smart," she said.

"I hope you are right," you mumbled, your mouth full. Despite the hibiscus bloom in her hair and the slit in her dress up to her tanned thighs, you did not desire her as you did in your office. She talked. She teased. She smiled, and you looked the other way.

"I love to look at the sea, the ocean," you told her. She sighed. You did not like the way she walked, the way she jabbed at the Keshi balls, the way she brushed her teeth, the way she pulled the curtains. You did not talk at the airport when waiting for departure. She left first. You said, "Bye." She did not answer. She gave her ticket to the attendant and did not look back. She did not look at you. You were glad. You went back to the bar for a whiskey on the rocks. The liquid burned your throat and then expanded in your warming chest. Good. Bad weather delayed your flight. Severe thunderstorm, the announcement informed you. You had another drink and watched rain wash the plate glass in front of the bar. Lightening tore through black clouds. A baby cried.

"A bad storm. Could become a hurricane," people said looking at computer models on the TV screens. "Let's get out of here as long as we can," an elderly man laughed, angling for the buckle of his seat belt when you sat finally strapped in a window seat. You pulled your cap over your eyes, feigning sleep. As he munched his pretzels the same noisy way Sally ate nuts in the dark, you knew it: you never loved her. You would tell her Monday morning. When you spotted the continent's shoreline, you changed your mind. As soon as your phone found a signal, you texted her: "It is over?" No answer. "It is over?" you texted again as you waited for your bag in front of the conveyor belt which squeakily presenting the same tattered suitcase—somebody pick me up, please, somebody pick me up, please. When the phone buzzed, you knew it was her. What? You read the message while wheeling your case through customs—nothing to declare. Your Chrysler sat covered in dust on the fourth floor of the parking garage. Maybe you should have stayed in Aruba. The phone in your pocket buzzed twice more as you worked your way through ramps into the sunlight. You stood your ground the next morning when she demanded an explanation. You watched her hips swing this way and that as she swaggered out the door past Lupe's desk.

You adjusted your tie before you entered the president's office. He motioned you to sit. The leather felt cool through your impeccably ironed trousers.

"You wanted to see me?"

"We have a storm brewing."

"I know. We may have to evacuate."

"I am not talking about the weather, Henry." The managing partner's voice lost its warmth, and his gaze turned grey.

"Ms. Kasper has filed a complaint of sexual harassment against you."

"What?" You felt your blood surge towards your neck. "She does not have a leg to stand on."

"Did you have sexual relations with her?"

"I did."

"Against company regulations? Look son, you should have known better."

"I know."

"What do you want to do now, Henry? This may nip you in the butt."

"It was consensual. I can prove it."

"I hope you are right. She strikes me as the kind of person who is capable of producing a stink."

"Could we transfer her? Somewhere abroad maybe?"

"If you are innocent, we may not need to do that."

"I am. We went to Aruba together. I did not drag her down there in handcuffs."

You knew she would fight like a cat, vicious and agile, and even though you would win, she would inflict damage.

Coworkers stood in front of the TV screen when you went into the lounge for coffee. The storm had turned into a hurricane. "I hope it will not be us," they muttered as they shook their heads and walked out with their mugs. Then the storm hit, and people fled with kids and grandparents, dogs and goldfish, with tanks full of gas and coolers full of water, beer, power bars, and trail mix. The parking lot was nearly empty, and it was raining horizontally when you checked your gun in the glove box and pulled out into the street. The waves lapped over the seawall, towered high and clawed at you, your windshield wiper wiping, wiping. Eeriness spread over the town, shops closed, drained of life, windows boarded, an occasional police car, the siren of an emergency vehicle, and then—right in front of you—blurry through the condensation on the glass: her truck. Wiping, wiping. You knew it. You knew that plain, white truck, its erratic turns, its abrupt stops. You knew. And you followed.

Later, much later, disheveled and drained, you checked into the last room in a motel off the highway somewhere in Alabama you did not know existed. The motel was overcrowded with evacuees glued to the screen; journalists stood in four feet of water in front of flooded homes. In worn slippers and laceless shoes, they dragged themselves to the ice machine like ghosts hoping to drown their despair and grief in Popov and Bankers Club. You, sitting on the edge of that king-sized bed, staring at the carpet, a mix of yellow, brown, and filth, wondering how all that could have happened. How? Rain hammered the pavement, and you sat at a sticky table in a restaurant with no name and ate chicken wings. The salad was limp and lifeless. You left it on the plate. You left the Alabama, drove to Atlanta through heavy rain, hoping for relief.

When the lights were back on, you went home to an empty house, reeking of mold and rotten steaks in the fridge, a gooey, greenish sauce already staining the kitchen floor. Why did you come back? What did you hope to find? You thought to call Sally, but you resisted. You would be all right. You dreamt of angry waves, clawing spray, walls of water carrying you away.

"I will be all right," you confirmed when you looked at yourself in the mirror, adjusting the yellow tie in the morning. "I will be all right."

The storm damage was minimal: tiles missing from the roof, a few blown-out windows, some flooding in the lobby. All the employees came back—except one.

"She should never have evacuated alone," people said. "We told her, but she never listened. Poor soul. The police found her white truck at the ocean's edge, but they never found her. Who in her right mind would walk along the beach in a hurricane?" They shook their heads.

You said nothing, ambled back to your desk with your coffee, ignoring Lupe's accusatory look. She was gone. It was all that mattered, and over time people would forget. Sometimes, late at night, you still see that truck drive in front of you on the way home.

Grace Megnet
Rigor

Every day I drag myself onto this treadmill and walk for miles and miles. The living room is so small that the treadmill takes up most of the space. I had to push the dining table to the wall to make room. Now the whole place looks so crammed. All I do is put one foot in front of the other: *one-two, one-two,* like a never-ending two step. I would have more fun walking outside and enjoying the sunshine, the flowers, and the wind in my hair, but I am too fat to walk outside so I get on my squeaky treadmill, choose "fatburn" from the program, and, like a zombie, wait for the dull noise of the turning belt to start. *One-two, one-two.* The machine flashes "weight" and I submissively punch in 218. Age: 43. I do it like a ritual, like a sacred duty. *One-two, one-two.*

After Mom's death, I decided to take care of myself, but I have only lost a meager two pounds in the last three months, and I am still wearing my XXL tee-shirt and these god-awful sweat pants. I want to wear a pair of Lulemon yoga pants and a fitted tank, old rose. I like old rose.

Walking does not seem to be the best way to accomplish my goal. I might get better results with kickboxing or spinning, but such strenuous exercise would probably kill me.

One-two, one-two.

Walking was easier when I watched TV. It distracted me, and I forgot that I was exercising. I used to watch the food channel—never a soap opera. My whole life was a sitcom, and watching it on TV only brings back memories I want to forget. I watched Paula Dean, y'all, cooking up a storm with the holy trinity, and frying chicken legs in a lot of grease, but since the TV broke I have only this grey wall in front of me. Who wants to stare at a grey wall?

One-two, one-two. And then I talk to you. Is it odd to speak to the dead? I do it all the time, especially on the treadmill since the TV is broken. I talk to you, Mom, and I wonder if you can hear me. I hate this grey wall, and it is all I see, the grey wall and your magnolia paintings. I hate grey. I should paint it sunny yellow or lime green, but that would interfere with your paintings. I like lime green. You hated lime green. And you would hate to see your magnolia pictures hanging so crooked and full of dust.

187

"You should dust your house, darling," you would say. "It looks so unsightly. I don't like dust on my paintings, it takes away from their luminous quality." When you had talked to me like that as a child, I wished that I had had lids over my ears. Now I am forty-three, and you still talk to me like that, especially when I am on the treadmill. You are dead, and I wish you would shut up. I remember when you decided to be a painter: it was during the summer when I turned thirteen. You bought art material from a mail catalog and screamed with excitement when the postman delivered the parcel. It all looked so mysterious when you unwrapped tubes of paint with names like alizarin crimson, burnt umber, venetian red, cerulean, cobalt, and viridian; brushes with long handles and bottles labeled *Copal Medium, Resin-gel,* and *Liquin.* First you painted at the kitchen table. Then, one day, you came home with this gleaming expression on your face which, as we knew only too well, spelled trouble.

"I saw this wonderful oak easel at an estate sale two blocks from our house. It was such a bargain," you said, and Dad had to drop what he was doing, jump in the truck and go get it. Dad, Fran, and I worked like slaves late into the night moving furniture and stuff to turn the master bedroom of our three bedroom house into your studio—how selfish of you, Mom—because it had the best light, you said, and because the easel fitted perfectly next to the window overlooking the garden.

"Mind the drawers. You are ruining the knobs. More to the left. You are hitting the door frame." You gave the orders, and we sweated.

Dad grumbled under his breath, (and you pretended not hear him) and later, in a stupor, he even cursed, but you never listened to him, certainly not when he was drunk, and there was nothing he could do, and he knew it. Fran's room became the new master bedroom, and Fran moved in with me.

I did not mind sharing a room with Fran, but I never really got used to the smell of linseed oil that came out of your studio, and with time, the linseed oil seeped into every nook of the house, filling it with a noxious odor. At school I would sniff my clothes worried that I, too, exuded this penetrating smell, which, to this day gives me a headache. Dad had to make you two large shelves for the back wall, which you loaded up with your paint supplies: neatly stacked canvases in racks and boxes with intriguing labels like "gouache," "acrylics," and "Winsor & Newton." You arranged the brushes like flowers in glass jars: sable and watercolor brushes in some, the sturdier bristle brushes in others—all meticulously separated by size. I saw you caressing them with your long fingers when you thought you were alone in the house. When we were at home, you locked the door and spent hours, sometimes whole days, in that studio. Dad became a real expert at frying eggs and cooking spaghetti for Fran and me. Dad got his calories in liquid form.

When the weather was nice, you preferred to paint outside; you called it *"plein air."*

"Plein air paintings are fresh and spontaneous," you chirped. "I want to paint like Monet painted his haystacks—colorful reflections of light dancing on the canvas."

Meanwhile, Dad locked himself more and more into his cage of booze; and you turned an elegant, deaf ear to his griping and his mumbled complaints about rheumatism and forced him to carry the heavy oak easel down the carpeted staircase into the garden.

"Put it under the magnolia tree," you ordered him. Sometimes you called him back when you changed your mind, and he had to put the easel in a different spot.

"The Impressionists were the first ones to paint *"plein air,"* you lectured. "They invented paint in tubes, just like toothpaste, which they could carry around. Michelangelo and Raphael could not go and paint in the fields with a bunch of glass jars. The Impressionists were also enamored with trains—Manet and Monet both painted the St. Lazare railway station in Paris—they travelled to the countryside with their paints in tubes and painted outside in the fields." I tried not to listen. "It is good to know these things. Cultured people know these things, darling," you told me.

You must have painted those magnolias at least twenty-five times.

"I love the smell of magnolias, it is so tantalizing."

I could not smell any magnolias. All I smelled was paint and turpentine. While you were painting, I was lying in the grass, watching the bugs scurry back and forth. You wanted me to study for that stupid Physics final, but I had tossed the book aside and inspected bugs and ants as they climbed up and down blades and flower stems. When you sat on a folding chair, I saw only your back in a patterned dress of light colors and your yellow straw hat. Your arm moved up and down as you scrubbed paint into the canvas with a large bristle brush, and the crickets echoed the sound of that scrubbing. Your strokes were broad and nervous, and splatters of paint fell on the ground and buried ants. Most of the time you forgot that

I was there, but in the few moments when you remembered, you kept nagging me:

"You should be studying and not lying there stealing God's time."

I did not quite understand what you meant by "stealing God's time." I asked you, but you did not answer: you were back "in the zone"—another of your funny expressions I never quite figured out. It must have been quotes that you remembered from your childhood and translated into English. You said other things nobody quite understood.

"These girls are prunes."

Fran and I thought nothing of it, but my friends at school laughed at your English behind your back. I felt humiliated and embarrassed when they asked me,

"Why does your Mom speak so funny?" or "Why doesn't your Mom speak English like you?"

I never told you, but I was always glad when you did not come and pick me up after school, and then I did not have to endure such questioning.

One-two, one-two. These pictures have been hanging in my house for a long time. I kind of like them even though I told you otherwise. I even like the memories of that afternoon. Well, I would have liked it better without your constant nagging, but that was just you. How strange that a trivial painting of a magnolia has the capacity to outlive us by hundreds of years, not to mention the stupid nail it hangs on, which will still be here after we are long gone. I should really dust it.

One-two, one-two. Time passes so slowly. I have not even covered a mile and already sweat is dripping down my neck, and my tee-shirt is starting to stick to my love handles. I will have to lose a lot more than two pounds for those to disappear. If only exercising were not such a torture, one day I might be able to feel at ease in my body and even look sexy. You often reprimanded me about my weight. You wanted me to look trim and proper. I did not care then, but now I want to lose my fat and be sexy.

"Sexy?" That was not even part of your vocabulary. Girls, and especially your girls, had to be modest, and if possible, even a bit bashful. I wonder how my husband would react if one day I had really sexy legs. They have shaped up a little bit since I started walking on the treadmill, but not enough for him to notice; at least he has never said anything. He never said anything either when they were fat, and I mean *really* fat. He is a good man. I am not sure you ever liked him. Not true. I know very well that you did not like him at all. You always thought I could have found someone more educated, someone a bit more cultured. But I was *fat*.

"Darling, don't you want to wait some more? You don't have to marry the first boy that comes along. There are lots of boys out there, and some of them are even wealthy."

My husband loves me as I am. He is good to me. You had to explain to him what *"plein air"* meant, and he did not know who Cezanne was, either. You humiliated him on the first day when I brought him home.

He was nervous and intimidated.

"I like to paint *plein air*." He looked even more puzzled then he blushed.

"Oh, you don't know what *plein air* means?" You said to him in front of everybody, "People with some culture speak French like me." I could have hit you. You despised him for his lack of interest in painting and all that was dear to you. You thought it was a pity that he could not afford to take me to Europe and France to see the Louvre and the Mona Lisa, and you told him that one, too. I am happy here, but you thought it was a character flaw if one did not want to see the world (and by this you meant "the Old World.")

Yes Mom, you wanted us to be perfect. When we were small, you liked to present your two little girls all dolled up on Sunday for church. You spent hours at the sewing machine making dresses for Fran and me. Even though we were not twins, you wanted us to be dressed the same, especially on Sundays when we hopped down the road like little puppets wearing identical red dresses with black buttons and white lacy cuffs which you had crocheted yourself, identical black jackets with velvet collars, identical Patent leather shoes and identical little red handbags. It took you ten long minutes to braid my hair, and I never told you that I wanted hair like Fran's. You had cut hers short because she would not sit still long enough for you to braid it; but even she had to tie two white ribbons in her hair to show off the signature look of your girls. We looked like one of your paintings come to life when we marched down the street on the way to church. We looked like Goya's *Royal Family of Charles IV*, you the queen and dad the king. Goya painted the queen evil and the king a moron.

"Don't run! Not on a Sunday. Not on the Lord's day," you scolded. "You will scratch the leather and spoil the shoes. Fran, did you hear me?"

Fran never listened and ran anyway. You could not stop her. You pulled her by the hair as a punishment. Dad, excited with his new Instamatic, took to a picture which shows Fran with a forced grin and an awkwardly crooked ribbon. My ribbons sparkled the way you wanted them: crisp, immaculate, and perfectly aligned. When I look at the picture today, I wish my ribbons were crooked, too.

One-two, one- two. There is another picture of me playing the violin at Jefferson High. You practiced with me for weeks.

"You can do this. Let's try again! I want you to do it! I want people to see how gifted my daughter is."

You had to tune my little violin and put resin on my bow because I was too small to do it myself, and we played that Handel piece again and again.

"Stand straight!"—"Put your chin up!" and you admonished me to concentrate and not tap my foot on the floor. The neighbors' kids were shouting and laughing as they were playing hide and seek in the yard. Fran was there, too. You had long given up on her playing any instrument.

"Fran has no talent. She is a tomboy and has ADHD."

The day of the performance, my hands were clammy, and I threw up my lunch in the school bathroom. I never told you. Mrs. Townsend, the teacher, was unusually nice to me; she even smiled and nudged me on:

"You can do this, darling," she said "Your Mom will be so proud of you."

I was six and the youngest kid on stage. I made two mistakes, and Mrs. Townsend started over again, but you clapped anyway. I remember that. You stood there and clapped and clapped when everybody else had long stopped. Heads turned and you smiled, elegant in your lemon yellow chiffon fabric dress with a wide leather belt. Your stiletto matched your lipstick. Next day in class, Mrs. Townsend mentioned my two mistakes, and I cried. She talked to me harshly a lot, especially when you were not there, and I sometimes cried myself to sleep at night under my blanket, but you never noticed. Fran was different. She kicked and screamed, and you could not control her. You cried sometimes.

"Fran, why do you make Mom cry?" I asked her when we were in bed.

"Because," is all she said.

When Fran fussed and did not eat the leek dish, you hit her with a clothes hanger.

"This is a special recipe from Julia Child, and it took me all morning to prepare," you said.

"I hate leeks."

"It is good for you."

"I hate leeks."

"Don't be ridiculous, Fran. Just close your eyes and think you are eating ice cream."

"Ice cream! Ice cream! This ain't no ice cream! This is leeks, and I hate this damn dish."

"Watch your language, girl!"

"I hate this damn Julia Child crap."

That's when you lost it. I could see the nervous twitch in your left eye—always a bid sign—and you hit Fran smack in the face.

"You can hit me as much as you want," Fran said very calmly, "I am not going to eat." At four o'clock she was still sitting at the kitchen table, and by then the leeks were cold.

"I wanted five, six children," you said more than once, "but after Fran..."

By now I am soaked in sweat and I want to give up, walk away and never look back; but instead, I keep on trotting, obediently putting one foot in front of the other, one—two, one—two, covering one mile and another and another. Maybe I should increase the speed, but I am afraid of a heart attack. I would like to run if I were not so heavy and fat. I wish I could run like when I was small.

Fran and I tried to run with the trains.

"Faster, faster!" Fran challenged. "Let's see if we can catch it!"

We ran until we were completely out of breath, and then we fell to the ground, rolling over in the grass, giggling. I could run all the way to the store and back, and on the day that I bought you the wrong kind of cigarettes, I ran the distance twice. It was raining that day and I was drenched through and through. You wanted the ones with filters. Fran was long gone by then to the other side of the globe, and she never came back. I still miss her. And I miss Dad. You always said that Fran killed Dad when she left, because he drank more and more to forget. I wonder if you ever believed yourself. Did you truly believe that Fran killed him? You *did* know that *you* killed him, didn't you? How could Fran have killed him *in absentia*? Were you really as blind as you were cruel?

You also made me bring that spoon back, the only thing I ever stole, a little keepsake from high school which I had taken from the cafeteria. You were furious.

"My girls don't steal. Not spoons. Not forks. Not anything. My girls don't steal spoons from the school."

It was not silver or anything, but you had me walk all the way back—six miles—to the school and six miles home. You did not want me to have it because stealing was a sin. I wonder if Fran ever stole anything or if she told lies? I never did.

Remember the Christmas cards you wanted me to make for you? I worked really hard on those. I loved the colored pencils: red, orange, yellow, but you wanted them in blue tones and white.

"Red and yellow are warm colors and Christmas is in winter," you explained.

You made me redo every single one of them. They were not good enough. They were not perfect. "Try harder," you said. "It is Jesus' birthday."

"Always choose the hardest! All for Jesus!"

And every night we prayed: "Dear Jesus, come again soon and take us all home with you." It was like waiting for Santa, but that Santa came once a year and I knew when it would happen. With Jesus, planning was more difficult. He could come at any time, and I did not want to be left behind. Jesus never came.

You are dead, Mom, and I am still talking to you. I saw you in the coffin. I touched your arm, and you were cold. I have long stopped praying, but I said a Hail Mary for you just in case—"pray for us *nunc et in hora mortis*." It was raining, and I remember the chrysanthemums. I don't like chrysanthemums.

Finally the belt slows down. *One-two, one-two*. The treadmill makes less noise and announces 'cool down' time—another five minutes and it will be over for today. I will check in the mirror, and maybe my legs will be sexier. Maybe there is a real me under all that fat.

Cheylyn LeBeouf
Doorway

It was nothing more than a doorway, framed by cracked, rotting timber. Opening out onto the front porch, it captured a small view of the world made more beautiful by a softly falling drizzle. Everything looked so green, bright and beautiful and reinvigorated by the summer shower. Parched earth eagerly consumed the moisture, reveling in the lack of heat which had been chased away by the roiling cloud cover overhead.

It was nothing special—nothing more than a common scene captured by a disintegrating doorframe. But, for the moment, it was the most intriguing view in the world. Much more beautiful, in fact, than the dilapidated house supporting that worn out doorframe. A single-wide trailer with yellowing wall paper and a sinking floor. Every few feet, outside light peered in through a hole or crack emerging between floor and wall. The bathrooms were little better than outhouses and stunk of piss and mildew.

Run-down. It was an optimistic view of the old trailer, and the characteristic word Kaia used to describe her childhood home in an effort to remain optimistic. Over the years, the memories of this place had built into a festering sore in the back of Kaia's mind; one which oozed and pulsed as she picked at it over and over. Despite her best efforts, it was part of her.

Staring out the open door to the beyond, breathing smoke into the muggy air, Kaia's mother sat rocking in her creaking rocking chair. Her willowy frame supported a regal posture and tilt of the head, with her long legs stretched out before her, ankles crossed. Those legs! So beautiful that even the varicose veins protruding from the skin did little to draw attention from their perfection. Her green eyes, muddied over the years, were cold.

"Time for tea, isn't it, Mamma?" Kaia asked, voice barely above a whisper. Her mother's presence invoked an almost churchlike reverence that kept Kaia's voice low and her movements soft.

The only reply was that incessant creaking and the hiss of exhaled smoke.

On her visits home, Kaia often ran the house. Her mother's legs prevented much movement, thus Kaia cleaned, cooked, and made tea. It was more than what her stepfather did in the hours not spent at the paper mill. Quickly and efficiently, Kaia set the water boiling and gathered the bags of Earl Grey that her mother preferred. A cracked china set, once impeccably beautiful, was the only thing left of her Grandmother, and Kaia treated it with care as she lowered it from a pantry shelf. What her mother drank from when she wasn't there, if she was able to make tea at all, Kaia had no idea, for there was no way she would have been able to reach it. The idea of that glorious china set, baby pink with ivory rimming both cups and saucers, sitting alone in the pantry unleashed a swell of despair, and in that moment Kaia was tempted to take it and run as far as she possibly could.

The shrieking of the teapot broke Kaia's reverie, and she snatched it from the burner. The tea pot was the only thing that had ever shrieked in her mother's presence, and it was the only sound which the distant woman seemed to welcome, for it signaled a tradition that, despite her destitution, she refused to surrender.

The cracks in the china had been messily doctored with glue turned brown from seeping tea. Every time Kaia used the set, she wondered if it would shatter like a dam with too much force behind it. However, it was like her mother, remaining strong despite the degenera-tion of its beauty and usefulness. And, when Kaia set the steaming cup before her mother, she noticed that it was handled as though it were the most valuable thing in the world. Her mother's full lips pursed, and she softly blew upon the steaming contents, creating ripples across the surface.

"How is it, Mamma?" Kaia asked tentatively while trying to cool her own cup. She was no fan of Earl Grey, but she knew that not partaking in the ritual would only result in a confrontation.

"It'll pass I guess." The rest of tea was spent in silence, the two of them staring out the doorframe. By now, the drizzle had picked up a little, turning into a steady rain. In the distance, Kaia could hear thunder.

Kaia cast a glance at her watch and saw that it was a quarter past four. Fred, her stepfather, would be home from work soon, and then she would head out before the storm worsened.

The empty tea cup was held out in silence, and Kaia rose to pick it up. She had already done the dishes, so washed these as well so as to leave nothing piled on the countertop.

"Do you want me to put this somewhere you can reach it?" Kaia asked as she carefully dried a saucer.

"No point. Fred'll only hide it when you're gone." Fred despised the tea set—despised any relics from her mother's former life. They were reminders of where she came from, and it was a kind of life he would never experience. Fred was illiterate, not due to lack of schooling, but lack of "book sense" and motivation. He was a man who worked with his hands, and his father had been the same way. Despite a good job at the mill, he was lazy and squandered all of his money on useless things rather than taking care of his home or his wife. Kaia hated him, more than she hated anything else. Somehow, she felt that it was Fred who was to blame for her mother's condition, though in actuality he was no more to blame than the neighbor down the road.

Fred's arrival was announced by the backfire of his old pick-up as he pulled into the yard. Kaia saw him through the window, his wide shoulders hunched against the rain, ball cap pulled low over his brow.

"Goddamn rain," Kaia heard him mutter as he stomped up the porch stairs, trying to shake mud from his boots. The rest he tracked with him into the house, not caring that Kaia being there meant the floors had been cleaned that afternoon. For a moment, his hulking image took up the entirety of the doorway, then he swung the door shut and a gloom settled over them despite the open windows. "Didn't expect yah here today, Kid," he said in way of a greeting, making a beeline for the refrigerator. It was the line he greeted her with every time she came over, as though he had expected her to stop showing up after the previous visit. Or rather hoped—Fred had practically kicked Kaia out the door when she turned seventeen. Pulling out a beer, he cracked the tab with a snap, taking a deep gulp.

"Yeah well I was due for a visit," she replied. Having finished drying the tea set, she folded the towel on the edge of the sink and returned the china to its pantry cabinet. Fred eyed it angrily the entire time it was out in the open, but he looked satisfied when Kaia shut the pantry door after putting it away.

Fred, having already finished one beer, reached in the refrigerator for another, setting the first empty can upon the counter. Kaia watched as leftover saliva and alcohol mixed in a puddle around the bottom of the can. Then, still trailing mud from his boots across the freshly cleaned floor, Fred squatted next to Kaia's mother, giving her a kiss on the cheek. Had it been any other couple, the gesture would have been sweet; it would have been something that perhaps eased the intense hatred Kaia felt for Fred.

However, between these two, it was an act of aggression. When their eyes met after that kiss, it was as though each were trying to set the other alight with one look.

"So, what's for supper, Kid?" Fred asked, rising. He belched.

Thunder sounded in the distance, and the sound of rain on the tin roof had quickened. "Whatever you decide to cook, Fred. I've gotta get home before this weather gets any worse." Kaia made for the doorway, grabbing her purse as she went.

"Ah so that's how it is. You come here, take advantage of our hospitality, but you can't even cook dinner. Typical, Kid. Typical." Fred snorted derisively into his beer.

Kaia felt a surge of anger well up within her. These comments were not uncommon, and she had come to expect them over the years, but they never ceased to get under her skin. Ignoring her stepfather, Kaia bent over her mother and placed a kiss on top of her head. She smelled as though she hadn't bathed in a couple days. Kaia made a note to add that chore to her to-do list next time she was over.

"Goodbye, Fred," she said harshly, escaping out the front door as quickly as she could.

Outside, it had grown dark, the cloud cover becoming more dense. The sky looked as though it were boiling, matching Kaia's mood as she climbed into her car and cranked the ignition. The view through her windshield was distorted from raindrops falling fat against the glass, and for a moment, they seemed to wash away the trailer. However, with a flick of the windshield wipers, it was back in full view. Sighing, Kaia backed out of the driveway and began her hour-long journey home.

The drive always left her with plenty of time to think after visits to her mother's. She had spent her life wondering what the story was that lurked in the solemn woman's past. Ever since Kaia had been a girl, her mother had been an imposing figure that said little in the way of conversation. Over the course of a lifetime, certain tendencies had become apparent that set Kaia's mother apart from the rest of the lower class, for she possessed an air of sophistication that was inherent to those of the well-to-do. Yet beyond those hints, Kaia knew nothing of the woman who had, for the most part, raised her.

There was one thing lurking in that trailer that Kaia longed for, and it was partly what kept her coming back for her monthly visits. Her mother's room stood within the shadowy confines of a hallway, and it was a room that Kaia had never seen. For as a long as she could remember, the door had been closed to any outsiders—even Frank had his own room and was barred from the mysterious sanctuary that stood on the other side of a locked door. Kaia could remember sitting in the hallway as a child, contemplating that door and what may stand on the other side of it. Periodically, even now, Kaia would try the doorknob in the hopes that it would be unlocked. However, she had no such luck, and no way of breaking in since her mother kept the key on a chain around her neck.

Kaia had often wanted to ask her mother about the room but had never got up the courage. She felt that if it were something her mother wanted her to know then she would have told her, or perhaps left the door unlocked. She had seen Kaia sitting in front of her doorway many times yet had never offered an explanation.

Kaia's thoughts were interrupted by her arrival home. Driving up to the gateway of Breakwater Bay, she entered in her passcode and drove around to her parking space. Shutting off the engine, she listened to the sound of rain on the tin awning for a moment, simply staring out the windshield. It often struck her how different her life had become from those days spent in her childhood home, and it was somewhat jolting to make such a transition in a single day. No matter how long it had been since she moved out, Kaia always felt that that place was her home and this was only a dream. Pulling up to her building was always eerie, and it would take a moment before she would realize that this was her home and she was no longer trapped in the web spun by her mother and Fred. Trying to shake the feelings and thoughts of her past, Kaia emerged from the car and hurried up to the door of apartment 105. The rain was icy as it hit her back, and she cursed the faulty lock upon her door that delayed her escape from the weather. Finally, she managed to free the deadbolt and rushed into the apartment, quickly shutting the door then collapsing against it. Breathing in the smell of home, Kaia kicked off her shoes and flicked the lights on.

The apartment was more than Kaia had ever hoped to call her own, and it had taken her a lot to get it. Though only a one bedroom, she was its first occupant, and it was a tidy, homey little place. The coloring was all neutral, and her furniture was of the IKEA variety. The kitchen was small but functional, and pumpkin spiced candles spaced throughout the apartment made her feel warm and secure. Her most prized possession, a plaque with her degree from Lamar State College-Orange, hung upon the wall across from the doorway, and it was the first thing she always saw when she came home. It was a reminder of all she had accomplished in the past six years since Fred had kicked her out.

Kaia looked at the clock. By now it was half past five and her uncle, his wife, and their two children were due for supper at seven. That morning, she had put a pot roast in the slow cooker, and the smell permeated the apartment. Mentally running through her dinner preparations, Kaia hurried off to the shower to wash away the grime of the day's chores.

* * *

The knocking sounded just as Kaia released the pot roast from its slow cooker prison. She could hear her Uncle Allen calling to her through the door, and she laughed out an "I'm coming! Hold your horses."

"Bout time, we're getting soaked out here," Allen declared with a smile, ushering his wife and children in ahead of him. Kaia hugged each in turn.

"Hey, Kaia," Danielle, Allen's wife, greeted. "Smells wonderful in here!"

"So, anything new?" Kaia asked, heading for the kitchen. It had taken longer to boil the potatoes than she'd expected, and she still had to mash them.

"Everything's good. Allen just got a promotion at work, so hopefully I'll be able to stay home with the girls now." Danielle followed Kaia into the kitchen and began peeking around at the food to see if there was anything she could do to help. Allen kept the girls, Lexie and Marie, in the living room.

"The stations are probably all out because of the weather, but you can find something for them on Netflix, Uncle," Kaia called to him.

"That's excellent, Danny," Kaia said returning to her kitchen conversation. She knew how much her aunt longed to stay home. They worked together as nurses at Baptist hospital, and the occasional night shifts made it hard for Danielle to keep up with her daughters.

Over the course of the last dinner preparations, Kaia's apartment became filled with laughter and conversation. She loved moments like this—moments when she truly felt part of a family. Allen and Danielle had been the people she turned to when Fred kicked her out of the house, helping her through the rest of high school and encouraging her to go to college. He was her mother's nephew, and he and his mother had often taken Kaia in when her mother went through phases where she didn't feel like being a parent. Allen was Kaia's brother, uncle, and father, and he was the only person who had been there consistently throughout her life. He had often tried to gain custody over her, but it wasn't until after he married Danielle that he had his own place and a well-paying job. Plus, there had always been that curiosity which had kept Kaia going back home, no matter how miserable she was during her time there.

"Dinner's ready," Kaia announced, and suddenly the tiny kitchen was very crowded. Lexie and Marie couldn't help declaring how hungry they were several times over, and Allen stared hungrily at the food as he patted his thin stomach. Danielle, perhaps the most patient person Kaia knew, was the only person to stay out of the kitchen, and Kaia doled out portions to greedy hands. She didn't have a kitchen table, not having the room for one, so they all gathered in the living room to eat as they watched a sequel to *The Little Mermaid* that Kaia wasn't familiar with.

"This is yummy," Lexie declared in her tiny voice, gravy dripping down her thin arms. Danielle, sitting beside her, moved to wipe it away with a napkin.

"This is yummy," Allen agreed around a mouthful. Kaia smiled. She enjoyed cooking and loved the feeling of a meal well done.

"So, Kaia, any men in your life?" Allen asked in the way of conversation. He often inquired into Kaia's love life, and she had come to know that it was due to worry over her being alone. He might have let off if she even made the small commitment of getting a puppy, but Breakwater Bay wouldn't allow that.

"No, not really," Kaia returned simply. She tried to encourage Allen on the subject of romance; because if she did he would probably try to hook her up with a co-worker or something along those lines.

"Hmmm," was all she got in reply. Marie shushed them as *The Little Mermaid* got herself into a particularly sticky situation. Danielle scolded her for shushing adults. Kaia shook her head and smiled.

The rest of the evening passed in a similar fashion. Kaia couldn't help but be in love with this small family, for they were everything that she had always wanted. And, when the time came to say goodbye, with the girls yawning and rubbing their little eyes, Kaia felt a twinge of sadness. Though she was younger than Allen and Danielle, she felt a maternal sort of possession over them and the girls, and she hated that she would be left here alone once they were gone. She wondered if this was what empty-nest syndrome felt like, and she suddenly felt very old.

"Thank you so much for dinner. It was wonderful," Danielle smiled, Lexie wrapped in her arms.

"It'll be our turn to cook next time," Allen said, cradling Marie in one arm and hugging Kaia with the other.

"Sounds good." Kaia opened the door for them and watched sadly as they passed the threshold. "Love you guys."

"Love you," they called back in unison.

Kaia closed the door behind them and slid the lock home. It had been a long, emotional day, and her exhaustion finally caught up with her. Danielle had helped her put away the left overs, and Kaia felt that the dishes could wait until morning. She perused Netflix until something caught her eye, hoping the noise of the television would help to ease the loneliness which had suddenly descended upon the apartment. Wrapping up in a blanket she kept thrown across the back of the couch, she curled up and barely made it through the opening credits before she was softly snoring.

* * *

Kaia woke the next morning feeling stiff from sleeping on the couch all night. Somewhere in the middle of the night, she had turned off the television so that the apartment now held a quiet stillness. It was a Sunday morning, and even the sounds of the city seemed still. Looking at her watch, Kaia noted that it was only seven a.m., and she wondered at the fact that, given her exhaustion the night before, she had awoken so early. Her mouth tasted rank and bitter, and she sat stretching only for a moment before going to brush them. The bathroom mirror allowed a glimpse of tangled blonde curls, and dark circles created half-moons beneath her honey-colored eyes. Teeth brushed, Kaia splashed cold water upon her face before returning to the living room. There, she could still smell the pot roast from the night before. She opened the blinds on all the windows, and sunlight lit up the apartment. Candles dissipated the smell of last night's meal, and music got her feet moving as she proceeded to do the dishes. Once that was done, Kaia was at a loss. She had somehow managed to get the whole weekend off from work, and she was unused to so much free time. Unsure of what to do, Kaia sat for a moment on the couch, enveloped in a warm ray of sunshine. Her eyes closed and she felt as though she were on the verge of falling...

And suddenly Kaia was seeing Allen and his family and feeling everything she had the night before. She felt the love and acceptance she had felt, and suddenly her mother's forlorn face flashed through her mind. Kaia felt an urgency to go to her mother, and without a thought, she threw on shoes and hurried out the door.

* * *

When Kaia pulled into the rutted-out driveway, she caught a glimpse of her mother through the open doorway. As usual, she sat in her rocker exhaling a plume smoke, and from this angle, shadows danced across her in strange patters. Fred's truck was gone; this being Sunday, he would be out fishing all day. Kaia was grateful for his absence and the alone time with her mother that it would afford.

"What are you doing here?" her mother asked in way of a greeting. As she rocked, the floor creaked beneath her.

"I came to talk to you," Kaia replied, planting a kiss atop her mother's reeking hair.

"You never come just to talk."

Today, the sun shone brilliantly, and the heat was already climbing. Kaia could see sweat beading on her mother's brow, and she could feel her own armpits growing damp.

"So, what did you come to talk about? I can't give you money if that's what you're asking for."

"I don't want any money, Mom." Kaia sat for a moment, wondering just how to express what she felt into words. Wondering how to ask her mother all the questions that had been building up over the years. "Why?" was all that would come out, and Kaia sat with her head down for a moment, unable to say anything else.

Her mother was silent for a moment, then she eased herself from the confines of that old rocker. Kaia rose and went to her, placing a supporting hand on her elbow. "Follow me," the older woman rasped, and Kaia watched with amazement and anticipation as they entered the hallway and paused before the door which had featured in so many of her fantasies. "I should've shown you this a long time ago."

Jim Sanderson

The woman's hands shook as she pulled her key from around her neck, inserting it within a deadbolt and freeing the lock.

Amber Placette
A Loss at Walmart

Damian always feared he would lose his son. He often dreamed of the release of Charlie's hand from his in a crowd, of losing sight of the top of the little boy's black head of hair, of watching the tiny red jacket and navy shoes disappear among dozens of others. Damian imagined some sweaty, swarthy individual with a windowless white van throwing the limp body of his son through an opened sliding door. He pictured an aisle in Super Wal-Mart, his cart full of hot dogs, pencils, and Christmas ornaments, as he spun in circles and yelled for his son.

It was all really ridiculous. Charlie didn't even wear a red jacket, and Damian had never thought to look at the color of his shoes. Furthermore, he had never seen an actual person driving a windowless van, at least not one that didn't have "Jack's Plumbing: Don't Take Your Crap to Anyone Else" painted on the side. And to lose a child in the vortex that is a Super Wal-Mart would be incomprehensible; some vested employee stocking water balloons would find the child before he or she could travel very far.

Damian knew that he must be suffering from some type of psychological problem. He had diagnosed himself via an episode of *Oprah* that showed how chronic fear is a manifestation of an underlying issue. Damian had even made a list.

Item one: a broken marriage. When he had met Kimberly in college, he did not love her instantly nor, did he ever grow to love her. Damian merely grew accustomed to her. He liked that he had a person who ate with him, slept with him, and called him daily. Whenever he grew accustomed to something, he was resistant to any change. For ten years, he had eaten at the same diner with coffee-stained counters and single functioning urinal out of habit.

It was that same lethargy that forced Damian to stay with Kimberly all through college, with her boring clothes and scheduled bowel movements. He was too comfortable to seek out a more suitable person. Having to *meet* someone and *build* a relationship and *share* details of his life-- frankly, it all consisted of too many action verbs and implied a great load of work. Kimberly was his very own sun; she was there regardless of whether or not he wanted her to be, and although at times it did hurt to gaze directly at her, Damian appreciated her warmth, her consistency, and her predictability.

Marriage was the next logical step. It was all very uneventful, and Charlie was the result of their honeymoon. After years of unprotected and preventable sex, the one time the couple was expected and protected in their union, a son was the result. Kimberly didn't want a child.

"I want an abortion," she had casually mentioned over breakfast one morning.

"I don't believe in abortion," Damian had responded.

"Since when?"

"Since that guy at the store passed out fake fetuses to every person in the parking lot. That really freaked me out."

"I don't want a fetus, even a plastic one."

"That's not your decision."

"If I have the baby, I'll leave it screaming in your arms, and I'll walk away."

"I dare you to do that. I dare you to have a baby and then abandon us both."

Apparently, that was the wrong thing to say. Kimberly plowed through her pregnancy, gave birth to a son, named him, and left three weeks after the birth. Damian felt like she was an Easy-Bake oven that had been broken after her first use. The divorce had been painless; Kimberly wanted nothing at all except some hideous hand-knitted afghan she had forgotten during her departure. That was five years ago, and Damian was positive he suffered from some form of post-traumatic, panic stricken, abandonment disorder.

Item two: a crappy job. At the beginning of his career as a high school science teacher, Damian had set realistic goals for himself. Get a Ph.D. Publish until someone noticed him. Teach college. Climb any ladder with decent rungs. But when Kimberly left, he abandoned his master's degree. The thing that irritated him was that it was all disgustingly typical. He was a young father with an infant who needed child care during the day and attention in the evening. He was every stupid person he saw at the grocery store with a calculator and coupons, looking for Kool-Aid and Hamburger Helper.

Therefore, he was stuck at his job. It wasn't even the miserable pay that corroded his mind like rust on a neglected car. It was the women. He was only one of two male teachers in his department, one of only a dozen or so in the entire school. There were no prospects among the women. They were all married, and they were all horrible. Each one of them had a face caked with Mary Kay products and apparently bathed daily in Elizabeth Taylor's newest scent. They were overly cynical, challenged in almost every area except fundraising and obsessed with fab diets.

The conversations were what really got to Damian. Day after day of endless chatter about their idiotic children who were all named after flowers or football players: Lily, Daisy, Peyton, Troy. Relentless information circulated about whose turn it was to restock the spoons or who was in charge of crustless sandwiches for the next party. Five years of it and Damian understood why students shot their teachers.

And the final item of his underlying problem: Charlie. Charlie was the source of every stomachache Damian had experienced in the past five years. He knew it wasn't Charlie's fault. Charlie hadn't begged him to date and then marry an unattractive person. Charlie hadn't asked to be conceived in a dingy hotel near a polluted beach. And yet, Damian felt a hybrid of love and regret when he looked at his son.

When his wife had first left, Damian had purchased a book entitled *A First-Time Father's Fears Fixed: A Guide to Raising Children Alone*. It was only $5.99 at the store. It cataloged what the nameless child was supposed to be doing at every month, how to respond to defiant behavior, and how to grieve the loss of a spouse and still celebrate the joy of a child. Damian studied it harder than any other text he had ever read. He wanted to follow rules so no one at any point could blame him if his child became a dysfunctional adult.

The only problem was that the book stopped when the child turned five. Damian had been free-handing everything for about four months, and it scared the hell out of him. He classified himself as a decent father. He cleaned and fed and spoke to his son, but it all had the very distinct feeling of a tongue passing over the hollow space of a tooth that a filling once occupied. Whenever he thought of himself as a father, it was like a reminder to get that filling fixed, that the awkwardness and discomfort could be easily remedied in a matter of time. He even programmed Charlie's eighteenth birthday on his phone.

Damian often wondered how anyone could love a child. He didn't mean the aggressive affection that causes people to have dozens of pictures of their kids positioned at every possible location they frequented but rather the quiet enjoyment of being with a person, the affinity of equal fondness. Damian knew no one could ever get that from a child. With every hug Charlie gave him, a line of snot was left on his shirt. Every time he patted Charlie on the head, Damian remembered the monstrous bouts of fever and vomiting he had endured and healed since the boy's birth. Once, he had even vocalized his thoughts to his son in the car.

"You know what, Charlie? You're like some piece-of-shit first car. You love that car, you know? But, damn, you'd love to just leave it by the side of the road too," Damian had said very carefully. His satisfaction lasted only the few seconds it took to look in the rearview mirror and realize that Charlie had fallen asleep.

* * *

Damian liked to wait until midnight to do the grocery shopping. The aisles were empty, the shelves were stocked, and he could easily convince Charlie to ride in the cart and sleep. However, on that night, Charlie seemed to have tapped into his inner spring of energy and insisted on walking beside the cart.

"You'll get tired and end up in the cart anyway," Damian warned.

"No. I won't," the little boy mumbled.

"Okay, but no whining. God, you know I hate it when you whine."

"I won't whine as long as I get Chiclets at the end."

They maneuvered around the store. Damian marked off his mental list effortlessly until he reached the special Stock-Up-and-Save section. He always became confused about what he had to buy in order to get something else free. This week it was a carton of eggs for a tub of cream cheese. He cursed as he shifted through the small freezer that held the containers of cream cheese; every one had that overly sweet strawberry flavoring swirled through it. Damian wanted just regular cream cheese and was determined to sift until he found it.

When he removed his head and shoulders from the crevices of the filthy freezer, Damian triumphantly threw the silver and white container into his cart and remarked how he must have been lucky to find the last one at the bottom.

Charlie naturally didn't respond; he was no longer anywhere in sight. The special section Damian occupied was at the center of the store surrounded by half a dozen different aisle openings. It was obvious Charlie had wandered down one of those, and Damian began to call out to him.

Five minutes later, Damian was losing his voice and growing increasingly angry. His son knew the store well enough to be able to find his way back to the cart. And if nothing else, Damian was screaming at the top of his lungs.

"Sir, what's the problem?" asked an older man in a red vest. His nametag read, "My name is Steven. It's my pleasure to help you!"

"Well, my son seems to have wandered to another universe," Damian confided.

"Uh-huh. No problem," Steven answered. Out of the great beyond of his belt, the vested individual retrieved a walkie-talkie.

"Alan, we've got a 212 in section eight. Make the announcement. What's your son's name, sir?"

"Charlie."

"His name's Charlie. Ten-four," Steven said as lowered the device. "Absolutely no problem. Happens all the time. Once a day usually."

"Yeah," Damian responded. "I mean, you even have a code and everything. And sections..." Damian made the mental notes that this man probably watched *Law and Order* religiously and volunteered for the neighborhood watch. His thoughts were interrupted by the overhead speaker announcing that they had a small boy unattended whose name was Charlie. If anyone found Charlie, they were instructed to bring him to a front register.

"Okay, sir, let's just head that direction. I'm sure your son is already there waiting," Steven concluded.

But Charlie wasn't there. Twenty minutes later, Damian called the police.

* * *

The police officer scribbled notes while Damian fiddled with his jacket zipper and answered questions.

"His name is Charlie...he's five years old...he's got dark hair, and it's short..."

"How about a picture? You got a picture?" the officer asked.

"Yes, I have a school picture, I think," Damian responded as he pulled out his wallet. He handed the small photograph to the officer who apparently was practicing free association through his writing as Damian had not said anything in the past minute. Damian finally had to ask a question to break the continuous note taking.

"What happens now?"

"Well, if we can't find him here, we gotta mark out the area. Uh, you know, send out an Amber alert. Light up the map..."

"What map?'

The man in the black uniform now exhaled loudly and finally stopped writing.

"The map of local predators."

"Oh." Damian nodded. The language was a babble of euphemisms. He wanted to ask the more obvious questions now like wasn't the area already "marked out" in maps, and shouldn't that list of predators always be lit up like a Christmas tree? But instead, Damian sat on a bench at the front of the store and tried to look distraught and nervous.

Normally, the situation would have angered him, the waiting and the interruption of a routine. But since he didn't have to really do anything, Damian felt surprisingly indifferent to the entirety of everything that was happening. The fear he had always fostered about losing Charlie was diminishing. Damian even felt somewhat childish for ever dwelling on it at all. Damian slowly reached a strange realization: he liked the attention and the movement that this incident had caused. He liked the hubbub of activity around him, the continual fetching of coffee by insignificant people and the reassuring sense that people were concerned about his feelings and yet unaware of them at the same time. The minutes passed quickly as the store went into a prison-like lock down and the doors were closed. There was talk of dogs being brought in to search the store, but Damian was more focused on the next move.

The disappearance of his son would certainly be an addition to his list of issues. It was this realization that began to fuel the insatiable thoughts in Damian's mind. If Charlie wasn't found in the store or in the time span of a few hours, a search would be organized. That search would continue for months. There would be a flurry of posters, press conferences and ribbons. Volunteers would come out of the woodwork like cockroaches to try and find a shoe in a field. There would be those ridiculous candlelight prayer circles where someone's jacket or hair always caught on fire, forcing the whole thing to end in a speech from the fire chief about the importance of candle safety. The next months seemed filled with nothing but tissues and torture if Charlie wasn't found because people would expect certain things out of a lost boy's father, and Damian wondered if he would be able to summon the anticipated emotions on cue. The only comfort was that eventually it would all have to end, even if Charlie was not found.

People gave up and forgot things, like what's her face who disappeared six months ago in Alabama. Damian couldn't remember her name, but she was never found. Suddenly, one singular thought made Damian's stomach heave to where he almost made a move for the trashcan by the door: he was somewhat relieved Charlie might be gone and forgotten. He didn't like the idea that his son might have been abducted by a local, now lighted, predator, but what if Charlie was just taken by a nice, partially insane, grieving mother. He was not enthusiastic about Charlie being in any pain, so Damian tried not to dwell on the particulars of his sudden absence. Damian entertained the thoughts of a certain pleasure in the role of father of a lost child. This could change his whole life.

He wouldn't have to go back to work. He would be busy appearing on television and running the foundation named after his son; he would be lobbying for harsher laws for kidnappers and writing a memoir. He was intoxicated with joy at not having to go to that place anymore. He might return to collect a few things and to watch the women whimper over him. He could probably even get out of buying girl scout cookies this year.

"Excuse me, sir," the policeman interrupted Damian's thoughts. "What about the boy's mother? Could Charlie's mother have taken him?"

"No," Damian answered quickly. "Not in a million years would she ever have taken him. She's always in bed by eleven. I mean, she knows she's heinous unless she gets her eight hours."

"Okay, then," the policeman accepted.

The thought of Kimberly made Damian realize something else: he could have sex again and not the stifled, towel-taped-to-the-door-crack sex either. Damian wouldn't have to worry about Charlie discovering some half-naked, surgically enhanced woman in his bed. He also didn't have to silence any type of exclamation as if he was still sixteen and doing it in the back of the auditorium during study hall. Damian could have full force, violent sex if he wanted. He hadn't had that kind of sex in years or ever if he was honest, but he knew that kind of thing existed. The point was that he could have it if he wanted now.

Damian wondered what kind of women he would attract in his condition. He hoped all the sad-faced women would eventually scatter when he revealed that Charlie's disappearance had left him wounded, unable to ever desire children again or even a meaningful relationship. This allowed him to be fully available for women who had tattoos and suggestive names like Candy or Essence. Damian would certainly not allow himself to become lazy as he did when it came to Kimberly. Damian understood that what he was thinking could be considered heartless, but it wasn't as if he had tried to lose his son in a supermarket. He couldn't help it if he was an emotionally bankrupt individual, and Charlie did not need to be raised by someone like that anyway. A child would be better off raised by someone who wanted him, someone who would risk time in a maximum security prison to have him. Damian was glad he had the mental dexterity to realize all this without the cloudiness of emotion that often turned logical people into full blown shit-for-brains.

Damian's train of thought was completely derailed by a disturbance on aisle four. He rose from his bench and moved in that direction where a swarm of people seemed have gathered. There was a sudden command for the crowd to part, and when it did, Damian recognized Steven, the supermarket security wonder, carrying his son. Charlie appeared to be half-asleep and content to be at the center of the gathering of searchers.

"Sir, we found him," Steven called through the crowd as if Charlie was the Christ child who went missing from the manager. As Steven maneuvered through the aisle and towards the register, Damian allowed something inside him to break. All the thoughts and plans of the past hour evaporated, and his face must have shown extreme disappointment, which thankfully is often mistaken for its cousin emotion of relief.

Steven managed to get to Damian and handed the little boy to his father. Charlie rested his head on Damian's shoulder as Steven continued to prattle.

"He was hiding on the diaper aisle. He must have crawled back behind the big containers of diapers and fallen asleep. Thank God I thought to check there. I mean, I know tons of kids who do that kind of thing..."

Steven's babbling, the chuckling of the small collection of police officers, and the other random individuals who stood around smiling like a sitcom family from the eighties all made Damian feel incredibly sad. Moisture began to form around the corners of his eyes, and he allowed himself to silently weep as the crowd watched. He cried because now he had to probably pay for his groceries, he would have to go back to work the next day, and his life was not changed. Damian cried for Charlie who was asleep in his arms, for Kimberly who had left him alone, but mostly for himself and what he now had lost.

CPSIA information can be obtained
at www.ICGtesting.com
Printed in the USA
LVOW10s0527201216

518043LV00001B/63/P

9 780991 532124